THE OCEAN DUMPING
QUANDARY

A Book in the Williams Press, Inc. Series
A grant from the E. A. Barvoets Fund assisted
in paying the costs of publishing this book.

THE OCEAN DUMPING QUANDARY

Waste Disposal in the New York Bight

Donald F. Squires

*The Sea Grant Institute of State University
of New York and Cornell University, Albany*

*This research was sponsored by the New York Sea Grant Institute
and by a grant from the MESA New York Bight Project, National Oceanic
and Atmospheric Administration, U.S. Department of Commerce*

State University of New York Press

ALBANY

To Marjory, Joel, and Larry

Published by State University of New York Press, Albany

Copyright © 1983 by The Research Foundation of the State University of New York State University Plaza, Albany, N. Y. 12246

Printed in the United States of America

For information, address State University of New York Press, State University Plaza, Albany, N. Y. 12246

Library of Congress Cataloging in Publication Data

Squires, Donald Fleming.
  The ocean dumping quandary: waste disposal in the New York bight

  Includes bibliographical references and index.
  1. Waste disposal in the ocean—New York Bight
(N.J. and N.Y.) I. Title.
TD796.7.S7   1983   363.7'28   82-19135
ISBN 0-87395-688-5
ISBN 0-87395-689-3 (pbk.)

10 9 8 7 6 5 4 3 2 1

Contents

List of Illustrations   vii
Preface   ix

Chapter 1. Perspectives of the Bight   1
  The Ecosystem   4

Chapter 2. The Margins of the Bight   19
  The Sandy Margins   20
    Man and the Coastal Fringe   27
  The Estuarine Terminus   31
    Man and the Estuary   35
    Modifying the Estuary   41
  Man's Boundaries   45

Chapter 3. The Resources   51
  Fishing   54
    Sportfishing   63
    Marine Plants   68
    Aquaculture   70
  Mineral Resources   71
    From the Bottom of the Harbor   74

Chapter 4. Peopling the Bight   78
  The Modern Era   79
  Developing Industry   82
  People and the Bight: Interaction   86
    The Case of Energy   87
    The Case of Water   93
  What Does It All Mean?   97

CONTENTS

Chapter 5. The Law and the Bight   100
Legislating Cleaner Water   104
Research—The MESA New York Bight Project   113

Chapter 6. The Bight As a Dump   126
Dumping in Perspective   128
Wastewater   131
The Sewage Sludge Problem   134
Industrial Wastes   136
Toxic Substances   139
Spoils of Dredging   144
Refuse   148

Chapter 7. The Costs of Dumping   154
Human Health   155
Aesthetics—The Floatable Crisis   161
Ecosystem Effects   166
Adapting to Man   170
The Economic Impact   173

Chapter 8. The Bight in Our Future   176
As Others See Us and We See Them   178
Where Are We and Where are We Going?   182
To Whom Does the Bight Belong?   188

References   193
Index   223

Illustrations

1. A perspective of the Bight — 5
2. Some representative plankton from New York Bight — 11
3. Some representative benthic invertebrates — 13
4. Some characteristic birds of the Bight — 17
5. Locator map of the New York Bight and the Hudson-Raritan Estuary — 21
6. Major channels of New York Harbor — 40
7. Some of the major commercial fishes of the Bight — 56–57
8. Principal commercial fishing areas of the New York Bight — 61
9. Major kinds of gear used in commercial fishing — 64–65
10. Some of the important recreational fishing areas of the Bight — 67
11. Growth of the population of the New York Bight coastal area — 81
12. The "Bill of Sale" for Manhattan Island — 83
13. Energy costs and illumination used: Candles to Gas Light — 89
14. Sources of wastes discharged into the New York Bight — 98
15. The "Sludge Monster" as created by George Huehnergarth — 108–109
16. Captain R. Lawrence Swanson, MESA New York Bight Project staff — 116
17. Dr. Joel O'Connor, MESA New York Bight Project Staff — 117
18. Some MESA New York Bight Project staff examining "floatables" — 121
19. The NOAA research vessel *George B. Kelez* — 124

20. Location of oil lease sales, major dumping sites and
     other uses of the New York Bight   138
21. Landfill along southern Manhattan Island   146
22. Garbage scows being filled at Manhattan   151
23. *Ceratium*, the small dinoflagellate plankter which
     caused the fish kill of 1978   168
24. Uses of the Bight—A Map   179
25. An essay by a sixth grader   183

Illustrations appearing on chapter opening pages show common fishes of the New York Bight.

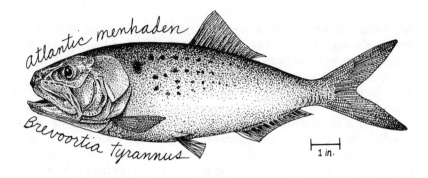

atlantic menhaden

Brevoortia tyrannus

1 in.

Preface

The story of the New York Bight region is rich in the relationship between man and ocean. For nearly four centuries the region's growth and development have been built on that relationship: first on ocean resources, later on waterborne commerce. A new chapter is being written today for tomorrow.

Where better to study the coastal ocean than off the nation's premier city. The City's front doorstep—a bit of the Atlantic Ocean—is one of the world's most intensively used coastal waters. Through the Bight have sailed mighty armadas of tall ships, steamships, ships of maritime commerce and war; millions of immigrants, and countless tons of goods going here and there. New York's coastal ocean, bounded by some of the finest sand beaches in the country, is used by millions of urbanites, suburbanites, and ruralists. Its shores are rimmed by high-rise housing, industry, suburbs and farms. It has been shaped, altered, used and abused in all manner of ways.

To the more than 18 million people living around the New York Bight, it is a part of our experience, sometimes a part of the reason we are living here: jobs, the opportunity to be near the ocean, or just because we grew up here. Its shores are the home of the cultural and financial center of the country, and shelter the world's busiest port, the largest concentration of people in the nation, the site of a great industrial complex. And, its coastal waters have gained notoriety for their sludge monsters, their fish kills, and other signs of environmental degradation. We have lately come to recognize the ocean's importance to us. The recognition is sad because the ocean has become the final repository—the final environment—of our pollution.

Short-sightedness is our problem. We avow that an individual's actions can't be important in the whole scheme of things. We remain resolutely unconvinced that the sum of our individual actions, the collective short-term gains we seek, affects the course of nature. Garrett Hardin wrote of this in his classic *The Tragedy of the Commons* (1) and showed that each of us, by our cumulative actions, affects the whole. Where better is this displayed than in the New York Bight?

And each of us tends to see our own goals and aspirations as paramount. Thus to the sportfishermen the rapacious commercial fleets are gobbling up the fish—particularly the one I was about to catch. On the other hand the commercial fisherman who pays his fee and earns his living from the sea, knows that all those unregulated sportsmen are catching most of the fish. We allow these visions of self-righteousness to lead us to immense contradictions. While using its fishery resources for food, we are poisoning some of them with industrial chemicals; while seeking the pleasures of the Bight to bring comfort and expansion into our lives, we burden its waters with sewage and other wastes we don't want to think about.

We have come to know, from the messages of Cousteau, Heyerdahl, Carson, and others, that man has affected the oceans far, far from land. We in this coastal region are painfully aware from frequent newspaper and television announcements of sullied beaches and fish kills that we have affected the New York Bight. It isn't the "Dead Sea" as portrayed by some; it is a place of enjoyment and is productive for our society.

The oceans are vast, but not so vast that we cannot contaminate them. We discard that which we do not want on our lands into our streams. Inexorably, these pollutions work their way to the rivers, into the estuaries, and into the ocean. New York Bight becomes different because here we move, by deliberate effort, much waste to the ocean by barging sewage sludge and dredge spoil as well as allowing the discharge of pollutants from pipes and other outfalls. Are our successes in creating the premier city of the nation to be signaled only in fouling an area of coastal ocean thrice as large as the State of Connecticut?

I have written this book for a number of reasons. First, the New York Bight, perhaps the most affected bit of coastal ocean in the nation, offers us an opportunity to learn about man and ocean environment interactions. Second, the most extensive study of this bit of ocean ever made has just been concluded—the National Oceanic and Atmospheric Administration's MESA New York Bight Project—and there are some new things to be said and new insights to be gained.

And, third, our interest has been progressively turned toward the ocean in the last decade so the time may be ripe to do something about its health and well-being.

Relationships develop and change with time. Because we are so much involved with living, we sometimes forget how yesterday is related to today and today to tomorrow. And, we may also forget that circumstances which govern our actions and behavior will change with time and may, at some future date, make the decisions of yesteryear seem inappropriate. Our use of natural resources is greatly affected by such perceptions. As long as a frontier exists, regulating the use of land doesn't seem necessary; as long as a resource is plentiful, or even available, moderation in its use doesn't attract our attention.

Our present relationship with the New York Bight is the product of over three centuries of interaction between ourselves and this coastal ocean. Many former decisions about the use of the estuary and the Bight would be thought immoral, or at least unwise, today. But the social, economic, and political setting in which those decisions were taken were very different. "What the public will stand for" today might not "play in Peoria" next year. In judging the character and nature of our relationship with the Bight, it is important that we weigh it in the context of that particular time and of the times and circumstances which precede.

For much of the past three centuries, the Bight was a seemingly limitless resource for all the purposes to which we put it. While, as we shall see, from time to time some section of the estuary was overstressed, overpolluted, or otherwise misused, there was always more. Now we seem to have reached some sort of crossroads in our relationship with the Bight. The signals are that human activities have directly affected this coastal ocean. The muddling around of the past had some cumulative effect, but mostly we have simply become sufficiently inventive, and numerous, to alter major segments of the natural environment. Our decisions then become more relevant, for their effects are more profound.

This is the perspective for this tale of ocean and man. I have tried to show the context in which decisions of the past were taken and how those patterns have come to affect our relationship with the Bight today. It is of little consequence to rail against combined sewers or some other factor affecting the estuary or the Bight today because, at the time, the decision reached was acceptable. We may change our behavior, we may improve our decisions through better understandings. But to change the results of past decisions requires a determination to do those things and spend that money required to undo that which was done.

To tell that story I will first define and describe the New York Bight. Then in successive chapters, I will chronicle the growth of population and industry. The increasing strain from pollution as the region developed will be apparent as we examine the use of the Bight's resources. How government and science have attempted to cope with that increasing pollution forms the basis for Chapter 5. Then I will explore the particular issue of ocean dumping, a highly controversial use of the Bight.

As society and the natural environment interact, the natural system may be stressed, extended, and often overburdened. While we quickly see the aesthetic impacts of debris, flotsam, and jetsam, other stresses may be exhibited in the ecosystem in very subtle ways. We have found indications, subtle changes now, but evidence that our actions have begun, at last, to pressure the Bight into reacting more strongly, responding not just superficially, but in lasting ways which may have effects for generations. Understanding these causes and effects may induce us to reduce the stresses and lessen our impact on the system.

The New York Bight has suffered not only as a result of the development of the metropolitan region, but in a sense, through the growth of our nation. This is not the result of actions of some other "they," but of the sum of actions of individuals, ourselves. By understanding this and by taking action, we can change what has happened. Because there are opportunities to rebuild our heritage, to enjoy the coastal ocean that shaped the development of the region, to undo those damages that have been done, this story is told.

Acknowledgments

This book was edited in its preliminary form by Marjory Simmons and the staff of the MESA New York Bight Project, who were its severest and most constructive critics.

John Dana, my patiently thorough associate, provided the extensive library research incorporated in this book. The veracity of citations are his; errors, the author's. Loretta Simon assisted with portions, particularly Chapter 5.

Dr. Joel O'Connor, MESA New York Bight Project, NOAA, was both the father and the godfather of the project. His continued understanding, support, and patient criticism have contributed greatly to the success of the work.

Much of the information compiled in this book came from the working papers prepared for the MESA New York Bight Project by the many participants in the Synthesis Workshop, Williamsburg, Virginia, in 1978. Some of those papers have been collected and prepared for publication. I am grateful to the insights and resourcefulness of these many contributors, most of whom are acknowledged appropriately in the text.

I am particularly indebted to those who with thought, diligence, and care reviewed the typescript. To Dr. Henry Regier, Institute for Environmental Studies, University of Toronto, I am particularly grateful for many insights and guiding influences. Mssrs. Charles Parker, Michael Kawka, Stanley Chanesman, and David Goodrich of the MESA New York Bight Project staff deserve special thanks for their constructive critiques and additions. Harold Stanford, Garry Meyer, and others of the MESA staff offered freely of their wisdom and collective guidance through the successive reworkings of the text.

Illustrations were done by Sharon Ellis from rough materials assembled by me and research assistants.

Finally, Captain R. L. Swanson, then head of the MESA New York Bight Project, sustained my work with his quiet belief that this book would be completed.

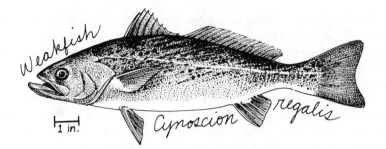

1 / Perspectives of the Bight

After a hundred leagues we found a very agreeable place between two small but prominent hills; between them a very wide river, deep at its mouth, flowed out into the sea; and with the help of the tide, which rises eight feet, any laden ship could have passed from the sea into the river estuary. Since we were anchored off the coast and well sheltered, we did not want to run any risks without knowing anything about the river mouth. So we took the small boat up this river to land which we found densely populated. The people were almost the same as the others, dressed in birds' feathers of various colors, and they came toward us joyfully, uttering loud cries of wonderment, and showing us the safest place to beach the boat. We went up this river for about half a league, where we saw that it formed a beautiful lake, about three leagues in circumference. About xxx of their small boats ran to and fro across the lake with innumerable people aboard who were crossing from one side to the other to see us. Suddenly, as often happens in sailing, a violent unfavorable wind blew in from the sea, and we were forced to return to the ship, leaving the land with much regret on account of its favorable conditions and beauty; we think it was not without some properties of value, since all the hills showed signs of minerals.(1)

With these words Giovanni da Verrazano, a native of Florence, generally accorded the distinction of being the first European explorer to reach New York, described its harbor as it appeared on April 17, 1524.

Almost a century later in 1609 John Juet, aboard Henry Hudson's *Half Moon*, wrote: "For to the Northward off us we saw High Hils. This is a very good Land to fall with, and a pleasant Land to see." He recorded "many salmons, mullets, of a foot and a half long a peece, and a Ray as great as foure men could hale into the ship" (2).

Most explorers sailing along the coast to New York Harbor commented upon the abundance of fish and birds, the sand beaches, lying low and glistening in the sun, backed by lush green forests, suggesting richness of resources and wealth for those who could exploit them.

Today, the appearance of the Bight is different. To be sure, seen from the Bight, the land may still show as a low white rim of sand beaches crowned by the green of forests indistinct through the salt haze lying low on the horizon. But it is now too often tinged brown with the atmospheric pollutants of industry, automobiles, and dwellings. On a calm day, its waters appear deep-blue to blue-black, its surface may be dotted with plastic castoffs of civilization. On the right course, great offshore drilling rigs can be seen in the southern Bight. Ships large and small; ranging from great tankers to small fishing boats, hurry across its waters. Nearer the mouth of the harbor, congestion of shipping increases, the low skyline of the forests is shattered by water and communications towers and high-rise dwellings, and the water becomes blue-green to brown. At about the point where spectacular views of lower Manhattan first became visible, there are clusters of hundreds of fishing boats—private and charter or party boats—favored fishing areas called Mussel Bank, Old Orchard Shoal Ground, and Tin Can ground (3). At night the lights of the City, reflected off cloud cover, "provide an unerring beacon to the seafarer seeking the harbor" (4).

More than 17 million people depend on the Bight; sport fishermen off New Jersey and Long Island every year spend over $250 million catching $90 million worth of fish (5); nearly 12,000 commercial fishermen harvest about $48 million (dockside value) in seafood every year (6,7). Its beaches and bays are lined with public and private recreation areas, marinas, boatyards, and the like, which are the basis for a $460 million annual expediture on Long Island's south shore alone (8).

The Bight is also a waste-disposal system for those same people and more. Municipal sewage, storm water runoff and industrial discharges from places as far distant as Albany, 150 miles up the Hudson River, find their way to the Bight. But some wastes are even more deliberately placed in the Bight and none of its uses have gained it more notoriety than this, the Bight as a dump. Of all the wastes dumped into the nation's coastal waters, more than 95% of the sewage sludge and 90% of acid wastes dumped from vessels were introduced into New York Bight waters (and an additional 48% of industrial wastes are dumped just beyond the Bight) (9). But these quantities are small in comparison to the volume of wastewater discharged directly or indirectly into the Bight, waters containing those materials flushed into sewage systems by people from their homes and their places of work (10).

The Bight is a major part of our nation's vast ocean transport system. Over 7,000 ships traverse the Bight each year carrying imports or exports between the nation's busiest port and places around the world. Tankers are the only means of bringing oil from the Middle East to the automobiles and homes of the northeastern United States at prices we can afford, and much of it is landed at the Port of New York. Except for giant containerships there are no reasonable means by which beef grown in New Zealand and Australia can be brought cheaply to McDonalds, Burger King, and other fast-food shops.

There are other uses of the ocean: seafood production, a source of minerals, space for recreation and esthetic enjoyment. Each of these is important to someone living around the Bight. But, perhaps, more important to all of us is the role that the ocean plays as part of our global environment. The ocean is where our oxygen is produced, where our fresh waters are derived, and where life itself began. We are a part of the ocean, just as the ocean is a part of us.

We should not forget that man lived in the New York Bight region for at least 9,000 years before European intrusion. In the short span of 354 years, from European settlement to today, all the changes from the way it was to what it is today have been made. In less than 4% of the time man has used the Bight we have polluted and contaminated its waters; overharvested its fisheries; intensely and often misguidedly developed its coastal lands; maldistributed its recreational opportunities; abused it as a dump; built and then let great port facilities crumble from neglect and disuse; and allowed a city of over 7 million people to be cut off from their waterscape by highways, buildings, and derelict automobiles.

In this same time we have done some marvelous things—built a great city and achieved wonders of beauty in arts and humanities. We have made the borders of the Bight accessible to millions of people so that they can enjoy the gleaming beaches and rolling surf. We have created the human pleasure of gratifying our curiosity as we poke along the docks and wharfs wondering at the fishing vessels and pleasure boats, as we board the party and charter boats to go forth to capture the denizens of the deep for dinner.

For other parts of the country, New York Bight is an important example of what can happen to the coastal waters off any city. Outsiders satiated with the superlatives New Yorkers love to heap upon themselves, will simply say that it's their problem. But it really isn't.

What has happened to New York Bight is not just another case of misuse, abuse, lack of concern, or other failings of "New Yorkers." It is the story of the interaction of Western progressive society and the ocean; a story rich in opportunity seized, in great development, and in the cost of these actions. Can we control our future to recover and preserve that which we value? What happened to New York Bight has happened elsewhere, and will happen again wherever people fail to reckon with the finiteness of what Buckminister Fuller called "our spaceship earth" (11).

The Ecosystem

"Ecosystem" is a shorthand way of describing a set of interactive, evolving and balanced physical, chemical, and biological relationships. If you poke an ecosystem in one place, it may well react someplace else. Ecosystems are dynamic, they move and grow and change and die. In the pages that follow, we briefly explore that particular ecosystem called New York Bight and find out how it works, where its life comes from, and how man fits into it.

Where is the New York Bight? It is an over 19,000-square-mile portion of the Middle Atlantic Bight of the North Atlantic Ocean. It is bounded by the New Jersey coast from Cape May to Sandy Hook and the southern shore of Long Island, N.Y., from Rockaway Beach to Montauk Point. The seaward boundary of the Bight is the continental shelf break, where the relatively flat, gently sloping, shelf drops sharply, at 495 feet, to become the continental slope. Distance from shore to shelf edge ranges from 93 miles to 114 miles (12).

New York Bight was formed through eons of geological time, but its present shape was sculpted by the last major ice advance of the continental glaciation. As the great Wisconsin period glaciers began forming, 40,000 years ago, the ocean began to retreat across the continental shelf. Much of the shelf was exposed until glacial melt restored ocean waters, starting about 15,000 years ago. Earlier geological events are obscured by a carpet of sand, gravel, and boulders pushed up by the glaciers and washed forward by their melt waters to the edge of the continental shelf. With the melting of the glacial ice, sea level rose rapidly until about 7,000 years ago when the present shoreline was approximated. Since then sea level has risen more slowly (relative to the land), about half an inch a century, and the shoreline creeps closer to the mainland (13).

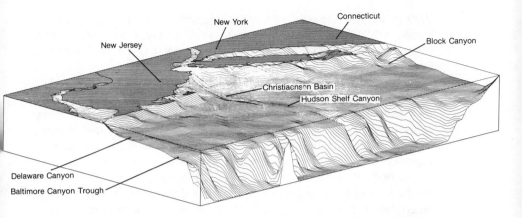

Figure 1. The New York Bight as it would appear if it were drained of water. Vertical dimensions are exaggerated so that slopes appear steeper than they actually are. The view is from the southeast. (Computer graphic prepared for the Sea Grant Institute by the American Geographical Society)

The Bight is itself a piece of the Middle Atlantic Bight which runs from Cape Cod to Cape Hatteras. If the shelf were drained of water, as it was during the continental glaciation, we would see that the New York Bight is separated from the rest by the Block and Delaware Shelf Valleys and is, itself, bisected by the Hudson Shelf Valley. When sea level stood about 480 feet lower than at present, the ancestral rivers flowed across the continental shelf and carved those valleys which are now virtually buried in sediments and covered by the waters of the Atlantic. There are other important features in the Bight's floor: smaller valleys carved by lesser rivers and streams; terraces and scarps which were formed at older shorelines while sea level rise hesitated; and, near the entrance to the port, a broad depression called the Christiaensen Basin (14).

As the glaciers began to melt and sea level began to rise, the shoreline began its retreat to the present position. Rising seas reshaped the carpet of sediments laid over the shelf into the ridge and swale topography which characterizes much of the floor of the Bight (15).

Rising sea level also shaped the sediments of the Bight into its shoreline, a shoreline shaped like a flexed arm. The upper and forearm are the shores of Long Island and New Jersey characterized by a low-lying fringe of barrier beach separated from the mainland by lagoons. At the elbow is a great estuary—that of the Hudson and

Raritan Rivers, separated from the Bight by the spit called Sandy Hook, a series of underwater bars such as Flynn's Knoll, Romer Shoal, and the East Bank, and the offshore bar called Rockaway Beach.

The carpet of sediments covering the continental shelf was reworked by the rising ocean waters. Existing features were eroded and a discontinuous sand blanket up to 30 feet thick was formed. Finer sediments were resuspended and either carried into the lagoons behind the barrier beaches or off the edge of the shelf. Some older lagoonal sediments are exposed from place to place on the shelf where not covered by the sand carpet. Today movement of sediments on the floor of the Bight occurs principally during storms when waves reach the deeper waters. Finer sediments seem to accumulate only in the topographic lows such as the Christiaensen Basin and in the fringing wetlands of the Bight (16).

The Bight lies between colder waters to the north and the warmer waters to the south. Nearshore on the shelf, colder currents flow southward, with the warmer waters of the Gulf Stream further offshore in the ocean, flowing northward. South of Cape Hatteras is the domain of the tropics; north of Cape Cod is the cold North Atlantic. The Middle Atlantic region has a marine flora and fauna which is a compromise between these two regimes—it is called the Virginian biogeographic province. Many species, particularly the fishes, move in great sweeping migrations up and down the coast from the Chesapeake Bay to the Grand Banks. The Bight thus shares some of the richest fisheries in the world.

As with all living systems on this earth, the sun provides the energy that drives conditions in the Bight. It (1) powers the winds that form the waves; (2) brews the ocean currents that sweep up on the shelf margins and break into eddies; and (3) provides the energy that microscopic plants use to convert carbon, oxygen, and other elements into larger molecules in the first steps up the long chain of organisms feeding one upon the other.

Out beyond the continental shelf edge is the great river-of-the-sea, the Gulf Stream, flowing northward from the Caribbean carrying immense amounts of energy in its sun-warmed waters, waters that make Great Britain warmer than Maine even though it is much farther north. But the Gulf Stream doesn't warm the coast of the Bight, for wedged between the shelf and the Gulf Stream is a counterflow, a part of the Labrador Current, carrying cold waters southward. The currents of the Bight though, are powered not primarily by solar heating as is the Gulf Stream, but by the tides and the winds that move across its waters.

Controlling the Bight is a temperate mid-latitude climate dominated by maritime air masses sweeping up from the tropics for 9 to 10 months of the year (the Bermuda High) and by Arctic air masses for the two most severe winter months (the Canadian High). Winds associated with these air masses move the waters of the Bight first one way and then the other (17). The result is what physical oceanographers call a *statistical* water movement—at any given moment the motion cannot be predicted, but over the long haul a general picture emerges (18).

Issuing from the Hudson-Raritan rivers is a plume of water which flows down the Jersey coast, its less salty, less dense waters flowing southward on the surface with a more dense, more saline return flow moving below into the estuary in response to tidal action. Over the middle and outer portions of the shelf, water moves generally to the southwest more or less parallel to bottom topography, and at speeds of about 2 miles per day. This pattern may be reversed for months at a time, particularly when there are strong persistent southerly winds or when there is low rainfall in the Hudson Basin. To the north and east close to shore there is a "semipermanent," poorly defined, low-speed gyre of water moving counterclockwise. But nowhere are the currents marked (19).

A most important effect of the wind on the Bight is to mix its waters. Solar heating, particularly in the summer, and other factors tend to cause density layers to form and the Bight becomes a watery layer cake. During the winter months, when the winds are usually strongest, mixing is almost complete, and the waters of the Bight are very similar from top to bottom in their temperature and salinity (which in turn define density), oxygen levels, and other factors. During the rest of the year, particularly during spring runoff, fresh, less dense waters float on top of the saline, more dense, shelf waters, and without adequate wind to mix them, form stratified layers of utmost importance to the behavior of the Bight (20).

The boundary between the upper warmer and lower cooler layers is called a *thermocline*. The thermocline is usually most marked in the inner shelf region where as spring heating and fresh water runoff occur, the surface waters become less dense relative to the colder, deeper waters. Winds are also less strong in spring and summer so that less mixing occurs. Close to shore, stratification is less marked because solar heating more completely warms the shallow water mass. Other boundaries may form where waters of different salinity (a *halocline*) or density (a *pycnocline*) are overlaid. Density is, of course, a function of temperature and salinity. When very pronounced layering occurs, the boundary between layers can have very important effects. Oxygen, contaminants and other dissolved materials mix, settle or diffuse slowly through the boundary. Many plants and animals prefer to stay above or below it and particles settling through the water column may be stopped, at least temporarily, at the boundary. In fall, as winds increase in intensity, stratification breaks down. Storm incidence in winter is high enough so that Bight waters are usually fully mixed.

The seasonal temperature cycle in the Bight is remarkably well defined. During winter months temperatures are the lowest, particularly near the coast. Minimum temperatures are usually reached in mid-January, averaging less than 2°C. By April, warming of the surface waters begins, particularly near the coasts, and by May solar heating is far enough along so that thermal stratification of the Bight has commenced. Surface temperatures of up to 22°C. occur during the summer, but waters at the bottom remain much cooler, sometimes less than 4°C. The seasonal pattern of water temperatures in the Bight, then, is of cool winter waters with relatively uniform temperatures from top to bottom as a result of wind-driven mixing and warm summer temperatures usually accompanied by stratification and considerable decrease in temperature from top to bottom (21).

Out on the shelf edge, differences in the temperature and salinity of waters over and off the shelf form a density front, a sort of nearly vertical boundary similar to atmospheric fronts. The shelf edge front can be very stable and persist for much of the winter. At its bottom, on the shelf side, is an accumulation of warm waters. This is extremely important to fishermen seeking the tilefish, a commercially important species that lives only in that bottom temperature maximum along the shelf edge. In the late 1800s, in one of the rare instances in which the front broke down and the temperature maximum dissipated, 1.5 billion tilefish died because of the cold temperatures they then encountered (22).

Another thermal feature on the shelf seemingly important in fish distributions is the pool of cold water that forms in the center of the shelf during the summer. It is believed that the cold pool makes it possible for some cold-water fish to survive in the Bight long after the other waters have warmed beyond the temperature tolerances of those species.

The sea is salty, but its salt content varies. Because we aren't dependent upon that salinity, we pay little attention to those degrees of saltiness. To many ocean creatures, saltiness defines the difference between places which can and cannot be lived in. The lovely starfish whose predation can decimate oyster and clam beds is a creature of saline waters; shellfish may live in brackish climes and when there, are out of the reach of the simple star. Others, such as the anadromous fish, live much of their life in the sea but seek out less saline places, such as the Hudson estuary, to spawn.

Salinity variations in the Bight are not defined as well as are those of temperature, for they represent a delicate balance between runoff of fresh water from the land, evaporation which increases salinity, rainfall which decreases it and the mixing of saline waters of the ocean and the Bight. In brief, anything which dilutes the Bight reduces salinity and anything which concentrates the salts increases salinity. Therefore, in general, salinity is lowest after the spring runoff and is highest in winter. The range in salinity of the Bight is from 32 °°/00 near the coast, to 35.5 °°/00, which is considered normal for the ocean, at the shelf edge. Of course, in and near the estuary and other sources of fresh water, salinities are locally less (23).

The essential ingredients for the maintenance of life are water, energy, and nutrients. The Bight provides the water; the sun provides the energy. From the land come the nutrients nitrogen, phosphorus, and silica. With these ingredients tiny single-celled plants begin the complex task of converting all of this, by photosynthesis, to living matter. These phytoplankton, diverse in kind and known as diatoms, dinoflagellates, chlorophytes and numerous other names, are extremely important to the oceans as well as to man, for they commence the chain of life that may eventually lead to your dinner table. Most higher life in the sea has phytoplankton as its ultimate food source. Also, carbon dioxide taken up by the ocean is converted, by photosynthesis, to the carbon of the tissues of marine plants, and oxygen is released back to replenish that in our atmosphere. Thus these primary producers are also critical in keeping the balance between oxygen and carbon dioxide in our atmosphere (24).

Man and phytoplankton relate in a very interesting way in the Bight. The most important external source of nutrients for growth of phytoplankton is from the open ocean; the second most important is from our sewage. How much of the nutrients available to phytoplankton in the Bight comes from the Atlantic oceanic waters transported over the shelf is not known precisely, but by indirect means it has been estimated that this source may be at least twice as great as all others. Yet, because the sewage sources are clustered together near the estuarine end of the Bight and are, therefore, more concentrated, their effects are more pronounced in and near the estuary.

As the weather warms and days become longer, phytoplankton population growth and reproduction are stimulated. Blooms, or patches of intensive growth occur, often with one species following another in sequence. Phytoplankton blooms quickly use up some or all of the nutrients in the water, making, in many natural situations, blooms self-limiting; once the nutrients are used up, the bloom ceases. But because the nutrients are continually replenished by the outflowing of sewage-enriched waters from the estuary, growth of the phytoplankton in the inner Bight occurs in great abundance.

Phytoplankton blooms in the Bight occur in greatest density near the mouth of the estuary and along the coasts. Bloom intensity may be so great that the waters become turbid, sometimes coffee colored. Because the phytoplankton are dependent upon light for their photosynthesis, blooms limit themselves by still further reducing light penetration (25). Where the bloom isn't so intense and light isn't a limiting factor, the nitrogen is usually the nutrient first depleted from the water and the one that becomes a limiting factor in controlling phytoplankton growth (26).

Feeding on the phytoplankton are small animals called zooplankton. In general, zooplankton are most abundant in spring near the shelf break and during the summer in the inner and near shore regions of the Bight (27). From 1,000 to 1,000,000 zooplankters may be present in a cubic meter of water in the estuary; as few as 10 to 10,000 per cubic meter of water near the shelf edge (28). The zooplankton, composed of many species of crustaceans, particularly copepods, and larvae of other animals, changes in character with the seasons. In general peak numbers are reached in summer and fall. Summer abundance is primarily related to an influx of larvae from other organisms commencing their reproductive cycle and from blooms of copepods. Fall peaks are due primarily to blooms of copepods. Zooplankton comprise the food for many species of fish. Their abundance and distribution may affect the distribution and occurrence of fish, but too little is known of the distribution of zooplankton to be able to draw parallels (29).

Living on the floor of the Bight are a group of animals called the benthos. Some benthic organisms are well known to us; for we catch them for food: shrimps, lobsters, clams, oysters. Others are food for fish as well as man. There are some whose role in the ecosystem is not as apparent, but is important: those whose burrowing in the bottom mix the sediments; those which process organic material and thus

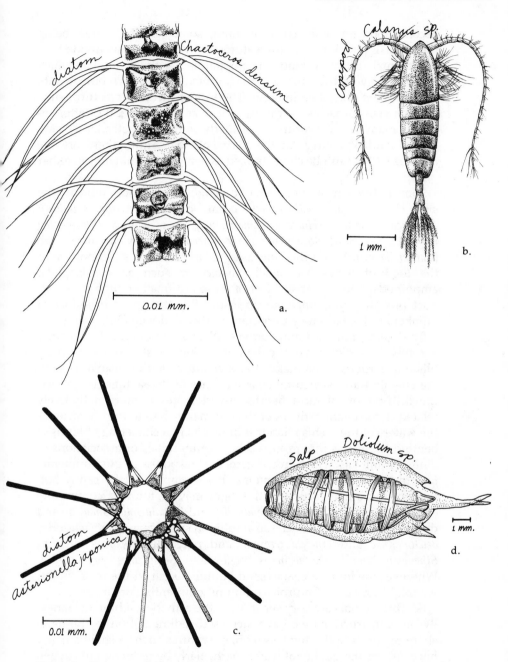

Figure 2. Common plankton of the New York Bight. Figures 2a and b are phytoplankton; figures 2b and d are zooplankton. (Drawings by Sharon Ellis)

become food for other creatures; and, some who by merely being there make places for other creatures to live. Zoologists divide benthic animals into two kinds. The epifauna are those animals which live primarily on the surface of the bottom. Those which burrow into the sediment are called infauna. The former includes creatures such as mussels, barnacles, shrimps, crabs, and lobsters; the latter includes many of the worms, particularly the polychaetes, and many clams. And of course, in the perversity of nature, there are the animals which can't be characterized as being predominately of either group.

Some of the benthic creatures of the Bight important as food are the surf clam (*Spisula solidissima*); ocean quahog (*Artica islandica*); American lobster (*Homarus americanus*); sea scallop (*Placopecten magellanicus*); hard clam (*Mercenaria mercenaria*); rock or cancer crab (*Cancer irroratus*); and the blue crab (*Callinectes sapidus*). Important in the food of fishes are small crustaceans such as the isopods, amphipods, and cumacea. Most of these are small enough not to attract our attention, only our curiosity. But they exist in sufficient numbers to be extremely important in the food web (30).

By digging burrows and tunnels other benthic animals structure and mix the sediments of the floor of the Bight just as the earthworm tills our gardens. This makes these creatures very sensitive to both the chemical and structural characteristics of the sediments. In fact, the distribution of most benthic invertebrates is more definitively related to the characteristics of the sediments than to the character of the water column. This relationship results in a clustering of kinds of benthic organisms into groups called communities or associations of kinds of animals which live together in response to environmental factors and their own interactions. For example, on the sandy bottoms of the inner portion of the Bight may be found a community consisting of the bivalves *Tellina agilis* and *Spisula solidissima*, a sand dollar *Echinarachnius parma*, the amphipod crustaceans *Protohaustorius deichmannae* and *Unciola irrorata*, and polychaete worms such as *Sthenelais limicola*, *Lumbrineris fragilis* and *Spiophanes bombyx* (31). Wherever medium to coarse sand bottoms occur in the inner Bight, we might expect to find this community of benthic organisms.

Benthic animals are very sensitive to the activities of human beings. By our constructions we have increased sedimentation in the near-shore region, smothering less mobile creatures such as shellfish, and have altered the quality of water, particularly by reduction of oxygen levels. While these impacts are severest in and near the estuary, the Bight's benthos has also been affected. The dumping of dredge spoils

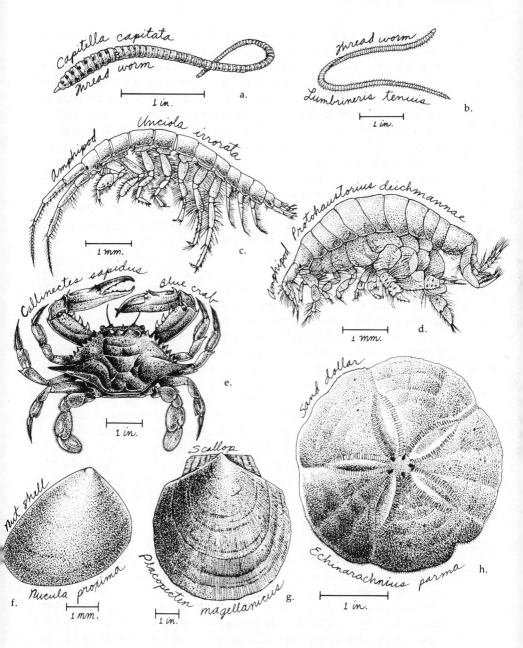

Figure 3. Some common benthic invertebrates from the New York Bight. Figures 3a and b are polychaete worms; c and d are amphipod crustaceans; e is a common crab; f and g are mollusks (clams); and, h is a sand dollar (echinoid). (Drawings by Sharon Ellis)

and sewage sludge changes the characteristics of the bottom sediments so that the organisms living where such alteration occurs may be smothered or unable to live. For example, fine, organically rich sediments collect in the Christiaensen Basin from the sludge dumping. These support a depauperate fauna consisting principally of large numbers of individuals of one species of polychaete worm, *Capitella capitata*. It is thought that this results from the high organic content of those sediments but may also be affected by low oxygen levels and/or toxic substances in the sediments (32). The absence of organisms such as the rock crab (*Cancer irroratus*) and the tube dwelling amphipods (*Unciola irrorata, Erichthonius rubricornis* and several species of *Ampelisca*) from the most contaminated areas of the inner Bight means that fish which might feed upon these organisms, and others which are associated with them, will also be absent.

More than 300 species of fish are known from the New York Bight, but few may be called "natives" or year-round residents. Most are transients, visiting seasonally. The fish of the Bight are species found, more characteristically, in the cool waters of the northern Atlantic or in the warmer waters of the mid-Atlantic. Although one study of about 250 species of shore fish of the Bight found that about 75% were tropical or warm temperate forms which move north of Cape Hatteras only in summer months (33), most ichthyologists would consider the Bight to be more northern than southern in its fish. For example, as few as 10 species may now be considered as "residents" of the Bight, if one defines residents as species which spawn there. Included in this group would be the dusky shark, snake eel, blueback herring, lined seahorse, striped bass, tilefish, scup, blackbelly rosefish, summer flounder, and windowpane flounder. The longfin squid, although not a fish, could also be classed as a resident (34).

Further, with seasonal shifts, the composition of the fish fauna changes extensively. In autumn somewhat over half of the fish present are "southern," and about a third "northern." In the spring, however, the northern and southern components of the fish fauna are more evenly divided (35). The reason that the Bight has so many migratory species, and relatively few kinds of fish that "characterize" it, is the great variation in water temperature which occurs through the course of the year. Surface temperature of inshore waters can range over 25°C. between summer and winter, while nearshore bottom waters may range over 20°C. When water temperatures rise in the spring there is an influx of warm water forms such as drums, jacks and bluefish, while a number of cold water forms such as cod, Atlantic herring, alewives, mackerel, spiny dogfish, and shad migrate out of the Bight to the north. As water temperatures begin to drop in fall, warm water species such as the summer flounder, butterfish, longfin squid, the hakes, and sea bass begin to migrate offshore toward deeper and warmer waters and to the south (36).

Because of this migratory pattern that brings a diversity of fish to the Bight, it has been an important fishery since the seventeenth century. Harvests have, however, been declining since the late 1930s, a result both of overfishing and the effects of pollution (37). Some of the important species of finfish caught commercially are the scup, weakfish, Atlantic mackerel, American shad, haddock, bluefish, summer flounder, winter flounder, yellowtail flounder, butterfish, black sea bass, Atlantic cod, and striped bass. Formerly fished intensively by the foreign fleets were species such as the red and silver hake, Atlantic herring, and squid. These may be increasingly harvested by Bight fishermen in the future. Menhaden, once accounting for much of the total tonnage of fish caught in the Bight, is fished for the oil made from its carcass. This fishery has been severely affected by overexploitation to the south and by restrictions placed on its harvest by well-meaning legislatures. Fishing for menhaden has been banned because many sport fishermen believe it to be a forage fish for such prized species as the striped bass and the bluefish and because the "bunker boats" which caught menhaden worked nearshore and often left an oily plume easily visible to beach-goers (38).

Some fish in the Bight suffer from fin rot and other diseases. Fin rot is the erosion of the fins and the skin around them, to the point where the fins are lost. Winter flounder are most susceptible. Of nearly 5,000 fish examined in one study, 14% of those taken from the inner Bight had fin rot while only 1.9% of those from other parts had the disease (39). Other studies confirm the relationship between the occurrence of fin rot and the dumping of sewage sludge and dredge spoils in the inner Bight (40).

"The New York Bight region not only has large, often spectacular, numbers of aquatic and terrestrial birds but also includes critically important marine and coastal habitats" (41). Among those bird habitats are nesting grounds for gulls, terns, herons, and rails; wintering grounds for ducks, geese, loons, grebes, and others and temporary refuges for migrating species. Over 400 species of birds have been observed in the Bight region. But it may be the phenomenal numbers of migrants in spring and autumn for which the Bight is most noted. One of the more unusual bird habitats of the Bight region is Jamaica Bay Wildlife Refuge, above which towers the skyscraper skyline of Manhattan. Bordered by the Boroughs of Brooklyn and

Queens and the Town of Hempstead, Jamaica Bay has over 300 species of birds, nearly half of all the species recorded occurring in the continental U.S. The Refuge is surrounded by residences of over 600,000 people (within 2 miles of the shore), with an overall density of 18,000 persons per square mile, and bounded on the east by John F. Kennedy International Airport. It has been used and abused as a sewage outfall and for garbage disposal, and dredged for a deep-water port. The 4,000 acres of remaining marsh are one of the world's most unusual birding areas (42).

Human activities, particularly destruction of wetlands and the general urbanization of the region, have had a pronounced effect upon bird populations. About 20% of the species breeding in wetlands have shown population decreases in the past 30 years. Others such as the Snowy Egret and the Glossy Ibis have increased greatly in numbers, presumably because of increased food supply at wetland landfills. Ditching of wetlands to reduce mosquito populations and later, the widespread use of DDT for the same purpose had enormous impact on breeding populations. Offshore marine birds seem to have a greater propensity for uptake of chemical contaminants. PCBs and other chlorinated hydrocarbons are often found in much higher concentrations in the flesh of these birds than in land birds. Poisoning by lead and mercury is also of concern in bird populations around the Bight. Oil spills can have a profound, although usually local, effect on water bird populations (43).

But birds also can affect man, and have done so around the margins of the Bight. Eastern Equine Encephalitis is caused by a virus transmitted by mosquitoes but birds may serve as a reservoir. This disease has caused the deaths of many hundreds of horses in New Jersey and New York, affects the commercial raising of ducks, pheasants, and other birds, and was, in 1959, responsible for 22 deaths among southern New Jersey coastal residents (44). Migrant birds seem to play an important role in transporting this disease and may be responsible for periodic epidemics. Local governments around the Bight have responded to the encephalitis hazard by extensive ditching of wetlands to reduce mosquito populations. Pesticides, particularly DDT, offered a less costly procedure which was extensively utilized. A result, prior to its use being banned in 1972, was widespread impact upon wetland invertebrate faunas and severe reduction in many bird populations. Even today it is believed that these wetlands remain an important reservoir of DDT and its residues (45).

1 in.

a.

Snowy egret Egretta thula

b.

Least tern Sterna albifrons

1 in.

c.

Herring gull Larus argentatus

1 in.

d.

Black skimmer Rynchops niger

1 in.

Figure 4. Some characteristic birds of the New York Bight region. (Drawings by Sharon Ellis)

Aquatic mammals were once abundant in the New York Bight region and formed the basis for an early whaling industry. As the whales were overfished, many whalers turned to shellfishing. Today, the Bight sees occasional marine mammals, but most are transients. Seals have been spotted in the Bight in recent times, and porpoises have been sighted in the Hudson River. Over 10 species of whale are recorded from the Bight, but of these, only the beaked whales (*Mesoplodon*) seem to be present with frequency (46).

Of all the species, however, *Homo sapiens* is the one that has made the most profound mark on the Bight. Although this species was once quite rare, it has grown in abundance. The lands surrounding the Bight everywhere show evidence of the presence of man, and although the ability of *Homo sapiens* to affect the oceans has been primarily at its margins and its surface, there is growing evidence that his capability goes further. Pollution-induced disease among marine organisms now extends to the ocean; occurrence of manufactured toxic chemicals such as DDT, PCBs and PAHs (petroleum aromatic hydrocarbons) are now global problems. We will now look at the relationship between that species and the Bight in greater detail.

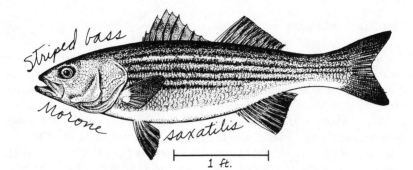

striped bass

Morone saxatilis

1 ft.

2 / The Margins of the Bight

Land creeps almost stealthily from beneath the waters of the Bight. No stout cliffs facing the onslaught of the ocean here: mostly a low, indistinct sand fringe backed by green vegetation almost obscured by the salt haze. New Jersey's highlands, the only relief from the flat landscape, were mistaken by early explorers for a series of islands standing out from the coast.

Shores loom more distinctly as you approach the neck of the Bight's funnel. But here the bottom shallows dangerously, for off the lower harbor a crescent of shifting bars and shoals extends from Sandy Hook to Rockaway Point, marking the terminus of the Bight and the beginning of the Hudson-Raritan Estuary. Once safely over the bars you are in a complex of protected waters—drowned river mouths—the debouchment of the Hudson, Raritan, and Passaic rivers, the estuary.

The Bight's boundaries then are the North Atlantic Ocean, the beaches of Long Island and New Jersey on the sides, and the Hudson-Raritan estuarine complex at the funnel or apex end. This chapter explores two of these margins—the sandy shores and the estuary—the points at which man and the Bight are in most direct and extensive contact. These margins are where different ecological systems and social turfs come into contact, fragile boundaries where delicacy and sensitivity are the keynotes. Has the heavy hand of man altered this delicacy? Shattered this fragility? The future of the Bight area may rest with the answers.

The Sandy Margins

Forming a broad V-shaped funnel that closes to the northwest are two chains of offshore bars and shallow lagoons backed by the mainland. On the northern side, Long Island's 118 miles of beaches stretch from Montauk to Rockaway Points incorporating such well-known colonies and playgrounds as the Hamptons, Fire Island, Jones Beach, and Coney Island. On the south, the Jersey Shore's 124 mile stretch extends from Cape May to Sandy Hook (1). Here are scattered the famous early resorts of the coast: Atlantic City, Asbury Park, and Long Branch.

Shores composed of beautiful beaches and submarine shoals are dynamic, uncertain, and hazardous in the face of North Atlantic wave and wind attack. A complex ecosystem of plants, invertebrates, and birds reacting to continual change in their physical environment of shifting sands, this margin is also the playground for megalopolites numbering over 19 million (2). The sandy vistas stretch back to the horizon to be replaced by the concrete canyons of the cities and the macadam creeks of suburbia. The beaches are a place for solitude, nature, or people watching, a place to sun and bathe and chase a ball. The beach is also the place where the enormous energy of the ocean's waves are absorbed by the continual movement of sand up and down and across its slope. Man persists in dwelling where he plays, but where there is capital investment there must be stability. How much are we willing to expend in a vain attempt to stabilize nature's dynamics? To counteract her enormous forces?

For almost two hundred years after discovery, the Bight's sandy shores were bypassed. An absence of protected anchorages, sparse water supplies, generally poor soils, little useable timber, a network of shifting navigation channels but mostly constant exposure to the full force of Atlantic storms made the shores unattractive. Only scattered life-saving stations, lighthouses, and beach fishing shacks disturbed coastal tranquility. By the late 1800s increasing affluence and easier transport made beach bathing popular for the growing populations of greater New York and Philadelphia. Coastal resorts grew up around oceanfront railheads and ferry landing points and gradually spread along roads radiating from such places.

Nevertheless, much of the Bight's shores remained undeveloped until after the second world war. Initially overrun by the wave of returning veterans seeking homes and aided in their search by now cheap gasoline and automobiles, it was then overtaken by a second wave of construction of leisure-time, second homes. Aided by high-

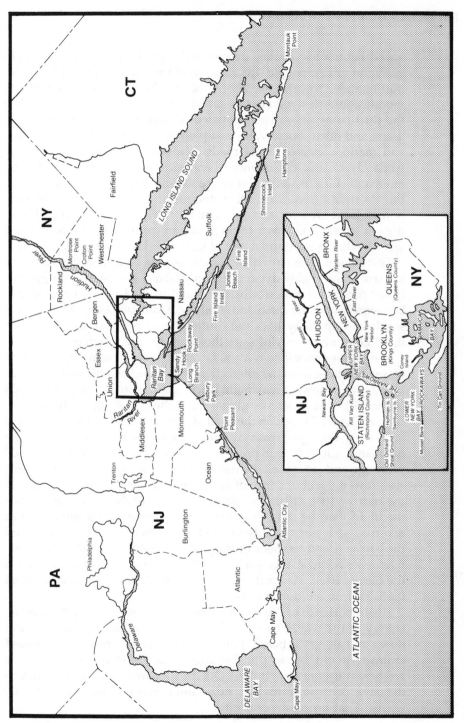

Figure 5. The New York Bight and Hudson-Raritan Bay Estuary Regions. (Map by Sharon Ellis)

speed automobile routes, decentralized job locations, and inexpensive land prices, people streamed out of the cities and moved, disproportionately, toward the shores of the Bight. Massive landscape modifications designed to facilitate coastal settlement and to stabilize the fluctuating shore were initiated. Dunes were leveled, wetlands diked and filled, boardwalks and piers extended, harbors expanded, and marinas created. New roads, bridges, and causeways crossed wetlands to link the offshore bars with each other and with the mainland. Groins, jetties, revetments and seawalls sprouted along the shore in efforts to contain diminishing beaches, to shield new homes from erosion, and to maintain navigation channels. Homes pressed closer and closer to the beach in competition for access and view. Today, a substantial part of the coastal fringe has been altered.

This sought after strip of land between the Bight and the continent is narrow and highly dynamic. Along most of the Bight's margin this fringe consists of a narrow barrier island with a lagoon or narrow bay between it and the mainland. Only at Montauk, Long branch, and southern Cape May does the continent come in direct contact with the Bight, and there bluffs are the characteristic interface.

The present shoreline is a good example of long-term dynamic processes resulting from the interaction of sea level change and sediment migration. Following maximum glaciation at least 15,000 years ago (3) sea level began to rise as glacial ice melted. It is likely that barrier islands formed far out on the shelf at the oceans edge and that, as sea level rose, they progressively migrated across the shelf toward the mainland. Close to our present sea level was reached about 3,000 years ago and since then the rise has been much slower. As the rate of rise slowed, an abundance of sand was accessible to wave action and the narrow strip of barrier island widened, probably mostly toward the Bight. For the last 600 to 1,000 years, however, the situation has reversed—a lesser quantity of sand is available to wave attack—and the barrier island has been eroding and migrating laterally. This situation arises because once sea level stabilizes, the only source of sand is the barrier itself. As barrier sand is carried laterally or offshore from the island, it is reduced in size.

The importance of the beach to the shore is in the dissipation of the energy of the waves by myriads of sand grains being rolled up and down and along the beach. But sand is lost in the process. Some sand grains wear out, become smaller and are carried into deeper water, or are blown up onto the dunes. Others are carried through inlets into the bays. Because of this loss, new sand is brought into motion by the waves. That process is erosion.

Movement of sand along the beach is called littoral drift. Most commonly, waves approach the shore at an angle. As a result, a part of the wave energy is directed parallel to the shoreline and carries sand along the shore. Because of the direction of prevailing waves, Long Island's beaches have drift to the west; on the New Jersey shore, north of the headlands extending from Long Branch to Point Pleasant, drift is to the north; and south of those headlands drift is to the south. Transport of sand by littoral drift results in the prolongation of spits at inlets and bay mouths. Sandy Hook is a classic example of such a spit, growing longer each year until finally its growth has been artificially stopped by dredging its growing tip. Such movement is vast—estimates at Fire Island Inlet suggest 450,000 cubic yards of sand are transported there each year (4)—this is roughly the quantity of sand which could be carried by a train of 4,500 gondola cars 200 miles long.

In areas where the barrier island is particularly narrow, storms may carry sand over the island into the bays. This process of washover is responible for the migration of the barrier island toward the mainland. As the island narrows, with less and less sand accessible to the waves, washover is increased; new inlets may even form where the washover is frequent.

Inlets interrupt the flow of sand along the beaches because the drift in part enters the bays and is lost to the flow. Artificial bypassing is a scheme by which such sand is dredged and replaced on the downdrift side of the inlet to continue the flow. When sand is lost to the drift system, there will be compensatory erosion downdrift of the point of loss.

Thus, there is a three-dimensional movement of the shore in response to the forces of winds, waves, tides, currents, and changes in sea level: a movement of the whole system toward the mainland. A building and tearing down of beaches and dunes goes on in response to natural processes: processes critical to us for we depend upon the barrier beach to protect the mainland from direct attack by the ocean and to lessen the effects of storm flooding. As we have built houses, communities and villages on the barrier bars we have exacerbated conditions, for property owners demand stability in return for their investment. As the offshore barrier system loses its ability to respond dynamically, its value as a natural barrier between ourselves and the ocean is lost.

Calculating the rate of change of the shore is a difficult task. Individual storms may massively resculpture beaches only to be followed by long periods of seeming stability. Winter beaches suffer more than summer because of the different frequency and intensity of storms. For example, parts of Sandy Hook have eroded as much as 70 feet per year over the past five years, although the long-term average is 17 feet per year. It has been suggested that the 1970s were twice as stormy as the 1950s, resulting in greater wave generation (5). A series of aerial photographs of the New Jersey coast used to calculate the longer term rate of change (6) showed that while rates varied from place to place, an average of 1 to 4 feet per year of erosion had occurred. Examination of historic charts and maps confirmed this as a long-term trend.

To slow erosion we have constructed great structures of rocks hundreds of tons each in weight or have driven steel piling into the sand. Emplacement of these groins and jetties entraps sand, preventing its migration in littoral drift. Wave attack results in down-groin erosion and a reduction in the sediment available for littoral drift. The result of groin construction is often that the profile of the shore is steepened and sediment is lost from the beaches to deeper waters. For many years we built these structures confident in the belief that they would halt the processes of nature. Orderly, fingerlike, projections of groins march along sections of the Bight's coast. But as we learned more of the mechanisms of shore erosion, we learned that stopping the forces of nature is not so simple. Today there is a counter movement. Many people, and government agencies, are reluctant to seek these expensive, and often futile, solutions to shoreline movement.

Except for its eastern portion, Long Island's coast is typified by barrier islands and landward bays. At Montauk the 60–70 foot high bluffs formed by the Ronkonkoma moraine are being rapidly eroded; narrow beaches extend from Montauk about 10 miles west. From Shinnecock westward, a barrier island separates the upland from the Bight. At Shinnecock Inlet the barrier spit has been shifting inland at about 2 feet per year for over a century (7,8). At Fire Island Inlet rates of beach change vary: 2 to 3 miles east of the inlet the beach receded 2,200 feet in the period of 1833 to 1956; 2 to 3 miles to the west of the inlet, there was a buildup of 1,200 feet in the same period (9).

New Jersey's shore differs from Long Island's in that glacial deposits do not supply the materials from which the beaches are formed. There are three differing segments of this coast: (1.) Sandy Hook, a barrier spit, at the north; (2.) the Highlands; a bedrock headland; and (3.) a southerly series of barrier beaches. The bedrock segment is about 16 miles long, extending from Long Branch south to Point Pleasant Beach. Here the beach is a narrow strip of sand beneath cliffs 10 to 20 feet high.

Sandy Hook, about 10 miles long, is a product of northward littoral drift. The hook has been breached at various times, but has been resealed either naturally or by man. Prior to the installation of a seawall, the spit was retreating at an annual rate of 7 feet per year with the sediment accreting at the end of the hook (10). The seawall, an armor of rock placed along the southern end of the spit, halted erosion, but some have objected to its appearance and the absence of beach. The hook has built out about 1 mile since 1760, but its growth has been terminated by channel maintenance dredging just off the tip.

South of Sandy Hook is a barrier island strip about 90 miles long. Its rates of erosion vary from 8 feet per year to accumulations of 2 feet per year, but much of the coast has been "stabilized" by man-made structures in recent years. Cape May was eroding at a rate of over 15 feet per year from 1842 to 1965 (11), a loss of 360 feet of shore.

Barrier islands are characterized by dunes 20 to 30 feet high formed by wind-blown beach sands. Gaps in the dune crests result from blowouts or washover. Behind the ocean-side beaches are primary, or first-line dunes: Landward of these may be wet swales followed by another line of dunes. Between the island and the mainland is usually a marsh or lagoon, called a bay. But all of these features are ephemeral and today's dune may be tomorrow's beach.

A variety of invertebrates inhabits the beaches. Historically, at least, sea turtles came ashore to lay eggs there, and terns and gulls nested on the strand above high water, especially on spits at inlets. Above extreme high-water line the first plants to appear usually are a few annuals such as seaside spurge and sea rocket. Beach grass is abundant on foredunes and serves to anchor them most effectively because it survives sand burial and spreads rapidly. After overwash in storms, incipient dunes are frequently formed when fragments of beach plants grow out of the organically rich drift lines, entrap blowing sand, and begin to increase in mass.

On back dunes and in swales shrubs grow with many species of herbaceous plants, often forming dense thickets of beach plum, bayberry, and poison ivy, the most common species. Shrub height is controlled by salt-laden wind spray that planes off the exposed tips of plants growing above the dune line. The tallest plants grow in the lee of dunes and in hollows. On barer areas, seaside goldenrod and beach heather are common. Small mammals and land birds are far more numerous here, especially when in spring and autumn migration thousands of songbirds concentrate on the barrier islands. Sands blown from dunes and overwash fans may engulf and cover low vegetation, leading to colonization by woody vines like Virginia creeper and poison ivy. Generally, the density and diversity of plant cover increases with distance from the ocean front.

Tucked away in interdunal hollows, or in the lee of large dunes, are maritime forests characterized by dwarfed and wind-shaped American hollies, sassafras, shadbush, with blueberries, catbriars, foxgrapes with herbaceous species beneath. The trees of these forests may be more than 200 years old and give a false sense of stability to the barrier island system. Deer herds may live here and in some places the very tallest treetops still support colonies of herons and egrets. Small mammals—foxes, mink, raccoons, as well as rodents and rabbits—all occur in numbers in this zone. Few stands of mature maritime forest still exist in the Bight, but there are notable examples at Fire Island, at Sandy Hook, Island Beach, and Little Beach Island.

Bayward of the maritime forest area, low stands of shrubs blend gradually into the high salt marsh (*Spartina patens*), normally flooded only during spring tides. Here live many marsh invertebrates and birds, and here breeds the infamous salt marsh mosquito. High marsh becomes the low, or *Spartina alterniflora*, salt marsh, flooded by high tides. Its productivity is a major source of energy transfer in the coastal estuarine ecosystem, and its tall grasses support large numbers of species and individuals of finfish and shellfish at various stages in their life cycles, as well as thousands of waterfowl, shorebirds, and herons which feed there.

Fresh water is especially critical on barrier islands—for man as well as for native flora and fauna. There is usually a "lense" of freshwater just beneath (or sometimes breaking) the soil surface, surrounded on the sides and below by salt water. This lense is accumulated rainfall on the island and is not connected with mainland groundwater. On larger islands the fresh water may be more or less permanent, on smaller ones highly ephemeral. Availability of soil moisture, water salinity, and depth to water table serves to determine types of vegetation and animal life on the barrier islands. Small depressions in which the freshwater table is at or near the surface for much of the year support bogs or marshes with various orchids, sundews, and pitcher plants. Such marshes are also the site of mosquito breeding and during the 1930s and 1940s were extensively ditched to provide drainage. In the 1950s and 1960s DDT and other insecticides replaced ditching in the attempt to control mosquitoes. The effects upon both invertebrate and vertebrate life in the wetlands were nearly disastrous. With discontinuance of the use of such chemicals, public health officials keep a close watch, for marsh mosquitoes may be a pool from which equine encephalitis is carried.

Man and the Coastal Fringe

When we use the coastal region, we may build structures: highways, houses, bathouses, boardwalks and other great works. These capital investments carry with them our unspoken message to nature, "Do not disturb." We modify the shape of the coast by leveling dune fields, widening beaches and constructing seawalls and groins to stabilize beaches. In doing this we fail to recognize the fundamental truth: we are seeking environmental stability in a system characterized by natural dynamic change.

Our approach to environmental stability is usually brute force. We build solid massive structures to stop the assault of the waves on the proverbial shifting sands, for nature designed a fluid system to absorb the energies of waves and winds. Each sand grain rolled about on the beach or the dune requires an expenditure of energy by wind or wave; the cumulative total is substantial—more than we can put forth with bulldozers and concrete.

Coastal geomorphology and the physics of beach dynamics are not yet exact sciences: reliable forecasts cannot be made of beach and dune behavior under varying weather, wind, and wave conditions. Nor is it possible to predict exactly what will happen to this behavior if engineering structures are placed to interfere with natural processes (12).

Problems arise when unstable barrier islands are converted into valuable real estate. Professor Joseph Heikoff described those difficulties and uncertainties involved in using structural solutions to attempt to stop the natural processes of shore erosion.

The U.S. Army Corps of Engineers was assigned the responsibility for protecting the nation's shorelines. One of its studies showed that part of Long Island's Westhampton Beach, west of Shinnecock Inlet, had receded 500 feet between 1940 and 1960. Since colonial days, the area had been hit by 126 severe storms. The maximum hurricane tide of record occurred in 1938, when 45 lives were lost. The Westhampton Beach project was part of a long-term program to rebuild the beaches and dunes from Fire Island Inlet to Montauk Point. About 34 million cubic yards would have to be placed initially, and about 480,000 cubic yards would be required annually to keep up with continuing erosion. Groins were to be constructed only if experience showed they were necessary. Their purpose would be to stabilize the fill, not to trap sand from the shore current to build up the beach.

The project was financed originally by a 52% federal contribution and 24% shares each by New York State and Suffolk County. A field of 11 groins was constructed in the middle of Westhampton Beach after a storm had damaged valuable properties there. Suffolk County, however, refused to pay the cost of dune reconstruction and the placement of beach fill between the groins. The results were predictable. Only eight months after the groins had been finished, they had robbed enough sand from the shore current to cause serious erosion to the beaches to the west of the groin field. New York State, Suffolk County, and the property owners persuaded the Corps to again go against its own design recommendations. Four additional groins were built to the west of the first field, but no dune and beach fills were placed here either. Again there was severe erosion further west, and a project was prepared to build six more groins. By this time, however, a new county executive had been elected, and he opposed further groin construction. He vetoed appropriations for the county share of financing on the grounds that more groins would only cause more erosion to the west, and that all county taxpayers should not have to support the property values of a few wealthy summer residents on Westhampton Beach. The project for the new six-groin field was abandoned in favor of a project of continual pumping of beach fill from the Atlantic Ocean bottom to replace beach sand lost by erosion (13).

No uniform policy exists among governmental agencies responsible for the shore region. For example, the U.S. Army Corps of Engineers, a primary actor in shore restructuring, has extensively studied the Bight's shores and made major proposals. These generally recommend maintenance of the existing shorelines and prevention of damage to human settlements by storm surge. Specifically, the corps recommends establishing and maintaining a high dune ridge to protect against coastal flooding. On the other hand, the National Park Service, a major steward of public coastal lands, maintains a philosophy that the shoreline system should function as naturally as possible. Its policies permit access while permitting natural modification. New Jersey has a state position on coastal erosion and has developed guidelines by which the coast should be managed. In general, these recognize the dynamic nature of the shoreline and stress a need to become less dependent upon beach protection structures. New York has also developed a state policy, but it relies upon its local governments to develop a stance: because of political influence at the local level, such stances may vary from time to time and place to place.

Housing developed rapidly in the sandy soils of the coastal fringe. Builders in these areas found that sewage fields or cesspools were highly functional for disposal of sewage. But development has now saturated the capability of the soils to absorb effluents, and runoff contributes to serious pollution of the lagoons and bays. Over 39% of New Jersey and Long Island coastal waters are closed to shellfishing as a result of sewage contamination (14). Construction of sewage-treatment plants creates a different problem. Many of New Jersey's and some of Long Island's treatment plants will export groundwater from the land to the ocean through pipes to ocean outfalls. Such exportation of fresh water lessens underground flows into the bays, resulting in higher salinities that may have a profound impact upon their productivity. Among other effects, increased salinities allow the entrance of starfish, highly efficient predators upon shellfish. And, existing sewage-treatment technology doesn't result in the removal of nutrients from sewage, nutrients which may be responsible for local eutrophication of bays.

As the sandy beaches and dunes were occupied, builders turned their eyes toward the extensive areas of marsh along the coasts. Before the 1960s there was little public awareness of the productive value of these "swamps" and they were quickly filled to create "new land" for homes and other amenities. Between 1964 and 1972, 17% of Long Island's wetlands were filled in and are now lost as productive areas (15). Before 1970, New Jersey was losing its wetlands at a rate of 1900 acres per year. After it had protected its tidal wetlands by state law, the rate slowed to 30 acres per year (16). Another destructive, but popular innovation is the "Florida canal," a means of creating a housing development in which homeowners can dock their vessel at their property. These long, dead-end, unnatural estuaries rapidly become stagnent backwaters quickly accumulating fine sediments and requiring continual maintenance dredging. Over 30,000 or more building lots of this design have been constructed on at least 10,000 acres along the enclosed bays between Cape May Point and Sandy Hook (17).

The margin of the Bight is constantly exposed to the natural forces that have shaped it, but nature is not always benign. A single storm can cause more damage in one episode than might occur over the lifetime of some property owner. While coastal erosion is most dramatic during winter storms, hurricanes are probably the largest single storm event occurring in the Bight. The track of these has, for about two decades, altered, so that their frequency is less, but the annual risk remains from 1% to 6%. With hurricanes and other storms come wind damage, flooding, and beach erosion. Despite continuing efforts to devise foolproof protection, loss of life and extensive property damage seem to inevitably follow. For example, the March 1962 northeaster killed 14 persons in New Jersey, injured more than 1,300, destroyed nearly 2,000 buildings, and damaged 14,000 others (18).

Disaster caused by a major storm is exacerbated by our short memories. Most of the people now living in the coastal region have not been through a hurricane. Each summer there is a massive influx of visitors to beach resorts, most of whom are not concerned about property protection and who have probably not experienced any coastal storm. Their interests and values are in making the most of their short stay. But older resorts such as Long Beach have become year-round communities and have populations who wish to preserve their properties. And too, senior citizens, the handicapped, and hospitalized persons who have special transportation requirements are all among the residents of the coastal fringe. There are few shelters on barrier islands; highways may be inadequate to handle an evacuation, as is demonstrated each weekend during the summer when the exodus of holidayers clogs traffic. The risk of raising false alarms during storm periods is more than some public officials can bear and there are signs that people who have experienced an early warning false alarm, such as the 1976 Hurricane Belle alert on Fire Island, may not be so willing to depart in the future.

The fact remains that each and every storm will bring some risk to life and property to the ever-increasing population of the coastal fringe. Eighty-four percent of the 280-mile ocean front of the Bight is classified as critically eroding (19). Five to six times a year an extratropical storm brings a storm surge with a height of 2 or more feet and its potential for causing flooding (20). And each threatens to be more expensive, for the residents of coastal regions are increasingly the more affluent members of our society, who build increasingly expensive structures.

Most alteration of the sandy margin of the Bight occurs because each of us seeks to protect our rights there. Property owners suffering erosion try to stem the course of nature in an ever more expensive battle. When costs escalate beyond their means they seek to transfer part of the expense to the taxpaying public. Recreationists seek access, and confronted by private lands, urge public acquisition of beaches and rights-of-way. Conservationists want to protect the disappearing habitats and the vanishing tidelands through governmental intercession. The public official, caught among all of these often conflicting desires, acceeds to the perceived greatest pressures. The choice may be the right one for the future, but the process of decision is largely luck, not knowledge.

The Estuarine Terminus

New York's qualifications [as a port] are evident, too, when you see it from the air. It might have been man-made as a port, so neatly functional is its shape and situation. On the northeastern coast of the United States, between latitudes 40° and 41° North, two large chunks of land stand out from the coastline like breakwaters. One is the flank of New Jersey, with its long line of reefs; the other is Long Island in the State of New York, a splendid boulevard, a hundred miles long, of sand, marsh, and grassland. These two land masses approach each other at an angle, and very nearly meet: they are separated by the entrance to New York Bay.

It is a wonderfully sheltered, secretive opening. Long Island protects it from the northern gales, the arm of sand called Sandy Hook reaches out from New Jersey to embrace its channel from the south, and the bulk of Staten Island stands like a cork in the middle. The mariner enters it sailing almost due west, but a few miles from the open sea he turns abruptly north, passes through the bottleneck of the Narrows, leaves Staten Island on his port side, and finds himself in the glorious security of the upper bay—gales and high seas left behind, even the sea birds domesticated, as he steams snugly between Brooklyn and Bayonne towards the comforts of the metropolis.

This is the lordly front door of New York—the carriage sweep. There is a kitchen entrance too, for between Long Island and the mainland there lies Long Island Sound, sixty miles of sheltered water linking the port with the Atlantic by a back route. This will also take a seafarer into the upper bay, via the tidal strait called the East River, while from the American interior the noble Hudson River flows into the Bay out of the north, mingling its icy fresh waters with the salt tide of the Atlantic. Diverse other creeks and rivers debouch into New York Bay, and all around are little islands, inlets, and spits, forming a watery sort of filigree upon the large-scale charts. (21)

At the end of the broad funnel formed by the sandy margins of the Bight is an estuary, the Hudson-Raritan Estuary. Here the fresh waters from the land, gathered into streams and rivers, flow into the Bight. There are other, smaller, estuaries around the Bight such as the Mullica River in New Jersey and the Connetquat River on Long

Island, but they are socially and environmentally insignificant compared to the Hudson-Raritan. Here, in an area of 155 square miles of complex geographic, ecologic, and oceanographic interactions, man has built the nation's greatest port-city complex. And, in the same area man's actions interact with and affect the Bight most profoundly.

Estuaries are important in the ecology of coastal waters because they are the dynamic and complex place where fresh and salt waters meet. Differing in their chemistry, their physics, and their biology, the mixing of these waters creates unusual environmental richness, diversity, and productivity. Estuaries are important in human affairs because their protected waters are easiest for human-scale relationships with the vastness of the ocean. For shipping and receiving of cargos, for the disposal of unwanted wastes, and for getting close to the water and the sense of calm and well-being the waterscape brings, estuaries are where people congregate. Of the 50 largest cities of the world, half are situated on an estuary, with another third located further up river from the estuary—only 7 are isolated from the coast. Each of these coastal cities shares the same problem: alteration and pollution of the estuarine environment is severe. The Hudson-Raritan Estuary is no exception, for here was fostered the development of a large population center and a vast industrial complex. We have profoundly altered the natural system which once existed there—by digging, dredging, filling, bulkheading, and polluting with sewage, metals, construction debris, industrial and chemical wastes, spills of oils and other chemicals—almost beyond recognition.

In an estuary the salt waters of the ocean are diluted by the freshwater flow of rivers which empty into it. Action of the tides also carries salt water up the rivers against the flow of fresh water. That portion of the river containing ocean salts is properly a part of the estuary. Tidal forces may cause tides even above that point of saltwater intrusion. This portion of a river, affected by the tides, but without ocean salts, is not a part of the estuary but is called the tidal river.

In a tidal river the water is sloshed back and forth by the tide and the flow of the river is no longer simply in one direction. The interplay of friction, which retards the flow of water near the banks and bottom, and tidal forces causes complex water movements. But in the tidal section of the river, over a period of several tidal cycles, there is net movement of water downstream. In the lower, estuarine, segment of the river, where salt waters from the ocean have penetrated upstream, a salt wedge is formed. Salt water because it is denser, stays near the bottom. Less dense, fresh river water flows out over the top. As the fresh water flows over the salt, it mixes with it and becomes more salty until, in the ocean, normal seawater salinity is reached. Even in the estuarine section, there is, over time, a net movement down the river.

Defining the Hudson-River Estuarine System is difficult to do with precision. It meets the Bight along the crescent of slowly shifting bars and interspersed channels between Sandy Hook and Rockaway Point. It includes the basin of the Raritan River to Bound Brook, New Jersey; the watershed of the Passaic River to Patterson, New Jersey; and the connection between Long Island Sound and the estuary, the East River. Comprising the estuary are the Lower Hudson River, Harlem River, East River, Upper Bay of New York Harbor, Newark Bay, the Kill Van Kull, Arthur Kill, Raritan Bay, Jamaica Bay, and Lower Bay of New York Harbor and all their tributaries. But where the estuary ends and rivers begin is almost arbitrary for that boundary continually shifts in response to freshwater flow, tidal stage, and other factors.

The Hudson River carries most of the fresh water flowing into the estuary, draining an area of 13,370 square miles. Not a large river as rivers go, the Hudson (thirty-first among U.S. rivers as measured by flow, ninety-eighth as measured by length) for the first half of its length is a river simply flowing in one direction, downhill. At the Federal Dam at Troy, the last dam downstream, the "tidal river" commences, for here is the "head of the tide." The wedge of salt water pulled upriver by the tides usually reaches upriver to a position somewhere about Poughkeepsie. Below this upriver encroachment of salt water, the river is a part of the estuary. The Hudson's numerous tributaries flow from the relatively undisturbed and forested lands of the Adirondacks and Catskills, as well as the agricultural lands of the Hudson Valley region. Its principal tributary, the Mohawk River, drains the fertile agricultural lands of northern New York. The Hackensack and Passaic Rivers which enter the estuary at Newark Bay and the Raritan, Rahway, and Elizabeth Rivers, which discharge into Raritan Bay, have a drainage area of 2,942 square miles.

The estuary acts as a catchment for natural and man-related materials originating both in its drainage basin and from spills in the port, from land- and street-runoff, and sewage and industrial wastes discharged from outfalls. These "additives" complicate the chemical composition of the waters of the estuary. Physical processes such as tides and tidal and wind-induced currents, freshwater discharge and storms, mix and muddle the waters so that the distribution of their properties is complex. Lying in the path of many of the storms that move regularly across the mid-Atlantic states, the Hudson-Raritan

Estuary is usually subject to storm conditions every one to two weeks during the winter. Because it is relatively shallow (depths of up to nearly 70 feet do occur) and has an irregular topography of shoals, banks, and ship channels, these mixing processes, let alone such matters as tides and circulation, are difficult to describe.

Estuary and Bight are connected two ways. The major connection is the opening over the bars between the Sandy Hook and Rockaway spits. The other, the "backdoor," is through the East River to Long Island Sound. The East River, however, is different from what we usually consider a river to be; in fact it is more properly called a tidal strait, for it connects two bodies of salt water.

Just as movement of water within the estuary, particularly the harbor portion, is complex, so to is the relationship of estuary and ocean or, in our interests, harbor and Bight. Because the rivers flowing into the harbor are adding water, there must be a flow from the harbor to the Bight. But it is confused by the surging of waters from tides, winds, and other forces. Less dense, less saline waters in the estuary flow outward on top of more dense, more saline waters from the Bight pulled into the estuary by the tides. Averaged over a tidal cycle, that is through both rising and falling tides, flow outward or seaward through nearly three-fourths of the width of the mouth of the estuary on the southern or Sandy Hook side, occurs principally in the upper 20 feet of water. Below this depth, water movement is into the estuary. On the northern, or Rockaway Beach side, in about one-fourth the width of the opening, there is a tidally averaged inward flow throughout the water column (22).

The other entrance to the harbor, the East River, has a very complex flow. Because of the physical complexity of the estuary, tidal ranges and times differ greatly from place to place (23). At Willets Point, at the southern side of Throgs Neck where the East River begins, the tidal range is about 58% greater than the range at The Battery, where it ends. Tidal phases occur about 3.3 hours later at Willets Point than at The Battery. Thus, at high tide at The Battery the water surface is higher than at Willets Point and the tide flows through the East River toward Long Island Sound—a flood tide. At low tide the situation is reversed and the flow in the East River is towards the harbor—an ebb tide (24).

These two tidal waves in the East River interact in a fashion such that water elevation in the river, during ebb flow, is about 0.45 meters higher than during flood flow. The cross-sectional area of the river during ebb flow is about 5% greater, because of the greater water height, which means that more water is transported during the ebb flow than during the flood. Further, because of these tidal factors, the ebb flow lasts longer than the flood, resulting in more transport from Long Island Sound via the East River to the estuary. These factors vary from day to day and season to season, and it is only by looking at accumulations of data over long periods of time that the average trend can be detected (25).

That picture of the connection of the estuary to the ocean is only an approximation of the complex reality. Why should we be concerned about this circulation process? Quite simply because although the principal sources of fresh water entering the estuary are from the rivers, we add an additional 2,442 million gallons a day from wastewater treatment plants (26), about 9 million gallons a day (on average) from storm water runoff (27), and lesser quantities from groundwater flows, seepage, and other sources. All these sources add pollutants to the estuarine waters. Some of the materials added are trapped in the estuary and become a part of the sediments, others undergo significant physical, chemical, and biological transformations, and some move directly out of the estuary.

Based on available information, it has been estimated that something in the order of 2,660 metric tons of suspended particulate matter are carried out of the estuary into the Bight each day. But, there is also something in the order of 2,630 metric tons coming into the estuary through the circulation mechanism described. The net exchange which amounts to 30 metric tons of particulate matter each day, or 10,950 metric tons per year, is a significant amount (28). The important difference, however, is that the outflow is significantly more contaminated than is the inflow.

The estuary acts as a trap for pollutants added to the rivers which flow into it and for those placed directly into it. The harbor region is highly polluted by all water quality measures. That pollution is transferred to the Bight in the form of a plume of water flowing out over the bars to the Bight, or into Long Island Sound.

Man and the Estuary

New York is the very image of a great city—towering skyscrapers, hustle and bustle, culture and commerce. The greatness achieved in this metropolitan region resulted in large part from its large natural harbor connected by the Hudson and Mohawk Rivers, and later by a system of canals, to the Great Lakes and to the heart of the nation. Waterborne commerce through this great port from all parts of the world could touch the industrial and agricultural centers of the developing country. New York Port dominated United States trade for over a century and around it developed industrial complexes. But unlike some coastal cities, the linkage between the New York metropolitan area and the sea has almost been lost in modern development.

From a colonial trade in furs and other products of wilderness to an economy stimulated by the region's developing agriculture, the port's commercial heritage commenced with a monopoly granted in 1678 to a few leading citizens for the bolting of flour and baking of bread for export (29). It is said that there were 3 ships, 8 sloops, and 7 boats in the harbor in 1678. Three hundred years later 7,166 ships called at the port, over 15% of all ships calling at the 11 leading United States ports (30, 31).

Early port development was concentrated along the East River where the Great Dock, Manhattan's first, was built in 1649. Because New York did not have to contend with the high tidal ranges so often encountered in European ports, its docks were simple affairs. A Glaswegian visitor of 1823 wrote:

> The slips run up a considerable way in the center of the buildings, as it were in the middle of streets; and being built or faced up with logs of trees cut to the requisite length, allow free ingress and egress to the water, and being completely out of the current of the stream or tide, are little else than stagnant receptacles of city filth; while the top of the wharves exhibits one continuous mass of clotted nuisance, composed of dust, tea, oil, molasses, etc., where revel countless swarms of offensive flies (32).

By 1840 the East River had 60 wharves; the Hudson 53. The East River remained the principal commercial area until steamboats and Hudson River traffic became important. The first wharves on the New Jersey side were constructed in 1847 and by the 1900s there was extensive port development in both Brooklyn and New Jersey.

The Hudson River, Long Island Sound, and other portions of the estuarine complex were the starting points for another kind of venture: steamships. Robert Fulton's *Clermont* first sailed from New York's Tenth Street wharf on her maiden voyage to Albany. The *Clermont* and her successors were successful largely because of the complex of sheltered waters in which they could sail. The Hudson River, without great tides or the strong current of the Mississippi or Missouri Rivers, was an excellent trial ground for the early steamers.

"Clinton's Ditch," as New Yorkers termed the Erie Canal, is often credited with contributing much to the rise of the Great Port by expanding the area it served. The port's earliest hinterland was the Hudson River Valley, and adjacent Long Island, New Jersey, and Connecticut. While East Jersey traded with New York via Raritan and New Brunswick, West Jersey was held in Philadelphia's commercial embrace: eastern Connecticut and eastern Long Island were in Boston's sphere. Linking the port with the westward pioneer movement played a key role in the port's commercial expansion. As early as 1724 surveyors commented on the possibility of a water level route westward from Albany to Lake Erie, avoiding the Appalachians. In 1818 New York's legislature appropriated funds necessary to commence construction. Pushed tirelessly by DeWitt Clinton, the Erie Canal became a reality and in October 1825 its 363-mile route was opened to commerce.

In creating the Cotton Triangle, New York Port was to cement its competitive position with all other Atlantic ports. To accomplish this triangular trade, New York financiers developed coastal packet lines linking the cotton ports of Charleston, Savannah, Mobile, and New Orleans with the European ports of Liverpool and Havre—but all passing through the Great Port. It is claimed that during the period of the Cotton Triangle, New Yorkers were getting 40 cents—in interest, commissions, freight, insurance and other profits—of every dollar paid for southern cotton. This "irrational" trade, which required hazardous coastal shipments in lieu of direct business with Europeans, seemed to prosper because New York had access to desired foreign imports and New England manufactures. These goods, concentrated in the Port of New York, were the basis for both the coastal trade in cotton to the port, and the Cotton Triangle (33).

It took two centuries for the port to achieve national prominence and most of a third before it surpassed London, Liverpool, and Hamburg in volume and value of traffic (34). By the Civil War, the Port of New York handled 70% of the nation's imports and over 30% of its exports, a balance characteristic of even today's port activities. The port reached its zenith in 1871 when it handled about 71% of the combined value of imports and exports for the nation. From that time on, its importance has declined and other commercial and industrial activities of the region outstripped port functions in importance to the City and its economy (35).

Today, neither the Erie Canal nor the Cotton Triangle is important to the port. Its hinterland has shrunk as rail and road transport have eased movement of goods from industrial and agricultural centers to other ports and as the nation's population has dispersed those other ports have developed their own competitive advantages. As with other ports, bulk movement of oil and petroleum products dominates today's lists of importations. Bulk cargos account for much of the volume handled by the port (87%) and most of that is oil based (77%), but New York is not a bulk cargo center as is, for example, New Orleans. New York Port commerce is marked by the high value of the imports received and by the very large amount of local traffic generated—more than half the local traffic of all ports in the nation (36).

For most of recent history, goods were moved on ships in what is called "break-bulk" cargo. Materials were crated, bagged, or bundled into the capacious holds of ships, shored up to keep them from shifting in transit, and off-loaded at appropriate ports of call. Tramp steamers, so called because they wandered without fixed itinerary moving in accordance with cargo manifests, were early displaced by "liners" that had regular routes and scheduled callings. Break-bulk vessels are characterized by the complex of masts, booms, and rigging or derricks by which slings or pallets of cargo are loaded. Today such vessels are becoming less common as they are replaced by ungainly container ships loaded with aluminum or steel boxes piled to startling heights.

In what has been one of the most dramatic technological changes in shipping since the invention of the steel hull, the packing of cargo into huge boxes, containers, dramatically altered concepts of marine commerce, ship design, and port configurations. Containerization of ocean-going commerce developed rapidly: in 1968, 18% of the port's cargoes were containerized; in 1978, 60% (37). This, the container revolution was pioneered in large part at the Port of New York and New Jersey.

Containerization moved the major activity of loading and unloading cargo from dockside to the place of manufacture. Large numbers of stevedores previously required to "work the ships" became unneccessary. Because the cargo arrived ready to load, and because large cranes were able to lift and place the containers on the ships in seconds, turn-around time for ships in ports could be measured in hours instead of days. Container ships now routinely take on cargoes in 8 to 12 hours that would have taken up to 4 months by older means. Instead of warehouses, containerization requires large open spaces. Between 30 and 50 acres of back-up space are required per container crane.

Anticipating and actively participating in the development of containerization, the Port Authority of New York and New Jersey made plans in the mid-1950s to develop containerport facilities. New York

City's waterfront, already studded with many new piers and warehouses, but destined to be never used, was congested, and truck traffic moved slowly while New Jersey's coast, slower to develop, had acres of low marshy land available for development. By 1962, the Port Authority, using sands dredged from the Lower Harbor, had filled 1,165 acres of marshlands for the Elizabeth Container Facility where 19 container cranes now service 22 container berths (38).

Shortly after the creation of the Elizabeth Container Facility, Port Newark was redeveloped to handle containers. These two now carry 75% of the port's container traffic; Howland Hook and Northeast Terminals on the New York side handle the remainder. New York's docks still are used for most of the break-bulk traffic, over 80% landing or departing from New York piers (39).

New York City clearly lost in this transaction. Of 42 city-owned piers on the Hudson River, many built just prior to the container revolution, 3 are used for shipping, 17 are vacant or demolished. Only two active piers remain on the East River. Twenty-five percent of the city-owned piers are now used for freight consolidation, storage, or parking (40). New Jersey also lost as trucks replaced rail as the principal land transport system to the port. Over a thousand acres of waterfront railyards lie vacant and derelict (41). The port is seriously plagued by the remnants of these obsolete and unused facilities and vessels along its shores and shoal waters. Aside from the danger to watercraft from deteriorating piers, piling, bulkheading, and rotting sunken hulks, which regularly and often unnoticed release drift into navigable waters, their existence destroys the esthetics and prevents full use of the shore area.

The U.S. Army Corps of Engineers regularly collects and disposes of drift material from harbor waters, but this does not cure the problem, it merely copes with it. The corps has recommended removing or repairing 2,230 derelict timber and steel vessels, 100 dilapidated piers, wharfs, and miscellaneous structures amounting to an estimated 23.6 million cubic feet of potential timber drift and debris (42). The Port Authority, New York City, and other municipalities along the estuary are now seeking new industrial development on these sites.

Further changes were to severly affect the port. Just as containerization revolutionized ocean freight, so the airplane caused the demise of the ocean liner. By the 1940s Pan American Airlines, flying out of the marine terminal of LaGuardia airport, carried increasing numbers of Europe-bound passengers in the great Flying Clippers of Juan Trippe. With the end of the war came new, large, long-range aircraft,

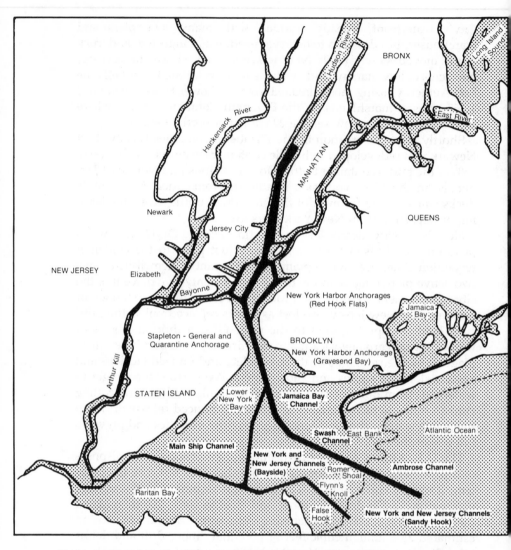

Figure 6. Major channels of New York Harbor. (Map by Sharon Ellis)

making mass air travel and transatlantic travel commonplace. In 1955, 700,000 transatlantic passengers left from the Port of New York; 20 years later that number was down to 61,500, and most of those passengers were on cruise chips (43). But even in the cruise business, the Port of New York can't compete. It is more desirable to fly to southern ports and board a tropical or Caribbean cruise than to spend two or three precious days fighting stormy cold weather to get to the southerly climes. While the City of New York, with the Port Authority, was developing the Consolidated Passenger Ship Terminal at piers 88, 90, 92, business was dying (the terminal is now mostly used as a parking facility) but traffic at the region's three major airports, all operated by the Port Authority, was booming.

The role of the port has not been limited solely to commerce. Between 1897 and 1954 16 million immigrants came to the United States through the port, most visiting first at Ellis Island. The reception of foreign born was not new to the port; from the earliest days, Manhattan had a cosmopolitan population. An early governor saw it as "another great argument of the necessity of adding to this Govermt the neighboring English Colonys, that a more equal ballance may be kept between his Matys naturall born subjects and foreigners which latter are the most prevailing part of this Government" (44).

In the 1980s nearly 90% of New York City's 191,300 acres is developed. A third of the land is used for housing, nearly a quarter for streets and highways and about 15% for recreation. Manufacturing facilities, institutions, garages, warehouses and other commercial uses occupy about 5% of the City's total area. Although patterns of land use vary from borough to borough, only on Staten Island is there significant undeveloped land.

By contrast much of the shoreline is poorly used. Rental rates for shore property and abandoned piers is sufficiently low that they can be used for parking, for storing abandoned vehicles, for tennis courts, or even lie vacant. Nearly 30% of today's shoreline of the City is devoted to manufacturing and industrial use, much of that in disarray. Little of the shore of the estuary is used for recreation and even less is natural or wildlife areas. There are about 18 miles of publicly owned beaches, 15 miles of which are open for use. Somewhat over 28,000 acres of wetlands remain in the City, over 25,000 of which are in Jamaica Bay (45).

Modifying the Estuary

Just providing the facilities required for port commerce meant changing the shore of the estuary. From 1634 when the Great Dock was constructed on the East River, bulkheading and dockbuilding—and mostly using the shoreline for disposal of fill and other wastes—have been changing the shape of the estuary. Ships have grown in size and draft with changing technology and the requirements of commerce. With increasing draft, channels were required to provide safe passage over the bars, through the estuary and to the docks. With this modification of the bottom of the harbor came the great movements of sediment and the residues of human habitation from various places in the harbor to other places.

Since early times humans have disposed of their wastes in and on the margins of bodies of water—dumping of street sweepings, garbage, excavation debris and other things at the piers was common in early New York (46) and continues to today with what we call "sanitary landfills."

> Since the first settlement of Manhattan Island in 1625, man has worked steadily to change the Hudson Estuary. Some of these changes were deliberate: shores were bulkheaded, and docks were built to make the estuary more useful as a port. Other changes were unintentional but inevitable; small streams were changed into covered sewers, and large streams into dredged channels and sometimes open sewers (47).

Little is left of the original estuarine shoreline. Exactly how much modification has occurred isn't known, for many of the changes haven't been recorded or even made within the framework of the rules and regulations. Much of the shore is bulkheaded or riprapped—some portions many times over. And, the City has grown by accretion. By 1966 about 20% of Manhattan, Brooklyn, the Bronx, and Queens were built on filled lands, about half of these were former garbage dumps or other waste-disposal sites (48). For nearly two centuries changes on the immediate waterfront were accomplished by filling to the heads of existing piers and building anew, extending the pier head line into the river. Between 1688 and 1862, the waterfront of Manhattan was moved 626 feet into the East River (49).

The expansionist scene has shifted now to the Hudson River where, in December 1973, Nicholas Perone tried to drive his dump truck on the West Side Drive but fell through instead. The Westway Project, a long discussed and debated scheme to construct 4.2 miles of new highway on the west side of Manhattan to replace a former elevated highway which collapsed almost a decade ago, may be constructed. If so, enormous amounts of fill will be added to the Hudson shore of the island, enough to build a six-lane highway (partially in tunnels), parks, housing, and industrial lands. All told, the full-scale project would add an additional 243 acres to Manhattan, 75 in parkland, 28 in land for other uses, the balance in roadways. That acreage is a 2% addition to the size of the island (50).

Early fill was street-sweepings and garbage carried by city cartmen (51). Cellar dirt, or the rock and soil removed for construction excavations soon became another material easily disposed of at the coast. For example, rock debris from the construction of 379 miles of underground subway tracks resulted in nearly 32 million cubic yards of rock (52). Other rock was carried into the harbor from foreign sources: scattered around the port are piles of ballast rocks brought in by the nearly empty sailing ships which would return full. The armored pier of Erie Basin, Brooklyn, was created from such ballast rock by an early enteprenuer. A former bartender of the Racquet Club had made an outstanding collection of European fossils from such materials. More recently, rubble from the London blitzes of the second world war, carried in the freighters returning empty, was used as fill for the F.D.R. (East River) Drive (53).

In 1866, at a cost of $750,000, two islands were created in the harbor by landfill operations. Hoffman Island, 11.5 acres in size, and the 2.5 acre Swinburne Island, were originally used for quarantine purposes (54). Other islands, particularly Rikers, Ellis and Governors, were added to (or eroded lands replaced by) rock fill taken from subway construction. About 100 acres was added to Governors Island to replace area eroded between 1625 and 1900 (55).

In recent times much of the material used in the construction of new land in the estuary has come from the harbor bottom. For nearly a decade (1966–1974), an average of almost 5.5 million cubic yards of sediment were dredged from the harbor bottom and used as landfill (56). From this mining came fill for such major modifications to the estuarine scene as the Newark and Elizabeth Containerports, the filling of the Hackensack Meadowlands and the construction of parts of the New Jersey Turnpike and Garden State highway systems. Some of the mining resulted in huge holes being left in the harbor bottom which have become local traps for fine sediments and which may lack oxygen in the bottom waters (57). Most mining, however, was associated with maintenance dredging of channels to provide access by larger and larger vessels to the harbor.

Sand moved along the margins of the Bight by littoral drift continually contributes to the shifting bars that separate the harbor from the sea. The flow of the Hudson River is sufficiently great to maintain some relatively deep channels, and for the first several centuries such channels were used by sailing ships to gain access to the harbor. The arrival of the *Great Eastern* on June 28, 1860, alerted all that these shoals had become a factor in the future of the harbor. By and far the largest vessel of her time, the *Great Eastern* drew 30 feet. There was considerable concern about her ability to call at New York, but after awaiting high tide, she was taken across the bar.

The first of the new breed of vessels, the *Great Eastern* touched off the dredging of Gedney and Ambrose Channels, the main corridors to the port (58). Gedney Channel, across the main bars, was dredged between 1887 and 1891. Ambrose Channel was authorized in the River and Harbor Act of 1889. Because there is continual movement of sediment into the channeled region, maintaining 32 miles of entrance channels and the system of 66 deep draft channels throughout the port has become a routine matter (59). By using reactor-produced radionuclides such as cesium and cobalt, from Hudson River-based nuclear power plants, it has been possible to determine recent sedimentation rates in the harbor. From 2 to 8 inches of riverborne sediment may accumulate each year (60). Yet the natural character of the Port is such that maintenance cost of the channels is proportionately lower than for most of the nation's harbors.

Once channel dredging became established, disposal of the spoil had to be regularized. the U.S. Army Corps of Engineers, the agency charged with maintaining the waterways of the nation, also became the issuer of permits for spoil disposal. In 1888 a site was established in the harbor and subsequently moved about as it and its successors were filled up. Since about 1940 sediments dredged from the harbor have been taken out to the Bight and dumped at the Mud Dumping Grounds. Over 1.9 billion cubic yards of harbor bottom have been moved by man since 1890 (61), an activity that constitutes the largest single source of sediment to the Bight (62). In the more than 35 years that the Mud Grounds has been used as the dumping site, enough material has accumulated to fill valleys and form underwater hills over 30 feet high on the continental shelf (63). These man-made hills themselves have now become navigational hazards.

Dumping dredge spoils at sea may seem to be harmless enough. After all, some say, the sediments came from the floor of the harbor and are just being rearranged, and such movement of sand is miniscule compared with natural events. But it is the magnitude of the operation: over the last decade, the annual average volume of dredge spoils removed from the harbor has been 8 million cubic yards (64); estimates of the sediment carried to harbor by river sediment load and littoral drift has been estimated to be about 85% of that dredged annually, the balance being new channel development and other sources of sediment (65).

What is different about the sediments from the harbor is their composition. The harbor has been, for many centuries, the settling basin for wastes from northern New Jersey and metropolitan New York and for materials carried down the Hudson River. Sediments dredged from the harbor are not often clean sand, but are fine-grained muds contaminated with industrial metals, petroleum hydrocarbons, synthetic organic compounds, polychlorinated biphenyls (PCBs), and toxic chemicals, and are rich in organic compounds. It is believed that the spoils moved from the harbor to the Bight constitute the largest single source of contamination by metals such as copper, cadmium, lead, and chromium, of the Bight region.

The margins of the estuary have been extensively modified by a more human spoil—garbage. New York City generates about 20,000 tons of refuse a day. For many decades "sanitary landfills" were the means by which this material was disposed of, and coastal "swamps", as wetlands were called by many prior to the era of environmental enlightenment, were a great disposal site. No one knows for certain how many wetlands were once located around the harbor. But of that original number, only 25 remain, with a total area of about 28,000 acres but nearly 25,000 of these are in Jamaica Bay (66).

Man's Boundaries

This chapter has dealt with the natural limits of the Bight; but there are other limits—the ones we establish. Mankind has a propensity for dividing things up. These manifold divisions of our globe, property and civil boundaries, are sometimes less than helpful. Different agencies may be created to carry out tasks within political units; and, as units are subdivided, so too are new agencies created. Layers of government result and communications become difficult. Many of the problems we confront in today's complicated world are larger than the jurisdictional units defined to cope with them a century or more ago. We have no effective regional mechanisms to deal with modern problems.

We have seen, in the case of shore erosion, that building a groin field required federal, state, county, and town decisions and financial participation (67). Later, with regard to sewerage and sewage treatment, we will see that joint actions between New York and New Jersey was, and is, needed—but is difficult to impossible to achieve. Some argue that we should organize ourselves to meet today's needs. For example, it has been suggested that many of New York City's problems stem from its irrationality as a political unit today. A larger jurisdiction incorporating the commuting region might be able to provide the required supporting functions and tax base. But, would such a unit be a city, a state, some new entity, or a jurisdictional basket case? Would such a unit, pertinent in today's world, be anymore relevant in some future time?

The Bight region was colonized in small settlements situated in grants of land made by kings of England or patents held by land speculators. These grew and became villages; soon towns were organized; then bigger blocks called counties. Some of the units, which once made sense, are now obsolete and mostly forgotten. Some mergers have occurred, some divisions. Even today easternmost Long Island seeks its own designation as Peconic County.

In 1883 the governments of Manhattan and Brooklyn had to agree to cooperate in order to build the Brooklyn Bridge. Fifteen years later, an agglomeration of 40 cities, towns, and villages, as well as the five parent counties, merged into the City of New York providing their pooled resources for massive new projects none could undertake independently. The results were more bridges and tunnels across the rivers, expansion of the subway system to the Bronx and Long Island, and establishment of regular ferry services. Northern New Jersey municipalities, however, would not join the movement for regionalism. There, separate governmental units, unable to muster funding, left coastal development such as port facilities, railheads, and the like, to private developers.

But it was clear that even the now broadened limits of New York City would be insufficient for development of the metropolitan region. Required cooperation was not made easy by the plethora of individual jurisdictions that had to be brought together. For example, the New York Bay Pollution Commission, established in 1903, sought unsuccessfully to involve northern New Jersey communities and state government. Conflicts emerging from that failure finally reached the Supreme Court. That august body declared that the problems would be better solved by "conference and mutual concession" and tossed the ball back to the states (68). The eventual result was the formation, in 1936, of the Tri-State Sanitation Commission, a body whose lack of success can be largely attributed to the fact that none of the participants ever gave up any sovereignty.

Similarly, congestion in the metropolitan area before the first world war called for joint New York and New Jersey solutions. Lack of common interests and outright antagonism led to the 1916 "New York Harbor Case" in which the Interstate Commerce Commission wrote:

"If we could overlook the fact that historically, geographically, and commercially New York and the industrial district in the northern part of the state of New Jersey constitute a single community; . . . and if we

were not persuaded that cooperation and initiative must eventually bring
about the improvements and benefits which the complainants hope to
attain through a change in the rate adjustment; then we might conclude
that the present [rail] rates result in undue prejudice to the people and
communities on whose behalf this complaint was filled. On the
evidence now before us that conclusion cannot be reached" (69).

In 1921 this decision led to the formation of the Port of New York
Authority (officially renamed in 1972 the Port of New York and New
Jersey Authority). But even as consent of the Congress, under Article
I, Section 10 of the Constitution, was being sought for the authority,
New York City was contending, in a blocking suit that "the
legislature of the State of New York had surrendered its sovereignty
or some part of it to the State of New Jersey" (70).

A study of the governmental units bordering the Bight and the
Hudson and Raritan Estuary revealed a total of 134 minor civil divisions (71). These ranged in size from the Borough of Teterboro, N.J.,
population 14, to the City of New York, population, 7,894,862 (72).
Two states, twelve counties, and 134 smaller units—that is a lot of
government; that is a lot of decision making; that is a lot of opportunities for things not to get done. In addition to these general-
purpose governmental units there are hundreds of independent
special districts providing schools, libraries, police and fire protection, garbage collection, street maintenance, water supply, elected officials, pet regulation, recreation, sewers, street lighting, planning,
and other services. Few of these have the same boundaries. We may
live in a half dozen or more special districts, often without knowing
it. Each of the minor civil divisions has considerable power to regulate
and control functions that determine man's relationship to the Bight.

Why are we reluctant to give up these local governmental units?
Mostly, as the eastern Long Islanders see it, to have the rights of self-
determination. And, too, some of it is history. In 1686 Governor
Dongan, an emissary of King James II, created a public trust of the
wetlands of the Towns of Brookhaven, Easthampton, Southampton,
Babylon, and Huntington. This action gave rights to the residents of
these towns to "fishing, hawking, hunting, and fowling" in the
wetlands—rights in perpetuity, a privilege continued and honored by
the constitution of the State (73).

Around the Bight, many governmental units go back to grants of
land made by the kings of England, sometimes further subdivided by
persons who may or may not have ever been there. Boundaries were
vaguely and imprecisely drawn, causing disputes to arise, some of
which have continued through the years until the present. For exam-

ple, litigation over the bottom rights in Great South Bay between Islip and Brookhaven sporadically arises, as it has for over a century (74). Few of these early boundaries bear much relationship to today's problems, questions, or urgencies.

Beyond the landward boundaries, there are jurisdictions in the Bight. Because these involve water surface, water column, bottom and subsoil rights, it is a three-dimensional environment even more complex than land. While the states and the federal governments share rights to the substrate and the water column, the surface of most of the Bight is international waters. There are special purpose economic zones that extend rights to resources out to the continental shelf and beyond. Within the Bight there are numerous international conventions and accords that have been reached with other countries: At least 10 affect the waters of the Bight (75).

Where the waters of the Bight lap onto the land things get complicated. Even the boundary we humans have set between water and land is contested. We define "extreme high water" as the reach of the highest tides; "mean high water," a sort of average place of the high tide, the usual seaward limit of private property; and "mean low water," a sort of usual point for low water. The mean high tide line and the mean low water line define the shore zone, a zone usually in the public domain. Mean low tide is also the point from which seaward measuring for other jurisdictions begins (76).

Moving away from the shore, first is the Territorial Sea, extending 3 nautical miles from the mean low tide line. It includes the air above, the sea surface, the water column, the seabed and the soil beneath. The origins of the Territorial Sea lie with the "cannon-shot rule," being the distance the old muzzle loaders could fire. Today the Territorial Sea is the jurisdiction of the states although the boundaries between the states extended out from shore are themselves litigated from time to time. Yet even in the Territorial Sea the "right of innocent passage" cannot be denied to foreign merchant ships and the federal government maintains a considerable interest in the Territorial Sea for defense and other purposes (77).

Beyond lies an area marked by parallel bands of "contiguous zones." The first of these is the 12-nautical-mile zone adopted by the U.S. in 1964. The 12-mile limit had much early importance in matters of waste disposal at sea, which is why many of the dumpsites in the Bight are located further than 12 miles from land. This importance has been diminished, however, by recent legislation, but most international conventions continue to recognize this zone as one in which nations may enforce sanitary regulations (78).

Yet another contiguous zone is the outer continental shelf, which became accepted as part of national sovereignty as technology to exploit it became available after about 1950. President Truman, by proclamation, established in 1945 a U.S. claim to the natural resources of the seabed and subsoil of the continental shelf. And in 1976 the Fishery Conservation and Management Act (PL 94-265) established the U.S. claim to the fishery resources of the shelf region extending to 200 miles from low tide and exclusive economic rights which encompass most of the Bight (79).

In the Bight, 14 federal agencies claim some sort of responsibility: Departments of State, Defense, Commerce, Interior, Health, Education and Welfare, Transportation and Housing and Urban Development; the Environmental Protection Agency, Federal Energy Administration, Federal Power Commission, Federal Maritime Commission, Interstate Commerce Commission, Energy Research and Development Administration, Council on Environmental Quality, Federal Power Commission, and the Nuclear Regulatory Commission. Of these, Commerce, Defense and Interior carry out the primary management functions; the remainder have some licensing, regulatory, or protection authority (80).

Five interstate organizations function in the Bight region: the Mid-Atlantic Fishery Council and the Atlantic States Marine Fisheries Commission are concerned with the commercial fisheries; The Port Authority of New York and New Jersey; the Tri-State Regional Planning Commission and the Interstate Sanitation Commission. Of these only the first has significant responsibilities over the Bight proper, the others being more or less land based (81).

Beyond the Bight and its contiguous zones are the High Seas that today are exclusive of the jurisdictions of any nation. But even as our ability to drill the very margins of the continental shelf is being tested, so too are the nations of the world eyeing the resources of the High Seas—and in the future they too may be divided up.

Europeans discovered the New York Bight to be a promising area for colonization. Successful outposts were established and gradual development of agriculture and commerce began. The strip of sandy beaches where Bight and continent come together was less hospitable than inland areas and so remained essentially untouched for several centuries, for here nature could be less than benign. In the great estuary, however, human activities could go on protected from the furies of the North Atlantic storms.

In time, technology developed the means by which the coastal environment could be overcome and hardy souls began pioneering the barrier island margins of the Bight. But metropolitan growth and crowding occurring around the estuary caused first the wealthy, then the masses, to look towards those beaches as a recreational resource. The automobile and cheap energy combined to make development of the coastal fringe economically possible. As the coast developed, we invested ourselves and our financial resources in relatively frail structures placed on a dynamic interface between ocean and land. Increasing amounts of financial and other resources have been expanded in the continuing struggle to overcome "the forces of nature" in protecting our summer homes and recreational facilities.

Realization has come slowly that this is an unequal battle. On the coastal fringe, mankind has not been the victor—our retreat is painful. Costs to individuals in the loss of their own personal piece of the coast is great and many are the attempts to place this burden upon the general public through tax-based programs of shore stabilization. But there is growing realization, and the public and their governments are tending to withdraw from this struggle. The coastal fringe will never again be barren of *Homo sapiens*, but perhaps our species and the rest of nature will be living more in concert than opposition.

But around the estuary, man was clearly the victor. Without the forces of ocean and atmosphere directly opposed, structural development went essentially unchecked. Where physiography and nature were not cooperative, they were overcome. The shape of the estuary was permanently changed. The sheer magnitude of the harbor made it seem, at first, too large for any personal action to affect. But we found that we could not use the estuary for every purpose, from recreational resource to sewer, and be pleased with the results. It was easier, for those who could afford it, and cheaper to move the sites of recreation outward to the coastal fringe than to rebuild the sewers and other infrastructure of the city. And so we turned our back on the harbor and built highways and industrial developments along its margins rather than places for people.

Here too change now seems to be occurring. Energy costs are higher, as are numbers of people. "Getting to the shore" is a chore. Waterfront revitalization is sweeping the nation and the Great Port is being rediscovered as an exciting and interesting resource. Will improved access to the shores of the estuary result in more investment in improving water quality? Will the costs to achieve this end be paid, given all the other demands upon our pocketbooks?

Bluefish
Pomatomus saltatrix
1 ft.

3 / The Resources

One of the most romantic but least understood uses of the ocean is as a source of natural resources. While fishing boats are scenic attractions and the sheer size and complexity of the offshore drilling rigs rank among the greatest of man's engineering achievements, what actually goes on beneath the surface of the water remains a mystery: a mystery engaging the continual attention of the fisherman attempting to lure an unseen, roaming creature to his hook with a bit of bait. Because the resources of the oceans are hidden by the restless waters whose vastness and intemperance protect them, they seem mysterious and different from those on land.

With unthinking ease, we muddle about with the environment that provides these very resources, often unaware of the contradictions inherent in our actions. While using the sea as a source of food, we also use it to dump toxic or noxious substances that may disrupt the chain of life in the sea. While dredging and maintaining deep channels for port commerce, we are, at the same time increasing soil erosion in the estuary's watershed, increasing the rate at which those channels fill in.

New York Bight is the setting for such contradictions. And, because we have used it for so many purposes over the last three centuries, its total productivity of resources may be suffering. Scientists are often unable to distinguish between the consequences of natural fluctuations and impacts of man-made interference on many resources. The very large scale of natural stresses and the long time span on which they operate make most natural events indistinguishable within our own short life spans. Natural processes have been forming the modern Bight for almost 15,000 years. On the other hand, we have been modifying its margins for only three centuries and for only somewhat over three decades have we had the awesome power of toxic chemicals with which to affect natural systems. In many ways we have had a tremendous impact on the Bight and its surrounding lands in this very short time.

The record can be easily traced in the shellfishery of the estuary. Clams and oysters have been in a state of decline almost since the time of European settlement. Early colonists acclaimed the abundance of shellfish, using their quality and accessibility as a means of attracting other settlers. Oysters, a particular delicacy, were once found in considerable abundance all over the estuary and up the Hudson as far as Ossining. Lower Manhattan was marked by oyster houses advertising Rockaways, Jamaicas, Bluepoints, and others, named for the various bays and inlets around the Bight from which they were taken. Charles Dickens wrote of New York:

> At other downward flights of steps, are other lamps, marking the whereabouts of oyster-cellars—pleasant retreats say I: not only by reason of their wonderful cookery of oysters, pretty nigh as large as cheese-plates (1).

But the twin evils of the fisheries—greed and neglect (overharvesting and pollution)—were about to strike. As early as 1715 the New York colony found it necessary to introduce regulations to protect the diminishing stocks of oysters in certain localities.

> Be it Enacted by the Governour Council & General Assembly & by the Authority of the same, That from & after the Publication of this Act, it shall not be Lawfull for any Person or Persons Whatsoever (Native free Indians only excepted) from & after the first day of May, until the first day of September Annually to gather, Rake, take up, or bring to the Market, any Oysters whatsoever, under the penalty of Twenty shillings for every Offence, to be recovered before any of His Mat'ys Justices of the Peace, who are hereby Authorized & required to hear & finally Determine the same, one half thereof to him, her or them, that shall prosecute the same to Effect, & the other half to the Poor of the place where the Offence shall be Comitted (2).

It was, in 1887, declared that "unless the pollution of the waters of the State is stopped, the planting of oysters in the neighborhood of large cities must entirely cease" (3). In the same year New York State's Oyster Protector was able to report that there had been earnest efforts on the part of oil refiners and other industries to reduce the volume of the "obnoxious effluents" then affecting the shellfish beds located along the Kill von Kull [sic] and Staten Island Sound (4). Not only were industrial and sewage pollutants affecting the oyster and other shellfish beds, but the physical disruption of the harbor bottom by dredging and dumping was causing changes inimical to shellfish. By 1915, the shellfish industry in the metropolitan area had effectively ceased to exist. Those shellfish beds that remained were so contaminated by sewage that they could not be harvested.

Recognition of the hazards posed to human health by contamination of the harbor waters, and particularly the shellfish beds, by human sewage came early but was slow to be acted upon. "Not until the 1890's was it realized that it was necessary to purify the sewage of its putrid, organic, germ-laden matter prior to its discharge in nearby waters" (5). Diseases, particularly typhoid and cholera, carried by contaminated waters had become a problem worldwide. For example, in England the first public health act dates from the Cholera year of 1848 (6). Outbreaks of typhoid fever attributed to contaminated shellfish were common in the Bight area through the early 1900s, reaching a peak of 1500 cases and 150 deaths in 1924 (7). Scientific study after scientific study of harbor pollution was conducted until in 1931 "a definite plan" for the construction of sewage-treatment plants was adopted (8). In 1979 still another plan was issued calling for the opening of 35,000 acres of shellfish beds (9).

Pollution or contamination of fishery habitats, although insidious and very destructive, can be easily comprehended. Overharvesting on the other hand is more subtle. Once a fishery is economically rewarding "more fishermen are attracted into the business, the individual fishermen try harder, and in a very short time the paradise of maximum economic revenue is lost" (10). Once the collective harvest effort exceeds the biological productivity of a species, the return to each member of the fishery decreases relative to the effort expended in the harvest. While greater harvesting efficiencies can be sought, the species reproduces only at its own rate. As a result, the stock "collapses": Reproduction fails to replace the harvest on a sustained basis. When such pressures are placed on species already affected or stressed by pollution or by disruption of spawning areas, the collapse can be precipitous.

We try to regulate or manage the fishery by setting catch limits or quotas for various species so that they are not overharvested; by establishing seasons during which fish can and cannot be caught we protect their reproduction; by keeping the fishery technologically inefficient, for example, by requiring the use of hand rakes for clamming instead of suction dredges, we reduce the amount caught by any individual; and in the end we may limit the number of persons who are actually allowed to fish (limited entry). These means are abhorrent to those who feel that they have a right to fully utilize a public resource. And therein lies the nub. The resources of the coastal ocean, with some exceptions in nearshore waters, are public. Various users do so with greater or lesser regulation and permission. Oil companies obtain leases and write voluminous environmental impact statements, commercial fishermen must obtain licenses and follow quotas regulating their catch, but sport fishermen need not. But each action is independent of the others. Fishing with or without a license has no interrelationship with a permit to dredge, dump, or drill. Yet, a fish caught is a fish caught; a dead fish cannot be caught. Fishing, dredging, dumping, drilling are all related through the effect each has on the ecosystem that is the New York Bight.

Fishing

Indians living around the Bight used the creatures of shallow inshore waters extensively for food and trade. Apparently harvested by a diverse variety of techniques including hooks, harpoons, spears, weirs, traps, seines, gill nets, and even shellfish tongs (11), fish served as a basis for wide trade. Even the purple lip of the quahog shell became a medium of exchange—wampum.

New England's settlers used fishery resources, particularly cod, as a base for early economic development. But, although many of early settlers of the Bight region came from fishing communities in Europe, fishing was of relatively minor economic importance in the New World, often serving as a sideline for farming. Exceptions were the whalers based in ports like Sag Harbor and Cape May. When the whales were overfished, however, Bight whalers tended to take up shellfishing rather than distant-water whaling as did the New Englanders. So, by 1679 there was an extensive Great South Bay oyster industry for the highly valued Bluepoints (12). Shad, sturgeon, alewives, striped bass, and turtles were heavily fished in the Hudson. Sturgeon became so important as a fishery that they were called Albany Beef (13).

Records on the Bight's fishery resource began in 1880, providing the basis for defining a series of evolutionary phases of its commercial harvesting (14). The first phase involved the taking of nearshore resources such as oysters, alewife, bluefish, American shad, and weakfish. These were easy to get to and required little technology to capture. By the 1920s, when offshore trawl fishing was introduced, these species were already in a state of decline presumably because of alteration of the nearshore environment and through over harvesting.

The otter trawl was introduced into the United States at the turn of the century and to the Bight after the first world war. With this gear, fisherman changed their habits, purchased larger vessels and the new nets, and set off to capture the haddock, silver hake, Atlantic cod, winter flounder, butterfish, and yellowtail flounder. This was the second stage of the fishery.

The third phase came when, during second world war meat rationing, the value of still other fish species such as Atlantic herring, red hake, and Atlantic mackerel was enhanced, and the fishing fleet pursued these species. The final stage, still continuing today, is characterized as concentrated fishing of temporarily abundant resources. The black sea bass, menhaden (a fish taken largely for its oil, used in industry), summer flounder, scup, lobster, and striped bass are the fish being caught.

In each of these phases, the target species were taken in increasing abundance until its catch declined. Harvesting effort was then shifted by the commercial fishermen to another portion of the resource. The picture then is a series of peaks in the tonnage of fish captured, followed by a decline; a shift to new resources, a peak, a decline, and so it goes. Overall, the New York Bight fishery reached a maximum of domestic harvest of about 315,000 tons in 1956, of which 87% by weight was menhaden; the greatest landing of food fishes occurred in 1939; since then, the picture has been of decreasing catches (15).

In the 1960s and 70s fishermen of the Bight (and of other U.S. coastal regions) avowed that the distant-water fleets of the Soviet Union, several European countries, and Japan were responsible for the decline of the domestic fishery. Those foreign fleets were impressive—large and numerous vessels, factory ships and the latest technology for harvest. While the quantities of fish taken were indeed prodigious, there is no clear evidence that the foreign fleets (which mainly fished offshore waters) actually competed with the domestic fishermen, who stayed largely close to shore, and indeed, several stocks were already in decline when the foreign fleets arrived (16). Yet this was a sore point and was hotly debated.

The controversy was resolved when the United States unilaterally asserted its rights to the fishery to a distance of 200 miles off the coast, an exclusive economic zone. The Fishery Conservation and Management Act of 1976 (P.L. 94–265) established a conservation zone in

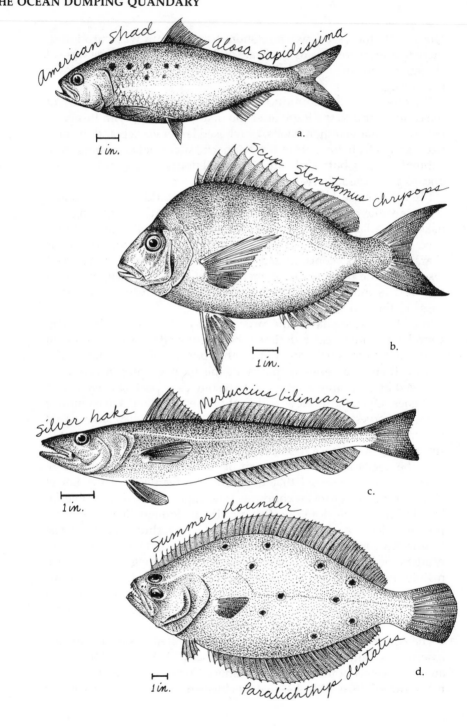

American shad   Alosa sapidissima

1 in.

a.

Scup Stenotomus chrysops

1 in.

b.

Silver hake   Merluccius bilinearis

1 in.

c.

Summer flounder

Paralichthys dentatus

1 in.

d.

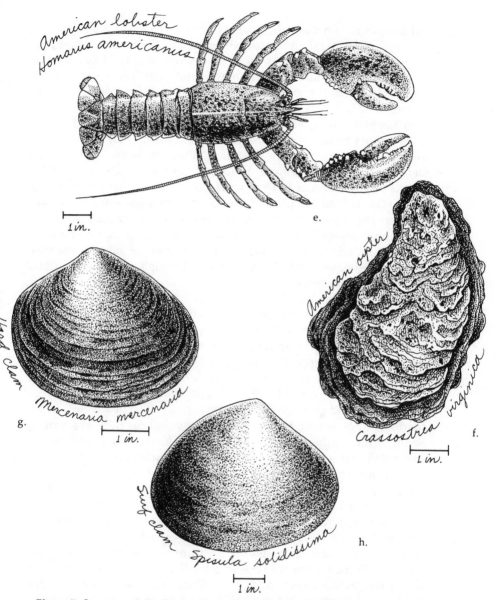

Figure 7. Some commercially significant fish and shellfish from the New York Bight. Fish include 7a. the American shad fished in the Hudson River; 7b. scup, once a leading commercial fish, now sought by both commercial and sport fishermen; 7c. silver hake, mostly fished by foreign fleets; 7d. flounder, one of the most sought commercial fishes (pictured is the summer flounder); 7e. the American lobster; 7f. the American oyster, once the predominant shellfishery; 7g. the Hard clam, recently the dominant shellfishery, but in serious trouble; 7h. the surf clam.

which this nation assumed responsibility for managing all species of fish except for highly migratory ones such as the tuna. Foreign fleets still have limited access to those stocks which were a part of their fishery, but not traditionally fished by our own fishermen, pending the time when the domestic fishery expands to fully utilize the resource.

While restraining harvest to safe biological limits, which permit each species to successfully reproduce and maintain the stock, is the central conservation issue, resource allocation is the real problem behind fishery management. Who is to get how much of what? In a democracy it isn't nice to shut someone out, as happens with limited entry. Our traditional attitudes toward property are also a hindrance. Because the creatures of the sea are seen as a "public resource" (or a common resource), no one owns them. And, because no one owns them, it is all right to exploit them. The dilemma of fisheries management is well demonstrated, in the Bight, through the management of the surf clam resource.

The surf clam, *Spisula solidissima*, is one of the most important fisheries in today's Bight. This clam is taken in tremendous quantities for use as minced fried clam and other processed foods. Its use for these purposes commenced in 1943 when a process was developed to remove sand entrapped in the animal during harvesting. The shortage of red meats and increased demands for protein during and following the war caused a rapid development of the fishery first off Long Island and then off New Jersey (17). By 1966 nearly 96% of the landings were coming from off New Jersey, but the fleet was moving south as the northern beds were depleted. In 1969 the surf clam was first harvested off Virginia and by 1972 production from off Virginia was greater than that from New Jersey. After exceeding even the historic high of New Jersey landings, the southern beds have been depleted and the fleets are moving northward again (18).

But the resource had been hurt. Total production from the New York Bight in 1976 had declined from 96 to 49 million pounds of meats (19). Why? Because more fishing pressure was being exerted. From 1965 to 1975 the number of vessels in the fleet grew from 68 to 99, and they were getting larger too (20, 21). Prices were also rising rapidly, tripling, for example, between 1975 and 1976 as supply grew short.

Further off shore lives another clam, the ocean quahog or mahogany clam (*Arctica islandica*), which can be used as a substitute for the surf clam for some purposes. While its existence had been known for a long time, it hadn't been fished because of a strong iodine flavor in its meats and because it couldn't be as effectively shucked by hand (22). But with the surf clam becoming scarcer and scarcer and prices soaring, science came to the rescue and removal of the iodine flavor was made possible. The ocean quahog became the "replacement" for the surf clam and its production soared. From landings of less than one million pounds a year from 1950–1968, the catch rose to 34 million pounds in 1980 (23).

This fishery is domestic—no foreign fleets have sought these clams. The species involved are sessile: that is, they don't move or migrate, so they should be relatively easy to manage. But they aren't being effectively managed. The Middle Atlantic Fisheries Management Council, established under the 200-mile-limit legislation, has been struggling to produce a management plan, as it is required to do under the law, for this species. Reductions in the fishing effort have been established by limiting the times a day and numbers of days a month each fisherman can go after the surf clam and ocean quahog. But someone is always willing to cheat a little and the resource suffers still further depletion (24).

But greed and selfishness are not the only factors affecting this fishery. Neglect, through pollution, has also taken a toll.

Extensive bacteriological studies were undertaken by the Food and Drug Administration in the late 1960s as concerns grew over the proximity of the Bight's surf clam resources and sewage sludge dump sites. These concerns were reflected in 1970 by the closure to clamming of a circular area over 450 square miles in extent. In 1974 that area was expanded to include most of the apex of the Bight (25).

In June and July 1976, a mass of bottom water deficient in oxygen and containing above-normal quantities of hydrogen sulfide formed off New Jersey (26). In July and August reports began to accumulate stating that both the surf clam and the ocean quahog in this area were dying in extraordinary numbers. Surveys undertaken that fall showed that in a 2600 square mile area about 90% of the surf clams died. That loss was estimated to be 62% of the total surf clam population livng off New Jersey. Mortality among the ocean quahog was about 25% of the total number. The result was a severe loss to the fishery and a nearly catastrophic loss to the surf clammers, for their landings decreased by 31% (27). While this kill resulted largely from natural processes, nutrient-rich waters from sewer outfalls, ocean dumping, and other man-made sources probably contributed to its severity (28).

Still an item only in the scientific literature, reports of abnormalities occurring in the development of mackerel eggs taken from the middle of the Bight provide a warning of perhaps another problem. Death, arrested development, and irregularities of development of these eggs has been tentatively linked with an as-yet-unknown toxic substance present in the waters (29). Are other species being similarly affected? What are the consequences to the fishery stocks? Surrounding such findings are many questions, all to be resolved before an assessment can be made.

The story of our management of commercial fisheries and shellfisheries is not one blemished with success. With too much government and too little governance, shortsightedness and a compelling readiness to blame the omnipresent "they," management fails to address the fundamental issues.

The major domestic problems of commercial fisheries in the New York Bight area are sociopolitical and economic, aggravated by wide fluctuations in abundance of individual resources from natural causes. To a degree the industry has been able to cope with resource fluctuations by using different methods of fishing.

Domestic fishermen in the area have been handicapped by restrictive state laws, usually justified as conservation measures, but in reality serving only to perpetuate inefficiency and increase the cost of locating and catching fishes and shellfishes. Some of this legislation has been passed at the insistence of recreational fishermen, who want improved access to certain living resources and a greater share of the catch (30).

There are many kinds of fishermen, more than there are of most crafts. Their gear and techniques are highly specialized and much of their success comes from knowing where the fish are and how to get them. That knowledge is not written in books, taught in classrooms, or even easily shared among fishermen. Baymen, draggers, longliners, lobstermen—terms describing skills few consumers and scientists know and appreciate—are the people who make their living from the sea.

Commercial fishermen, as a group, are rugged individualists whose conservatism may stem from a life of hard, exposed work always fraught with the danger that is a part of working on the sea. Fishing has always been a clannish activity, but new trends may change that with unknown social consequences. Larger corporations are entering the fishery with new and larger vessels and are crewing these, in some instances, from outside the traditional fishing community. Economic pressures to exploit the resources formerly harvested by the distant-water foreign fleets is causing introduction of training programs and new technologies. These may have the effect, again, of opening what has been a closed occupation.

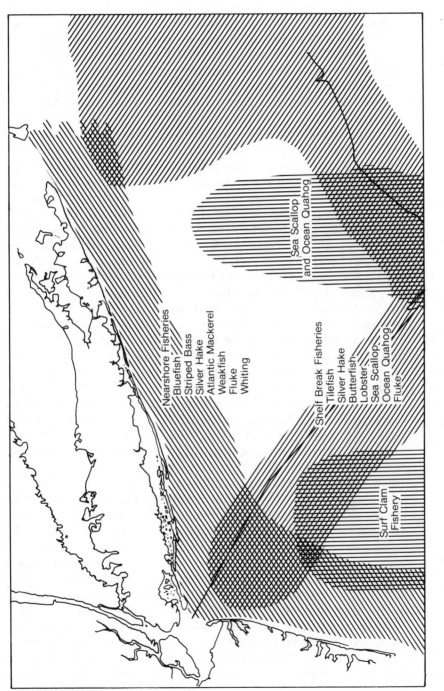

Figure 8. Principal commercial fishing areas in the northern New York Bight. The intent is to show the most actively fished areas—the fisheries are neither solely in the areas indicated, nor are unmarked areas not fished. (Modified from Davies *et al*, in Squires and McKay, 1982)

Nearshore Fisheries
Bluefish
Striped Bass
Silver Hake
Atlantic Mackerel
Weakfish
Fluke
Whiting

Shelf Break Fisheries
Tilefish
Silver Hake
Butterfish
Lobster
Sea Scallop
Ocean Quahog
Fluke

Sea Scallop
and Ocean Quahog

Surf Clam
Fishery

There are over 11,000 people who claim to be commercial fishermen of the New York Bight—5,156 working at it full-time; 6,395 part-time (31). Over 5,000 people work about half the year round converting the fish caught to some kind of product in the seafood processing firms in New York and New Jersey. Over 4,000 people are engaged in the wholesaling of fish, countless more in the retailing of products and fresh fish.

Gourmands of seafoods around the Bight are among the most avid in the nation. A study recently completed for the Port of New York and New Jersey Authority shows that consumption of seafoods in the metropolitan region is nearly twice that of the national average (32). Per capita consumption of fish and shellfish in the United States has risen over the past decade, from 10.6 lbs. in 1967 to 13.4 lbs. in 1978 (33). These data are based on commercial catches and do not include seafoods caught by recreational fishermen, nor the probably substantial amount sold or given away by commercial fishermen at the docks. Most fish are consumed within a narrow, 60-mile-wide coastal strip of the country. Fresh fish, still the largest selling form in a day of the fast-food shops, are an effective limit to distribution because of spoilage problems. The heavy emphasis of Bight fishermen on the fresh fish market contributes greatly to their problems for not only are they at the whims of seasonal migrations of fish stocks, but also shifting consumer demands and vacillating prices.

Harvesting of fish is complemented by a complex of processing, wholesale, and retail businesses producing, marketing, and selling canned products (17 plants), industrial products (6 plants), fillets and steaks (18 plants and numerous filleting houses). The largest wholesaling operation for seafoods is the Fulton Fish Market which handles 450,000 pounds of fresh fish each day (34).

Few changes have occurred in the seafood industry in the last fifty years. Ships are slowly modernized, but are a pale comparison to the factory ships operated by the foreign "distant-water" fleets—most still lack refrigeration, relying on ice to hold the catch. Few of the catching, storing, and shipboard processing techniques which led to high quality seafoods abroad can be undertaken on the small vessels of the Bight fishery. Further, the smaller vessels operate as day boats, remaining near shore, or short trip boats and as such are unable to reach the resources once harvested by the foreign fleets.

Marketing of seafoods has changed little too. Dominant in setting prices and in volume of sales is the Fulton Market, formally known as the Fulton Market Wholesale Fishmongers Association, Inc., founded in 1821. Still operating without refrigeration, the market is crowded pandemonium, as boxes of fresh fish are moved about the market by stevedore hook and handtruck (union rules forbid the introduction of forklifts) and sold both retail and wholesale. Today the Fulton Market is a picturesque anachronism and much diminished from its former status. Rumors abound that it is used to launder moneys derived from other less wholesome enterprises and that it is controlled by organized crime. The market is currently being investigated by the FBI and the Internal Revenue Service and numerous indictments have been made (35).

Sportfishing

Heaviest users of the Bight fishery are the recreational fisherman: those who do the fishing, those who operate the charter boats and party boats, those who sell and service private boats, and those engaged in all the supporting businesses and industries, including the tourist trade. About 2.5 million sportsmen fished the waters off New York and New Jersey in 1979, a number greater than the total of sport fishermen in the five New England states (36). From periodic surveys of the recreational fishery, data on which are not systematically collected, there is substantial evidence to suggest that in this region the recreational fisheries took three to four times as much food finfish as the commercial fisheries and in some species the proportion is much higher (37).

Sportfishing is big business: sportfishing is a major factor in the use of the commons. John L. McHugh, distinguished student of the fishery, has concluded, "The most worrisome prospect for the future of the fisheries of the New York Bight is whether adequate controls can be placed upon the recreational fisheries" (38). Thus far recreational saltwater finfishing does not require a license in either New York or New Jersey. In some areas, and among groups like the party-boat organizations, licensing is vehemently opposed. Licenses are issued, however, for some recreational shellfisheries.

Recreational fishermen come from most segments of our society. White males would seem, from such data as exist, to dominate the sport. However, women and members of minority groups—particularly blacks and Hispanics of the New York metropolitan area—are also fisherpeople, especially in party or head boat fishing, where many fish for food as well as sport. Food fishermen from urban areas who fish from the shores of the estuary are most affected by the pollution of the harbor for the fish they catch are often contaminated. But we know almost nothing of these urban fishers: who they are,

a. Otter trawls are among the most important fishing gear used in the New York Bight region. The broadly conical net is held open at the forward end by "otter boards" or "doors". The net is tied closed at the "cod" or narrow end. It is emptied by cutting the ties. Principal species fished by otter trawls are yellowtail flounder, silver hake, winter and summer flounder and scup.

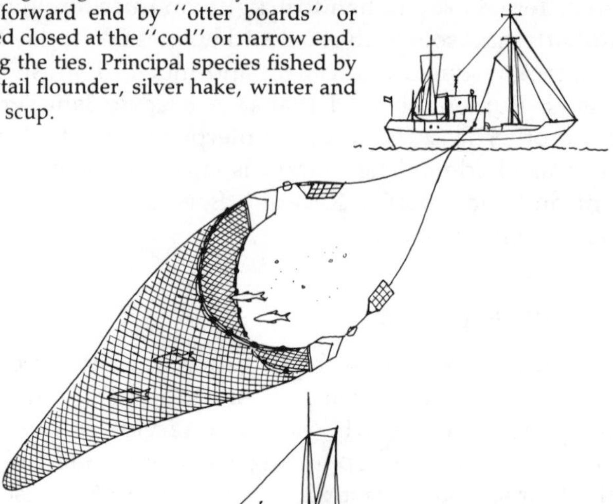

b. Purse seines are worked by one or two vessels which tow a large encircling net which may be over 1000 feet long, around a school of fish. The school is captured by closure of the bottom of the net which forms the "purse." This technique was once very important, particularly for the menhaden fishery.

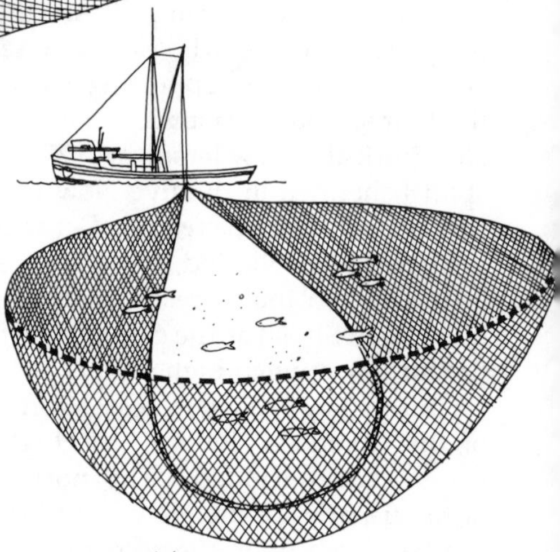

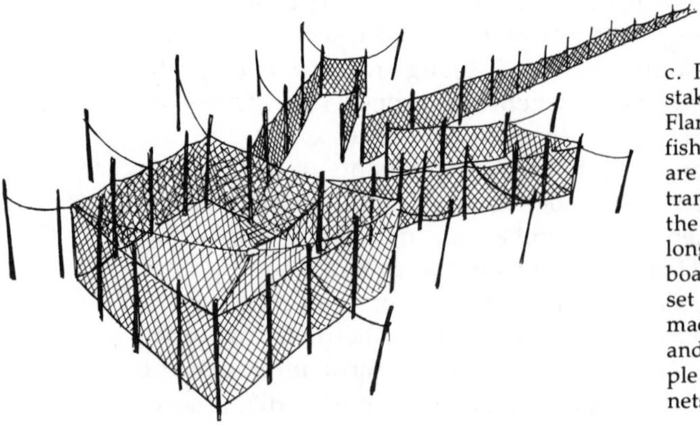

c. Pound nets are held on stakes driven into the bottom. Flaring "leaders" direct the fish into "bays" in which they are trapped by the narrow entrances. Fish are removed from the bays by dipping them with long-handled nets into tending boats. These nets are usually set close to shore. Atlantic mackerel, weakfish, bluefish and menhaden are the principle species taken by pound nets.

Figure 9. Typical fishing gear. (Drawings by Sharon Ellis)

d. Pots are traps constructed of wood, net or other materials which have a narrow entrance at one end. The pot is baited and then set on the bottom to attract carnivores such as lobsters and crabs. A buoyed line attached to the pot allows for recovery.

e. Gill nets work by entangling fish in the mesh, catching them behind the gill covers. Mesh size is designed to allow the head of the fish to pass through, but not the body. Nets may be stretched from stakes or from buoys, or may be drifted out in long lines. Weakfish and bluefish are often caught this way.

f. Haul seines are, in smaller versions, known as beach seines. They are hauled out, by boat, from the shore and brought back to shore, encircling the fish. The net is then hauled onto the beach. Weakfish, bluefish and striped bass are a principal catch.

g. Nearshore shellfish, particularly in the shallow nearshore bays, are taken by hand tonging or with long handled rakes. Oysters, once the principal species caught in this fashion have all but disappeared. Now the hard clam is the principal species.

what they catch, and why they fish. Most studies of anglers have looked at more affluent fishers of nonpolluted waters.

Most sport fishermen work from boats: nearly 70% of the fish caught by mid-Atlantic sport fishermen in 1979 were taken from private or rented boats; about 11% were taken from charter and party boats, about the same as that from man-made structures such as bridges, piers, and docks (39). In 1975 there were 259,000 individually owned outboard motors in Nassau and Suffolk counties and the five boroughs of New York City (40). There are about 300 marinas, boat launching ramps, and other facilities to cater to the boating angler along the Atlantic coast from Montauk to Cape May (41).

In 1976 there were 103 party boats and 154 charter boats operating from Long Island. The party boats ranged from 42 to 130 feet in length, carried an average of 70 passengers a trip, fished year round and an average of 6 days a week. Charter boats were smaller, averaging 42 feet in length, and carried an average of 12 passengers. Party boat fishermen sought flounder and mackerel in the early season, fluke and bluefish in midseason, and cod, blackfish and flounder in the late season. Interestingly, charter boat fishermen sought flounder and cod in the early season, bluefish, shark and fluke in midseason, and bass, bluefish and blackfish in the late season (42).

All of this supporting activity generates income. Direct angler expenditures off the south shore of Long Island and New York City was estimated in 1976 to be $96 million. If the value of the fish, at retail prices, is added in, the value is $147 million (43). For that same period, the value of the landing by commercial fishermen for the same was about $4 million.

Sportfishing is a big business. Sport fishermen are numerous (and vocal). And, many sport fishermen view themselves in competition with the commercial fisherman for the same resources. The dialogue is rancorous and the solutions offered to lessen conflict sometimes politically less than constructive. For example, a recent editorial in the *Long Island Fisherman* stated:

> The trend on the coast is very clear: that commercial fishermen will gradually have to move out of the inshore grounds in favor of recreational activities. Already Florida and a few other states have passed legislation that helps to initiate this process. In this same editorial section we have quoted from learned papers the same point of view and thus it seems the wave of the future (44).

Our fisheries are a commons. Our society has not come to grips

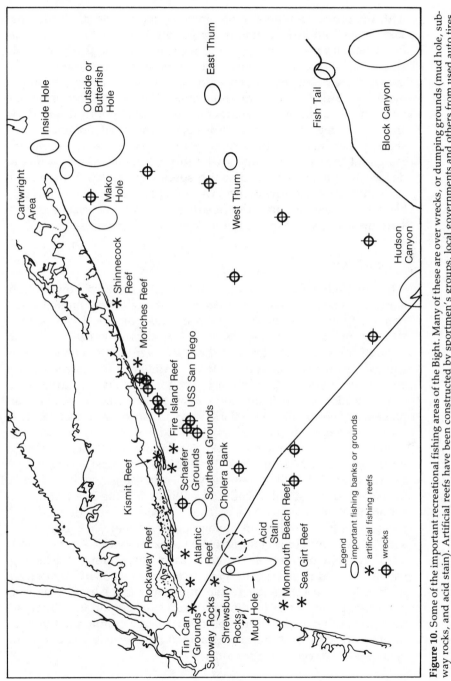

Figure 10. Some of the important recreational fishing areas of the Bight. Many of these are over wrecks, or dumping grounds (mud hole, subway rocks, and acid stain). Artificial reefs have been constructed by sportmen's groups, local governments and others from used auto tires, rock debris, or other common materials. Recently fly-ash and scrubber sludge wastes compressed into blocks have been used. (Modified from Davies *et al*, in Squires and McKay, 1982)

with the problems inherent in commons, for as Garrett Harden has said, "Freedom in a commons brings ruin to all" (45). Commercial fishermen, licensed and regulated, argue that left alone, there would be no management problems. But, as we have seen, there are too many, too efficient fishermen who now have the ability to harvest more than is produced by reproduction of the stock. Sport fishermen (and shore subsistence fishermen), unlicensed, poorly understood and lightly regulated, are increasingly vocal about obtaining their share, which is already the largest for many species. And, around the margin of the Bight are others who through their actions pollute or destroy habitats in which some fish species spawn. And, clinging to our concepts of self-governance, we attempt to solve a commons problem which extends half the length of the Atlantic seaboard on a state-by-state basis. We are not making notable progress.

Marine Plants

In the United States we have only begun to learn how to fully harvest the sea. We see this reflected in the relatively limited selections of finfish and shellfish found on most menus. Many species taken from our waters are destined for overseas cuisine; eels and mussels are two examples. But there are even more diverse uses of aquatic organisms than as direct food. Marine plants, seaweeds, may be increasingly important in our future for a variety of purposes.

Avid readers of labels on food containers will find the word "carrageenan." Found in a wide variety of substances from toothpaste to yogurt, carrageenan is used in the food industry as a thickener, stabilizer, and gelling agent. Extracted from red seaweeds, some of which are harvested off New England's rocky coast, carrageenan, worth over $50 million annually is increasingly obtained from overseas sources (46), but could be cultivated in the Bight or its surrounding shallow bays. Agar is another food additive derived from red seaweeds. It is used in biology classes, where it is called agar agar, as a nutrient broth for microbiology experiments. Agar is widely used by bakers and confectioners as a suspending, thickening, stabilizing, and gelling agent. Finally, algin, which is mostly derived from kelp, is used in the textile and paper industries, where its emulsifying and water-holding properties are important. There are numerous other pharmaceutical and industrial compounds derived from seaweeds. Most are now provided by overseas sources or are synthesized for economic reasons.

An emerging potential use for marine plants is the ocean farming of seaweeds for energy. This is a kind of solar energy in which sunlight is biologically fixed so that it may later be converted into a storable form of energy such as alcohol or methane. In this process, the biomass or some form of plant material is harvested and then converted by bacterial decomposition or fermentation into the fuel and nondigested residues. The process is not new: the use of marine plants and potentially very large-scale digestion is. The attractiveness of marine biomass, as opposed to the use of corn, wood, grasses, manures, and other materials being considered as feedstocks, lies in the availability of large surface areas of the ocean not being used for other purposes.

A small experimental kelp farm has been built on the west coast, the first step in what is envisioned as a huge biomass farm over 100-square-miles area. Research now going on in New York has determined that several of the seaweeds native to the east coast have a yield great enough to make them attractive for biomass conversion. In the waters of New York Bight, large amounts of nitrogen and phosphorus—the fertilizers of plant growth—may compensate for the cold. If so, then the nutrients added to the coastal waters from sewage outfalls could become an asset for at least energy production (47).

Early settlers used "salt hay" or *Spartina*, growing along the wetlands shores, as fodder for their herds and for a variety of domestic purposes. While cropping of these plants for their fibre content has been considered as a modern enterprise, the environmental values of these tidal plants outweighs their potential as a resource. Some other marine plants may become so abundant as to be a nuisance. Eelgrass, *Zostera*, is one such example. While vitally important for the maintenance of a shellfishery (the exact reasons are not well understood; however, during the 1930s when eelgrass beds were decimated by a wasting disease, so too were the shellfisheries of Long Island's bays) eelgrass can clog waterways and interfere with boating. It has been shown that eelgrass can be used as a source of fibre for paper manufacture (48).

There is a temptation, with marine plants, to introduce those species which have a high value in one place to another just as we have moved terrestrial, agricultural, species about the globe. But in so doing, we could unleash the enormous natural capabilities of reproduction of the plants in the absence of their natural predators and find that the valued species becomes a horrendous problem.

While such transplants of exotics are often ascribed to foreign parts, there is a local example of a seaweed become problem, *Codium fragile*. This seaweed, sometimes called the oyster thief, is thought to have originated in Japan, but became rapidly spread (by growing on the bottoms of ships?) in Europe and the United States. It was first found in the northeastern United States at East Marion, Long Island, in 1957. By 1961 it was well established there and spreading northward, and to New Jersey. Its transport from Long Island to Cape Cod is thought to have been through the movement of shellfish from one region to another. Today, *Codium* is a nuisance, clogging fishermen's nets and shellfish harvesting machines as well as accumulating on beaches in odiferous windrows (49).

Aquaculture

Aquaculture, or as it is sometimes termed, mariculture, is the wet equivalent of agriculture. It is the growing of marine organisms under controlled conditions, the improvement of stock for greater yield and higher quality of produce: it is the change from a hunting and gathering marine economy to an "agricultural" economy. Aquaculture is an ancient skill practiced with great success in the Orient. It is less well known in the United States, where a complex of institutional barriers has inhibited its development.

Around the margins of the Bight are small practitioners of aquaculture. These are, primarily, shellfish farmers who have learned to spawn oysters and clams in hatcheries and to supplement the natural sett of these shellfish by the hatchery spawn. Some of these firms have been in operation for over 50 years and have gained great skill. More recently, there is renewed interest in the potential of aquaculture, with new and diversified shellfish and finfish culture appearing around the Bight. But aquaculture remains an enterprise for the future (50).

With aquaculture comes a fundamental change in the nature of the fishery commons. As the introduction of agriculture fenced, with strife, the Wild West, so too must aquaculture "fence" the fishery commons. Investments in aquaculture mean expenditures for the "farm structure" which will support and contain the cash crop. With this investment will come the desire to exclude unwanted trespassers and poachers. Exclusivity inevitably requires land rights in the form of ownership, leases, or other arrangements which permit the exclusion of others. The fishery commons is conducted over underwater lands which are, in the main, publicly owned and controlled. The struggle to permit the right of private use of underwater lands and the water column above to the exclusion of commercial and sport fishermen, recreational boaters, and others, will be the struggle of the latter part of the twentieth century.

As with most major changes, the beginning of aquaculture has commenced slowly. The economic and biologic pressures are such that aquaculture will, in the final analysis, win. The wild fishery is now being harvested near its maximum overall, and with many species, overharvested. Increasing yield of these species will come only from aquaculture which will become more and more profitable as scarcity increases prices. The beginnings are present. Rafts, cages, and nets are being placed in the nearshore waters of the Bight for the cultivation of seaweeds, shellfish, and finfish. The New York State Legislature has called for the development of a state aquacultural plan similar to those of many other states.

As engineering skills are developed, the capability to construct and maintain larger and larger structures in the more hostile environment of the Bight proper will be achieved. As biological skills are developed, new strains of marine plants and animals will be developed which grow faster, and which, perhaps, like the tomato, will assume a square shape for easier packing.

Mineral Resources

There is more than fish in the sea. The potential of the mineral wealth of the ocean floor is of increasing interest as reserves of petroleum, metal ores, and other terrestrial resources become exhausted. The ocean floor, hidden from us by overlying waters and sometimes inaccessible because of the high costs of exploitation, will, in the near future, come within our grasp. Technology to permit the exploitation of the continental shelf, the next frontier of public lands, exists or is being developed. Here, again, the issue is the management of a common resource for the benefit of all. For example, can mining and oil and gas production take place without damage to the fishery? There are no certain answers; we may not know how to do it.

Energy consciousness has spurred a resurgence of interest in oil and gas from wells drilled on the continental shelf. Offshore production had been, to people around the Bight, something happening in foreign lands, such as Louisiana, California, the North Sea, and the East Indies. The revelation that there might be oil and gas off the shores of the Bight caused great excitement as well as consternation.

If there is petroleum in the Bight region, its presence results from geological activity beginning some 250 million years ago. The great plate of continental crust containing present-day North America, Europe, and Africa, then began to break up and separate along a fracture line which is now the Mid-Atlantic Ridge. The enormous stresses causing that separation also caused great blocks of the shelf to rise or fall. Where they were pushed down, depressions now called the Baltimore Canyon and the Georges Bank basin formed. Sediments carried by rivers were spread upon the continental shelf in thin sheets, but the basins accumulated more sediments, particularly fine-grained, organically rich materials which are the requisites for the still imprecisely understood process of petroleum formation.

As sediments accumulated, their weight caused the basins to continue to sink and deepen, allowing still more to be deposited. In the Baltimore Trough the thickness of this accumulation is 41,000 feet, while over the adjacent shelf the blanket of sediment is only 2,600 feet thick (51). This process took millions of years.

Proper thicknesses of sediment, with enough organic matter, followed by application of sufficient pressure and heat, is the recipe for making petroleum. Once made, however, the gas or oil would migrate through the rocks and be lost unless trapped in reservoirs. Finding those reservoirs is a critical art of geological exploration—an art at which the successful oil companies excel. Finding appropriate "structures," as the reservoir situations are called, is one phase. A second phase is determining if there are supplies of gas or oil in sufficient quantities to permit the development of a production field. That step requires exploratory drilling.

In the summer of 1976 the New York region caught oil fever. The stock market had palpitations—Texaco announced that one of its wells showed gas, possibly in commercial quantities. By 1981, over 25 exploratory wells had been drilled, all but two dry; hopes for a major oil find were disappearing. One of the "wet" wells had a test-flow rate of 18.9 million cubic feet of gas a day, a flow rate suggestive that a promising commercial gas field could be developed (52).

Leases sold in late 1979 and through 1981 have been for tracts on the shelf-edge side of the basins, new territory for most oil companies. Not only are the depths in which exploratory drilling would be undertaken greater than before, but the shelf edge is also unstable, subject to slumping—hardly the place to locate very expensive drilling rigs. There are also some very important environmental questions to be asked about development of oil or gas production in such tricky settings. These are under investigation.

Once oil or gas in commercially significant quantities is found, then production can commence. This is a long process involving the siting of production wells, their drilling, and establishing the means to transport the gas and/or oil to shore. Production would, if the pattern of most fields is followed, peak in the first four or five years and then gradually fall off until, about 20 years later, production would cease (53). This scenario is important to remember, for on it hinges some of the stronger arguments for not developing potential Bight region hydrocarbon fields.

While visions of oil riches dance in the heads of some, others have visions of oil-blackened beaches and damaged fishery resources. Long Islanders have responded to the possibility of offshore oil fields with great concern. The basic argument is that spills of oil fields would wreak havoc on a recreational industry economically far more significant to the region and the nation than the potential value of the petroleum. Displacement of a deeply rooted industrial and commercial infrastructure of beach and water recreation, sport and commercial fishing by a short-lived exploitation of a single resource does not make sense to many. That argument proceeds along the lines that fishing has been going on for over two centuries; oil production might last for only 20 years but could ruin fishing for some long time. Long Islanders are more concerned about these issues than people along the Jersey Shore for the reason that winds and currents would put oil from a continental shelf blowout on Long Island with a degree of certainty while New Jersey might be spared. Resolution of the argument is still to come.

Energy is critical to the Bight region—critical because almost all of it is imported, much of it from Middle Eastern oil fields. Studies have suggested that the possibility of major oil spills is higher from tanker collisions than from production problems of offshore wells. Sullying of the beaches of New Jersey and Long Island is a reality, not only because of the large, dramatic oil spills such as those at Amoco Cadiz or Santa Barbara, but also because of the small, incidental spills caused by people like you and me. One estimate of the sources of oil in the ocean concludes that:

29.8% is from tankers and tank barges
29.4% is from improper automobile crankcase oil disposal
17.3% is from other shipping
15.3% is from industrial machinery waste oil
6.1% is from refineries and petrochemical plants
2.1% is from offshore oil production (54).

Oil spilled from tankers and tank barges come from the cleaning of tanks (although prohibited), from small accidental spills, and from somewhat larger spills not always accidental. And, every sailor on every ship who finishes cleaning the ship after being in port and tosses his oily rags in the ocean just can't see how this pollutes a large ocean. Our insatiable appetite for automobiles affects the ocean. That little extra trouble to take our crankcase oil to the gas station for disposal sometimes causes it to be disposed of down the storm drain and into the river, into the estuary, and finally into the ocean.

From the Bottom of the Harbor

While the excitement of potential oil fields stirs our imaginations there are other important, but prosaic minerals being extracted from the Bight: sand and gravel. These minerals form the foundations of an urban society built of concrete on lands reclaimed from the coastal ocean and its estuaries. It is a fact that the Lower Harbor of New York is the world's largest sand mine. From 1950 to 1975 over 116 million cubic yards of sand were mined, an average of 4.66 million cubic yards each year (55). This is the equivalent of a hole 1 mile square mined to a depth of a five-story building each year.

Where does it all go? Most of the sand mined from the harbor is used for filling marsh and marginal lands. The great complex in the Hackensack Meadows of New Jersey, the New Jersey Turnpike's northern extent, Port Elizabeth, Newark Airport, and Battery Park City—are all built on sand mined from beneath the harbor. Today, tracts are being marked for mining more than 13 million cubic yards required as the construction of Westway, the replacement for the collapsed West Side Drive in Manhattan, moves ahead (56).

Fifty years ago, Long Island appeared to be a never-ending source of sand and gravel. Great mines levelled terminal moraines hundreds of feet high. Barges carried the aggregate materials to local ports all over Connecticut, metropolitan New York, and New Jersey. But as Long Island suburbanized, houses were built on the sites of future pits; supply became critical. Nearly a decade ago the geologist for the State of New York correctly stated that terrestrial sources would be very limited in 10 years—and that is now (57).

Mining in the harbor does have its negative side, however. Removing sand has the effect of deepening the harbor, if only locally. Such deepening has the effect of changing the circulation of water within the harbor and of altering the direction of wave attack on the shore. These two factors, in combination, can result in enhanced erosion (58). During the peak years of mining in the 1960s, sediment was removed from the harbor at a rate faster than it was being brought in by littoral drift from Long Island and from New Jersey (59); deepening was occurring.

As we have seen, maintaining the channels of the harbor requires dredging, which creates spoils. At present those spoils are disposed of at a dumpsite in the ocean. Some of the spoils are highly contaminated with heavy metals and halogenated hydrocarbons, among other things, and should be disposed of in some other fashion. It has been suggested that one such means of disposal would be to backfill the holes created by mining with the contaminated spoils (60). These pits, when nearly filled, could then be capped with clean sediments protecting the harbor environment from the contaminated sediments. This means of accomplishing several objectives simultaneously has a lot of attractions and is currently the subject of large-scale experimentation (61).

In the longer term, however, sand and gravel for fill and for construction aggregate will have to be obtained from outside the harbor. This is now a technological problem, for there are no dredges in the area large enough to do the mining. Further, even if there were, they could mine many years' supply in just a few months, a situation not economically attractive to industry for it requires expensive stockpiling. The metropolitan region is fortunate, however, for the glacial apron that extends from land to the edge of the continental shelf is a great carpet of sand and gravel. If sites are judiciously selected, which do not conflict with fisheries, there should be enough aggregate to last for many centuries to come.

Wherever we have looked in the ocean, the twin evils of greed and neglect were present. Greed has led to overharvesting of the living resources: the catching of fish beyond the capability of a stock to renew itself. Neglect has usually shown itself by using the ocean for disposal of wastes cheaply, a shortsighted process which may have long lasting effects on other resources.

Our fishermen are ruggedly independent. Each is harvesting from the commons—many are completely convinced that the little bit he takes won't affect the whole. But the history of the New York Bight fishery, documented in excruciating detail, is one of the overharvest of one species after another. When a common resource is being overused, it is often best for a third party to arbitrate, usually government. In the presence of perfect knowledge, governmental management schemes might work, but our knowledge is far from perfect.

Further, the tasks of regulation are complicated by our having divided the face of the globe into jurisdictions which have no relationship to the animals or plants which share this planet with us. Thus, towns, counties, states, and federal governments, in varying degrees, for various purposes and with hugely different competencies, bear the task of regulating the commons.

The evil, neglect, is insidious and pervasive. In a later chapter we will examine in detail the problem of pollution of the Bight. Increasing evidence is accumulating that pollution of the ocean is having an effect upon sea life. The effect may not be immediate death but rather subtle chronic or long-term changes. For example, the noise we make in the ocean with ships and submarines, explosions, and drilling and so on may have affected the ability of the whales to communicate over distances. Males and females may not be finding one another for reproduction, lessening steadily the size of their population. Some chronic effects may be expressed in lower rates of growth of individuals, by the presence of lesions or tumors, through loss of use of sensory organs which guide fish in their migrations, or by affecting the way a fish will interact with its own kind, with predators, or prey.

The effects of pollutants may also reach to man. Beds of shellfish or schools of fish may have a "tainted" taste from petroleum or other substances in the water. In the 18 September 1978 issue *Sports Illustrated* magazine reprinted, on the hundredth anniversary of its appearance in the *Spirit of the Times*, the following:

> Like rumbling sounds of distant thunder, an occasional report came to the office of the *Spirit*, to inform us that the gas factories were ruining the quality of eels and bottom-biting fish throughout the East River. But as the great body of anglers made no complaint, we made no note of the subject. But within the past year a more serious injury to the fishery around Manhattan has presented itself, the waters having become impregnated by the refuse from the kerosene refining factories to such an offensive degree, as to have not only deteriorated all bottom-feeding fishes, but the striped bass as well have become so permeated by the offensive refuse as to be unfit for the table. This is a great damage, for there are many who made bass fishing near New York their only recreation (62).

Perhaps nowhere is the "Tragedy of the Commons" better displayed than in our oceans. Resource management has not come to grips with this problem. While some argue that our laws cause inefficiency, particularly among fishermen, others would offer compelling evidence that our fishermen are already too efficient! This argument would offer as social justification that inefficient fishing offers greater opportunities to more people to earn a marginal or better living, while an efficient fishery would offer better economic return to fewer individuals.

But if allocation and utilization of a single resource is difficult in this commons, how then are the multiple resources of the commons to be allocated among the various different users, some of whom are mutually exclusive, others of whom are merely seen as being "bad." To each user, freedom of the seas is seen as a preeminent requirement. Thus the fishermen argue that all of the Bight is hunted by them and that outer continental shelf oil development, ocean dumping, ocean farming, and mineral resource exploitation would all, individually or collectively, result in loss of economic return. Only merchant shipping escapes direct attack, perhaps because it came first.

As our use of the oceans increases, the most central problem will be development of means to avoid, or lessen, the dispute which emerges from each new proposed development. Fishermen, or other users, should not be forced to a position of retreat before other interests; rather means must be sought by which various exploitive uses can be conducted within an orderly framework. But here is a central difficulty. Dumping of wastes in the ocean is a destructive use which may preclude all others. Our society showed for nearly three centuries its unwillingness to support environmental cleanliness. In the past several decades we have moved to improve the quality of the air, our drinking waters, our streams and rivers, and even the coastal ocean. Most uses of the ocean are dependent upon a quality of that environment—only dumping does not.

Tilefish

Lopholatilus chamaeleonticeps

1 ft.

4 / Peopling the Bight

Ecologists have made a parallel between human communities and individual organisms. In this analogy our transportation systems, such as highways, railroads, and pipelines, are comparable to a circulatory system carrying nutrients to the cells and wastes away from them; communications devices and networks become a kind of nervous system keeping all parts of the community and organism in touch. Such parallels are most pertinent to great urban centers and justifies calling cities superorganisms. A city may be seen as a giant creature, dependent for its existence on the proper functioning of each of its parts and all of its cells. But such a complex is not self-sustaining, for a concentration of humanity like New York City is dependent upon the resources of the region, the nation, and the world for its sustenance. Sometimes this dependency can be frighteningly real. Water supplies, food, the essentials of life, may be available only through the complex of regional farms, transportation, and marketing systems. Disruption of these connections by natural events or social disorders can be life threatening.

The area around the New York Bight—the most densely populated and industrially developed coastal area of comparable size in the United States—can be looked at as such a superorganism. This region is dependent upon imports and exports for its existence: raw materials, energy, food, water, and other essentials are imported; finished products and a variety of wastes are exported. This dependence upon imports and exports will be further explored as we look at the examples of energy and water.

As people settled around the margins of the Bight they brought different attitudes, objectives, and technologies to their use of the land

and water resources. At first, the physical character of the land defined both the way in which people lived and the quality of their life. As technology increased, man's ability to affect his physical environment, to alter the limits imposed by the physical characteristics of the land changed. "The over-all character of an area depends to a large extent upon what man wants to do, how he does it, and what technical skills are at his command" (1).

People apparently appeared upon this virgin continent 20,000 to 30,000 years ago. Although primitive by today's standards, these pioneers brought toolmaking abilities with them. The continent, awakening from the ice cover of the Pleistocene glaciers, was rich in large mammals like the wooly mammoth, the giant sloth, large caribou, and elk, providing an abundant food supply for the early hunters. They moved rapidly eastward from the west coast, arriving at the Bight region about 11,000 years ago, or perhaps even earlier, leaving their mark only in the few fluted, bifacially flaked points from their weapons, usually called Clovis points. Perhaps these early people, making their brief visit, had the first impact—the extinction of the large ice-age mammals (2).

The Modern Era

The first documented impact of man on the Bight region came with the introduction of agriculture. Archaeological findings provide evidence that sometime after 1,000 A.D. the cultivation of maize, beans, and squash commenced. Agriculture meant the development of semipermanent villages and the clearing of forests: accounts of early European explorers refer to large clearings for the planting of maize. An early governor of New Netherland, for example, reported what were apparently abandoned Indian fields at a number of places on Manhattan Island, one containing about 140 to 180 acres that could be "plowed without much clearing" (3). Indians also burned the woods to make clearings and to thin out the underbrush to make hunting easier.

> They cultivate no wheat, oats, barley, or rye . . . The grain which they raise for bread, or mush or sapaen, is maize or turkey-corn, and they raise various kinds of beans . . . tobacco for their own use . . . Of manuring and proper tillage they know nothing (4).

Specialized life patterns quickly developed: Long Island Indians learned to catch shellfish and finfish for food and the medium of exchange, wampum; the Oneidas turned out flint blanks for arrowheads; the Algonquins stripped birchbark in great sheets to construct lightweight canoes. These specializations resulted in widespread trade among the various tribes with journeys of 1,000 miles or more not uncommon. Talc from the Virginias and magnetite from Arkansas can be found at the sites of Indian villages in the Bight region.

While Indians were largely dependent upon local game and agriculture for their sustenance, they were sampling the fruits of trade between nations. Water routes facilitated this trade both with other tribes and increasingly with European explorers. But, man was still linked closely with the environment, dependent upon nature for existence. Population densities in the Bight region in those times reflect that linkage between humans and the environment. Coastal tribes were estimated to have been more populous than inland settlements largely because of the abundance of nearshore seafoods which supplemented traditional game and agricultural food sources (5).

As developing agriculture fostered the growth of settlements, local environments were stressed. Game around the settlements was hunted out and the hunters of the tribes had to go farther and farther afield. Local cultivation sapped the soils, requiring more cleared forests. As each settlement expanded, contact was made between tribes. Warfare resulting from such contacts and squabbles over rights to the resources may well have been a controlling factor in growth of early populations (6).

It is probable that, recorded in the sedimentary record of the Bight, is evidence of soil erosion resulting from this primordial clearing of forest lands. It is certain that from this time forward, erosion in the watersheds of the Bight has been steadily increased by our modification of the terrain and the vegetation. Increasing sediment loads of streams and rivers began a process of altering the configuration of the land and character of the flora and fauna: Man's reshaping of the planet and its environment had begun.

A great reduction in the numbers of Indians resulted from contacts with the European settlers, specifically arrival of the Dutch. Introduction of disease, massacres, and general dispiritedness severely reduced the Indian population from 1650 to 1750 (7). Population density probably decreased in this period but soon recovered as the European immigration commenced. The enormous density of human habitation we see today in the coastal metropolis of the Bight is the result of the influx of immigrants that began in 1624 with the settlement of 8 men

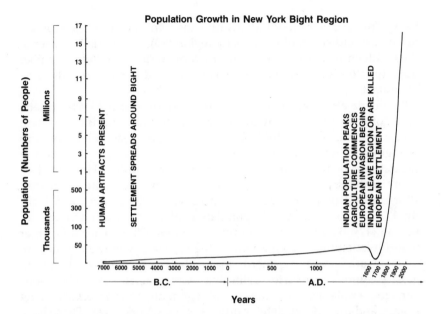

Figure 11. Population growth in the New York Bight coastal area. Indian artifacts date at least to 7,000 B.C. Indian populations grew slowly to a maximum until just before European settlement. Then disease, wars and out-migration resulted in greatly diminished populations. Explosive population growth of the European settlers followed. Note scale changes in population.

at New Amsterdam (now New York), and 18 or so families at Fort Orange (now Albany) (8).

The Dutch came, explored, and established outposts. They brought with them tools and knowledge that accelerated alteration of the environment. More important perhaps, the Dutch settlers came with the clear expectation of developing a trading economy—one in which the natural resources of the region were exploited in exchange for the importation of technology. Availability of transportation, the ships in which they came, signalled the advent of one of the most important changes in the way in which Bight residents lived—the transport of food, materials, and energy over great distances. The Dutch came originally to exploit the land; their home was Holland. But they found that the New World was much like home and they began to settle. As they settled, they took up agriculture, and their values changed; home became the New World and they tended the land as they had in Holland.

In 1647 Peter Stuyvesant reported that "there could not be in the whole Province, 250, or at farthest 300 men capable of bearing arms" (9). As the numbers of Europeans grew, the toll on the Indians was heavy. By 1675 very few Indians remained anywhere in the Hudson Basin east and south of the Albany region (10). By the first quarter of the eighteenth century the European population exceeded in number the estimated 60,000 Indians who had inhabited the region at the time of contact.

By the 1640s English settlers began arriving from Massachusetts and Connecticut; they settled the eastern end of Long Island. Then, "on a summer day in 1664, four British frigates swooped down to change New Amsterdam into New York" (11) and a new period in the settling of the Bight had begun. England, unlike Holland, had many unhappy prospective immigrants, and population growth, slow under Dutch rule, began to increase rapidly under the British. By 1770, New York City's population of 33,000 exceeded that of Boston (12). By 1810, with a population of 96,000 the City was larger than Philadelphia and had become the largest city in the nation (13).

New York, on the northern side of the Bight, is now the second most populous state after California, with a density of 367 persons per square mile. Forming the coastal region are New York City, Long Island, and the "downstate" portions of New York State. These have a total area of 4,014 square miles, a population of over 11 million and a density of 2,820 persons per square mile (14). If we add to that the rest of the Hudson Basin, where development directly affects the Bight, then there are an additional 1,700,000 persons, or about 74% of the population of New York State (15).

On the other side of the Bight, New Jersey, the fifth smallest state in the union (7,521 square miles), is the ninth most populous and the most densely settled, with 975 persons per square mile (16). From the industrialized and populous northern counties which are a part of the metropolitan region, the Garden State coastal region extends southward in ever less congested areas to Cape May on the north of Delaware Bay.

If we consider just the coastal rim of the New York Bight, there are 14.1 million persons living in 134 minor civil divisions. Approximately 50% are residents of New York City, 18% live on Long Island, and 32% reside in coastal New Jersey (17).

Developing Industry

We have grown greatly in our numbers and we have become immensely sophisticated in our technology.

Anthropologist Bert Salwen suggested that "the human popula-

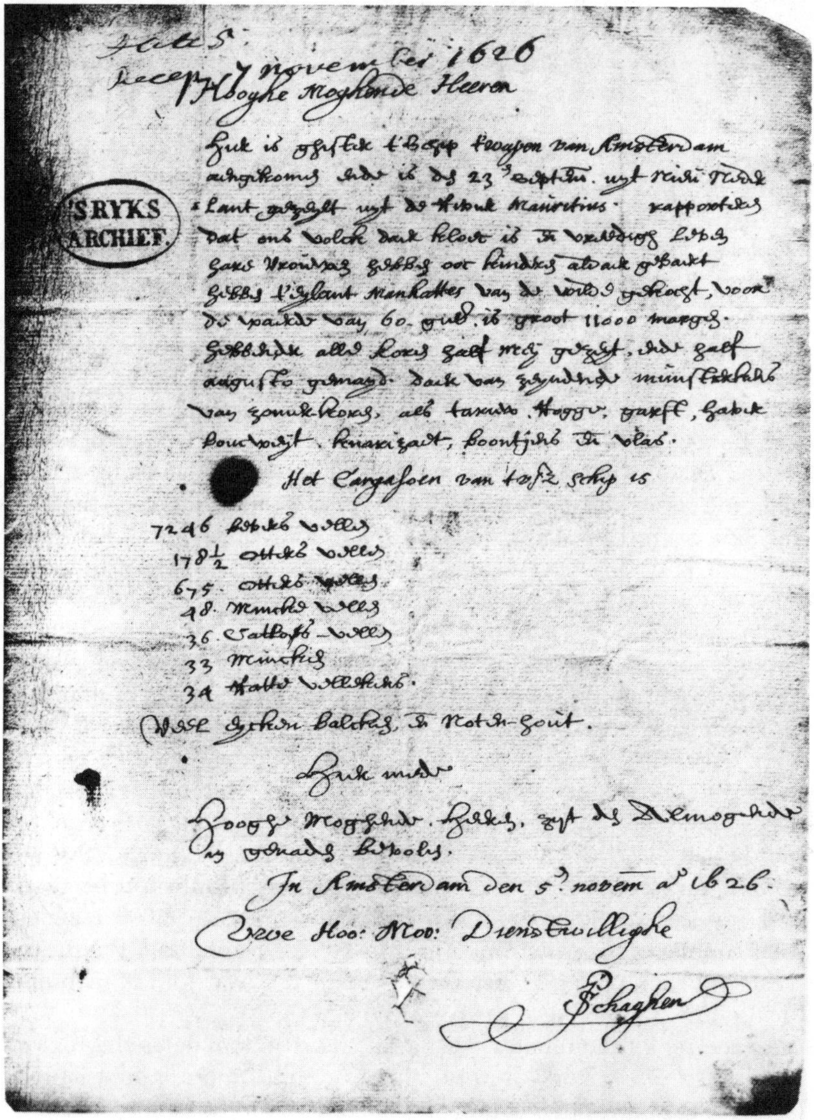

Recep. 7 november 1626

Hooghe Moghende Heeren

Hier is gisteren tschip t'Wapen van Amsterdam aengecomen ende is den 23 septemb. uyt Nieu Nederlant gezeylt uyt de Riviere Mauritius. rapporteren dat ons volck daer kloeck is en vreedich leven haere vrouwen hebben oock kinderen aldaer gebaert hebben t'eylant Manhattes van de wilde gekocht, voor de waerde van 60 guld. is groot 11000 morgen. hebben alle koren half mey gezayt, ende half augusto gemaeyt. daer van zynde monsterkens van zomerkoren, als tarwe, rogge, garst, haver, boeckweyt, knarizaet, boontjens en vlas.

Het Cargasoen van tvoorsz schip is

7246 bever vellen
178½ otter vellen
675 otter vellen
48 minck vellen
36 catlosse vellen
33 mincken
34 ratte vellekens

Veel eycken balcken, en noten hout.

Hier mede

Hooghe Moghende Heeren, zyt den Almogende in genade bevolen.

In Amsterdam den 5e novem ao 1626.

Uwe Hoo: Moo: Dienstwillighe

P. Schaghen

Letter of P. Schaghen announcing the purchase of the Island of Manhattan from the Indians, 1626

Figure 12. The "Bill of Sale" for Manhattan Island. This letter to the Hague, by P. Schlagen, reports information carried on the ship "Arms of Amsterdam" which sailed from New York September 23, 1626, on the purchase of an "unimproved" Manhattan Island for the "value of 60 guilders" (about $24.12 at the time). In 1978 the full value assessment of land and buildings of Manhattan was over $26 billon (Squires, 1981). (Letter reproduced from copy in O'Callaghan, 1853)

tions of the Hudson Basin region, since 9,000 B.C. have never, until *very* recently rated (conservation) of resources high among their culturally shared values. Rather, each society . . . has tended to live up to the carrying capacity of its habitat, using the technologies at its command" (18).

The technologies of modern society are incredible, developing out of the inventiveness of man searching for more and better ways to make things and to change the shape of the world. Using water power and wood as sources of energy, metals were smelted and tools fabricated. Around the developing margin of the Bight, these creative energies were harnessed and refined and, together with the natural attributes of the region that made trade easy, fostered the development of an extraordinary industrial complex.

The metropolitan region of New York City, northern New Jersey, and Long Island has been called the linchpin of the northeastern United States. The 3,900-square-mile region has a labor force of 7 million people and over 400,000 business establishments. This area has 32% of the population, 34% of the employment, 38% of the personal income, 29% of the value of factory sales, and 30% of the retail sales of the northeastern United States (19).

New York City is the hub of the region and is home for most of the nation's largest accounting firms, commercial banking companies, national broadcasting companies, advertising firms, and communication companies. Seventy-eight of the Fortune 500 companies have New York City addresses; more than 2,000 firms listed in Dun & Bradstreets' "Million Dollar Directory" are located there. In this complex of 16 million people, $42.5 billion dollars in retail sales were expended in 1977, about 6% of the nation's total (20). The city has become large enough to sustain an enormous production of goods and services for local consumption, the work of 378,000 business establishments. The metropolitan complex of Manhattan, the Bronx, western Brooklyn, and western Queens is the heart of the manufacturing area, with 63% of the capacity (21).

As the region dominates the Bight, the city dominates the region. Manhattan (New York County) alone provides more industrial jobs (396,000) than any other county in the nation. But the pattern is rapidly changing (22). Multistoried loft buildings that were once the site of manufacturing are rapidly giving way to other office structures. The clothing trade is still the mainstay of industry here, providing 43% of the jobs; printing and publishing provide 29% (23).

Beyond the city, along the concrete ribbons of highway extending out to Long Island are light industries, 7,900 in all, providing 308,000 jobs. Much of Long Island is a bedroom community for commuters to New York City. But beyond commuting range remain Long Island's farms and fishing villages. Suffolk County is New York State's premier agricultural county. With 9% of its land area under cultivation, the county produced agricultural products worth $65 million in 1974—the highest value of any county in New York or New Jersey (24).

Northern New Jersey is a large producer of chemicals. Oil refineries, containing about 4% of the nation's capacity (25), and other petrochemical industries are an important part of the coastal industrial complex. Textiles, electrical equipment, machinery, and paper products are also important. Most development has occurred in the northern part of the state where a commuter population, in addition to an industrialized corridor, has created a population concentration. Here, in a belt 34 miles long and 14 miles wide, extending from southern Bergen County to Perth Amboy in Middlesex County, is 66% of the industrial employment of New Jersey, with 8,100 plants employing 439,000 people (26).

But there is more to New Jersey, the Garden State, for 20% of its land is still in truck gardening, producing many of the fruits and vegetables consumed in the metropolitan region. Along its coast are fine beaches and old resort areas. Fishing remains an important industry.

Development of the Bight region's economy was fostered by its network of waterways and a major, central port, facilitating waterborne movement of materials in and out of the region. Also important to the area's development was ready access to abundant energy in the form of wood and water power.

But, as the nation grew, the port of New York lost its centrality and others came to claim their share of the commerce of the nation. Accompanying this shift, and perhaps stimulated by it, has been a gradual movement among the region's manufacturing industries toward "transport sensitive" products. Abetting these changes were increasingly high land, labor, and tax costs (27). Increasingly important in recent years has been the dependence of the region on imported petroleum for its energy—a dependency that has further stimulated the flight of heavy industry from the region. With the exception of petroleum refining and the associated petrochemical industry, there is little heavy industry left. Medium and small manufacturing firms are diverse and to a great extent produce for the large local market the city provides—sometimes referred to as Metromarket.

The rate of growth of local industries has levelled off, possibly because population growth in the region has slowed and perhaps peaked. But, although the rate of growth of the region is slower than the national average, the metropolitan region still dominates national manufacturing with a little over 8% of the total (28).

Yet the port remains a significant element in the region's economy, because since the 1950s it has increasingly become a regional port. Over two-thirds of the international commerce through the port originates in or is destined for the local area. In 1976, 72% of the exports and 88% of the imports passing through the port went to locations within 300 miles of the port (29). Imports are most significant in the port's trade; 61 million tons were brought through the port in 1977 (30). Exports in that same period were only 6 million tons. Seventy-seven percent of the imports are petroleum and petroleum products (31).

Exports, although accounting for only a small share of the total commerce passing through the port, are important to the area's economy; 43% of the exported materials originated within 25 miles of the port (32). About 12% of the nonlocal market manufacturing employment was directly related to the production of manufactured goods exported. During the 1972–1976 period there was a 41% growth in export-related employment in the Bight region, while total manufacturing declined 15% (33).

Originally linking the port with the rest of the nation were the waterways, particularly the Hudson and Mohawk rivers and Long Island Sound. These sheltered passages were supplemented by the development of canals, and then replaced by the railroads and most recently, highways. All these follow the same general course, for the pattern of settlement was laid out by the waterways and all subsequent forms of transportation have merely served to link the existing centers of population, markets, or manufacturing points.

Highways are now most important to the movement of goods and people. Railroads, once so very important in the region's economy, are being revived under the stimulus of energy costs; they may again play a significant role in the region's economy.

People and the Bight: Interaction

Striking changes have occurred in the Bight region since humans first appeared. Much has altered solely because of the huge increase in numbers of people living here; most of that change has happened in the last 50 years as population numbers doubled and redoubled. Technology has also greatly modified the face of the region. Introduction of automobiles, of new materials permitting ever higher buildings to be constructed, of heavy machinery which can literally reconfigure the shape of the earth, all these and more have been peculiarly European innovations for the region. From a heavily forested, sparsely populated area, the area around the Bight has become the center of the megalopolis and a part of the industrial corridor.

The kind, and rate, of change has occurred both because of increased numbers of us and our capability to extend our impacts through the use of tools and machines. "Future shock" has become a way of life (34). And change has affected the relationship between us and the ocean: the same ocean which is a part of the reason our region is what it is.

Historically, development of population and industry was linked to the port and its ocean connection. But a variety of factors have eroded this linkage. One might postulate that as the connection between the region and the ocean was weakened, that the value ascribed to a healthy oceanic environment was lessened. To fully explore that hypothesis would require a book of its own. We can, however, make some tentative forays into that inquiry by looking at how the region handles some of its most vital needs—energy and water. The purpose of this exploration of the linkage between energy, water, and the New York Bight is to see how the development of a population center and an industrial complex, all of which occurred on land, affected the ocean. It must be remembered that these are only two examples; others could be cited.

The Case of Energy

To run our complex of manufacturing and commerce and to sustain the enormous number of people inhabiting the metropolitan region requires vast quantities of energy. For the first two centuries of its human development, the Bight area's energy requirements were right there—wood and water power. But as more convenient and versatile forms of energy, particularly oil, became available, patterns of use changed. Today, the Bight region is an importer of energy, much of it oil, most of it from extraordinary distances.

In 1974 New York and New Jersey ranked forty-sixth and forty-fifth, respectively, among the 50 states in gross per capita energy consumption (35). This relatively low requirement results from a combination of factors which characterize the region including the prevalence of lower energy consumptive light industries and commercial activities, greater use of mass transit and fewer persons per household (36). However, New York ranks first, and New Jersey third, in consumption of oil—and all of its imported (37).

Imports of energy to the Bight region have increased over the last three centuries. But what comes in must also go out, so we may safely assume that the region is increasingly exporting some end product of its energy consumption—some in productivity, some in the form of wastes. Some of that "export" is seen locally: oil spilled from the armada of tankers bringing it to our shores, sullies our shores. But other exported wastes are sent further away, exported in the form of air pollution. This pollution results in contamination of the ocean, and, in our own contribution to the global problem of increasing atmospheric carbon monoxide, the so-called greenhouse effect.

When early European settlers arrived in the Bight region, they marvelled at the forests surrounding them, for those of their home countries had been cleared. "All cabin dwellers gloried in the warmth of their fireplaces, exploiting their world of surplus trees where a poor man, even a plantation slave, could burn bigger fires than most noblemen in Europe" (38). But the city's forests were soon cleared and by the early 1700s wood was being brought to the 12,000 people of Manhattan by as many as 50 wood boats a day coming from Long Island and the Hudson and Raritan valleys (39). As many as 20,000 cords of wood were needed each year to heat mid-eighteenth century New York City (40).

The wood fires of Manhattan created a lot of ashes which were carried away, under a city ordinance of 1675, to designated dumpsites along the waterfront (41). Accumulations of ash and other debris along the piers grew, requiring their being dredged. Clearing of the forests for wood greatly increased soil erosion in the entire watershed leading to shoaling of the estuary, resulting in more dredging.

Emerging industry also sought energy. For some enterprises, such as metal ore smelting, wood or charcoal would do. But for other industries, particularly the mills, water power was the answer. For all, location by the rivers and streams was essential for the transportation of energy, raw materials, and finished goods and to the carrying away of wastes from the processes. Dams sprang up along the rivers, and while they aided in catching sediment, they interfered with the spawning migrations of some fish, particularly the once prevalent Atlantic salmon. Northern New Jersey had abundant water power and water transportation, so an industrial complex began to develop there. Once started, that complex continued to grow, in many new

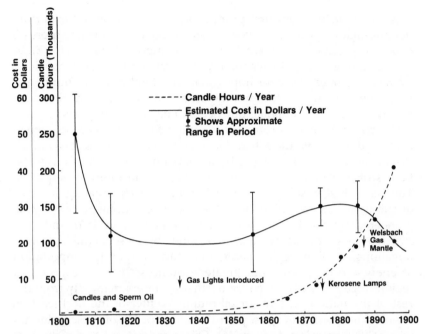

Figure 13. Costs for illumination in the metropolitan region in the 18th and 19th centuries. Early costs were very high—illumination tended to be one candle per room. Improvements in lighting were principally in gas illumination and then electrical lighting. Sharply increased lighting requirements after 1860 are thought to have resulted from the introduction of free libraries.

forms, as different kinds of energy besides water power became available. Industrialized northern New Jersey might not have come to be had it not been for water power.

As the industrial revolution rolled on and steam engines were introduced, coal began to replace wood. The transition, which occurred between 1850 and 1895, was hastened by the development of the railroads, for they provided the means to move the coal—and the steam locomotives themselves were a major consumer of coal.

Coal, burned in increasingly greater quantities in the boilers of the city for both steam heat and electrical generation, created enormous quantities of ash. Disposal of that ash in the ocean was simplest, cheapest, and expeditious for a city surrounded by water. By the 1960s as much as 110,000 tons of ash were carried yearly from generating plants to the Bight for dumping (42). That is about a fifth of the weight of rock and debris removed in 50 years of excavation for the city's entire subway system.

Then came oil. Oil was discovered at Titusville, Pennsylvania, on

August 27, 1859. From first production we became an oil exporting nation—that is, until about 1946 when we began to consume more oil than we produced and we became oil importers (43). The Bight region, though, has always imported its oil either from domestic or overseas sources. Despite hopes that the Bight's outer continental shelf might contain petroleum deposits, few ever thought that such production would eliminate our dependency on oil imports.

The nation changed from coal to oil quickly. Oil was more convenient, it didn't have the ash and soot and dust problems of coal. Further, coal was disadvantaged by its dependence on rail transportation; strikes of miners or railroad workers could interrupt supplies. The oil industry sidestepped such problems by creating its own distribution system—pipelines. Transoceanic shipment of oil was pioneered by the British, who first shipped oil in 1861 and constructed the first tanker in 1863 (44). Aided by these technological innovations the Bight region became dependent upon the importation of energy from greater and greater distances. In this respect, the region, together with the entire northeast, differs markedly from the rest of the nation. The major oil-refining center of the northeastern region is northern New Jersey. In 1972 the capacity of those refineries was 592,000 barrels a day (45, 46). Oil provides New York City with 71% of its energy compared to 44% for the nation (47).

With increasing amounts of oil being transported in the Bight region, an increasing amount is spilled. Something like 11% of the world's annual total of petroleum products moving by sea passes through the New York Bight, posing a substantial potential hazard to the region's sensitive fishery and recreation industries (48). Between 1973 and 1978, over 400,000 barrels of petroleum products were spilled in the nearshore waters of New York as a result of vessel accidents, 93% of the total spills reported nationally (49). About 320,000 tons of oil and grease enter the Bight annually, mostly from municipal waste waters and in dredged materials carried from the harbor to the spoil disposal grounds (50). If 50% of that oil and grease had come from petroleum products such as used automobile oil, then about 4% of the world's spilled petroleum is in the New York Bight (51).

As the coming of oil spelled the beginning of the end for coal, oil also prevented natural gas from becoming a significant source of energy for the Bight region. Natural gas was first exploited in 1821 at Fredonia, N.Y., and the first pipeline, made of wood, was in that city (52, 53). But natural gas didn't reach the Bight region until the late 1940s when the "Big Inch" and "Little Big Inch" pipelines were purchased from the government and converted to transport Gulf coast natural gas (54). Before that time, manufactured gas, made from coal or oil, had been in use. The New York Gas Light Company, incorporated in 1823, was the second manufactured gas company in the United States. Although New York City was the first to require street lighting (in 1679, every seventh householder was required to place a lamp in a window or to hang a lantern outside), it wasn't until 1827 that Broadway, lit by gas, became the Great White Way (55).

Until the mid-1800s, most homes were heated by wood, although coal was increasingly sought as a replacement fuel. Gas for space heating was introduced in 1910, following the invention of automatic ignition and thermostats (56). The oil burner became the new, hot item for home heating in 1920 and rapidly displaced coal because it put an end to the hauling of ashes and effectively competed with gas for a complex of economic reasons.

By the 1860s the principle of the free public school system had been adopted in at least the northern states and more and more people were learning to read. Reading required better light than that needed for domestic tasks and suddenly there was a demand for better illuminants (57). By the first quarter of the nineteenth century manufactured gas could provide better lighting, but because of the difficulty in its distribution, then limited to pipelines in the major cities, its use was not widespread. By 1875, kerosene lamps were available but within 20 years they succumbed to competition from the new Welsbach gas light mantles. Gaslight, in turn, was replaced by the incandescent lamp (58).

Thomas Alva Edison invented the incandescent lamp in 1879 in Menlo Park, New Jersey, and by December 1880 the gas lights of Broadway were being replaced by electric (59). In 1882 the Edison Electric Illuminating Company opened a generating station in New York City: Edison Electric and New York Gas Light went on to become Consolidated Edison, the giant utility so reviled by New Yorkers.

America clasped electricity, the most convenient of all sources of energy, to its bosom. At first coal was burned to make the steam to drive the turbines to drive the generators, but with growing concern for air quality, the generating stations, particularly of the metropolitan region were converted to oil. By the mid-1960s, coal was all but gone from the Bight region and oil was king.

Just as schools and literacy increased the demand for home illumination, the automobile spurred the demand for gasoline. By 1900 over 4,000 automobiles had been built in the United States (60); in 1909 Ford's Model T was rolling off the production line, and

Americans took to the road. Between 1925 and 1955 the number of motor vehicles tripled, and the demand for gasoline increased sixfold (61).

Petroleum currently provides about half of the Bight region's energy but, by contrast, only a fifth of the nation's needs (62). Most of the oil used around the Bight is for steam-electric generation of electricity: about 10% of the nation's electrical generating capacity is located on its shores, 35,000 megawatts in 1972 (63). In addition to its greater than national average use of oil for making electricity, the region is more dependent on gas turbines (for 22% of its electrical capacity) and has a higher proportion of nuclear generation (18% versus 4%) than the rest of the nation (64). In the Bight region, 34% of the electrical energy goes to household and commercial uses, 28% for transportation, and 10% for industry (65).

With oil in short supply in the late 1970s, much attention was being given to reintroducing coal for steam-electric generation. Coal's production of materials deleterious to the atmosphere requires that the combustion gases be scrubbed to remove sulfur. That process yields vast quantities of "scrubber sludge," a calcium sulfate slurry. A 500-megawatt power plant can consume over a million tons of coal a year, producing 600,000 tons of ash and scrubber sludge (66). Disposal of this material presents a massive logistic (and economic) problem. An obvious solution is to dump the material in the coastal ocean just as had been fly ash, the very fine air-borne combustion product first controlled by the utilities.

But, it has been found that scrubber sludge and fly ash can be compressed into blocks having structural integrity and from which metals, sulfur and other substances leach slowly, if at all, in seawater. Such blocks could then be used for constructive purposes. At present, "coal waste" blocks have been placed in the Bight, off the south shore of Long Island, to form an artificial fishing reef (67). Results are encouraging.

Burning of fossil fuels results in more than ashes, or oil spills. The coastal area from Cape May to Connecticut has been estimated to annually produce 8 million tons of carbon monoxide, nearly 2 million tons of hydrocarbons, 1.5 million tons of nitrogen oxides, 1.2 million tons of sulfur dioxide and 350,000 tons of particulate matter (68). Much of this matter ends up in the ocean as the atmosphere is cleansed by rainfall. Most of the rest ends up on land and then finds its way to the ocean.

The Bight may be, someday, a producer of energy. Oil and gas may be found beneath its floor; biomass for conversion to alternative energy may be grown at its surface. But at present the Bight is a medium for transport of enormous quantities of energy to its shores: energy which is then used to power the social and industrial complex around the Bight, to modify its shape and dimensions, and which then alters the quality of its atmosphere and waters.

The Case of Water

In today's society fresh water presents three different kinds of problems: getting it in sufficient quantity for all its uses; keeping its quality high enough so that it is safe for us to drink; and, disposing of it once it has been used. We drink it, wash ourselves and our belongings in it, cook in it, water our gardens, use it in a bewildering variety of manufacturing processes, and waste it. Mostly, however, we use a lot of water just to flush away the waste products of our bodies, our dwellings, and our places of work.

> Early man seems to have lived by the waterside: the oldest palaeolithic implements are found in the river gravels. Whether he bathed or not, he had to have water, and because he had as yet no means of bringing it to his dwelling, he made his dwelling by the river bank (69).

As the size of communities grew, the next problem emerged: water quality. If water supply and waste disposal weren't well separated, a contaminated water supply resulted. After several major epidemics which spectacularly reduced the numbers of people, the message came home. But the task of maintaining water quality becomes increasingly difficult as the size of communities grows. At the scale of cities, purveying pure waters is not simple. The quantities required and the problem of separating wastes and supplies is so complicated that great water supply, sewerage, and sewage treatment systems are required.

Manhattan's early water supply was never assured. The hard rock of the island made the water table shallow and easily polluted. Yellow fever epidemics in 1821 and 1822, a cholera epidemic in 1832, and disastrous fires in 1828 and 1835 resulting from inadequate water for firefighting were spurs to the search for alternatives to shallow, and contaminated, wells as a source of water. After much discussion and political maneuvering, the 37-mile Croton Aquaduct was completed in 1842 and water from Putnam and Westchester counties was imported into the city. Parallel aqueducts were added through the years, until by 1944 over 250 miles of tunnels were carrying water to

New York City from the Catskills and the Delaware Basin (70).

With abundant, clean water from the Croton, hydrants and fountains became commonplace. New Yorkers rushed to install indoor bathrooms and other running water amenities (71). New York City, like many other older American cities, does not meter its domestic water customers (only commercial and industrial users are metered and they account for only about 25% of consumption) (72). As is so often the case with "free" goods, use increases because there are no incentives to conserve. Consumption of water rose to 190 gallons from 154 gallons per day per person between 1960 and 1980 (73). This consumption rate is among the highest in the nation, more than double that of the Soviet Union and more than 20 times that of Great Britain (74). It is estimated that between 8% and 15% of the water delivered daily in the City is lost through broken pipes under the streets and in abandoned buildings (75).

But water use is a problem elsewhere than just in the cities. Supply systems were constructed early in the region's history and are piecemeal and not integrated. Most were not designed to cope with the prodigious quantities of water consumed by modern living replete with dishwashers, automatic washing machines, coin-operated car washes, and huge entertainment and industrial complexes. Northern New Jersey has experienced a 30% increase in water use demand since the 1960s although its population growth has been negligible (76). But the Meadowlands sports complex in the Hackensack Meadows alone uses 500,000 gallons a day (77).

Long Island's water supply comes from the porous Pleistocene sands and gravels of which the island is formed. These are an excellent reservoir in which to collect rainwater and are estimated to contain a 500-year supply (78). As the island's population grew, the outtake of freshwater from shallow wells began to exceed input and many wells were penetrated by salt waters from Long Island Sound or the Atlantic Ocean. In the mid-1930s, amid growing realization that Long Island was indeed an island, unconnected with mainland sources of water and difficult to bring water to, a program of recharging of surface waters was instituted. Today, the island is dotted with enclosed excavations of various sizes that collect the surface runoff waters that then trickle downward into the aquifers underlying the island.

New Jersey's water supplies are based on river, streams, lakes, and later reservoirs constructed by small water supply companies. In drought situations in both the 1960s and 1980s, these fragmented distribution systems were found to be inadequate. But supply is not the problem, for the Pine Barrens of central New Jersey have rich, un-tapped supplies of groundwater.

Even as the Croton Aquaduct was under construction to provide the city with a new water supply, there was parallel debate on what to do with the used water that would result. The problem was simple: water brought into the homes of the city would result in an almost equal amount running out of them. Chronic overloading of cesspools and other disposal systems quickly occurred and groundwater supplies were contaminated by sewage, increasing the dependency upon imported water (79). With more and more water being imported, the local water table rose and low-lying spots were flooded.

Sewers were first constructed to carry away surface drainage and storm waters, while domestic wastes and fecal material were carried away from clogged cesspools by buckets and horse-drawn carts (80). Although "night soil" was not supposed to be disposed of in street drainage, it was. But increasing growth of the city population and the introduction of piped-in water necessitated change from past practices. By the mid-1800s, many cities were following the European practice and combining surface drainage and domestic sewage disposal into a combined system (81). This mixing of domestic wastewater and rainwater running off streets and buildings resulted in what is called, in today's technical parlance, "combined sewers," which make up 70% of New York City's sewerage. Storm drainage, or runoff, usually doesn't require treatment: if it does, the treatment is different from that for sewage.

The problem with combined sewers arises with planning for quantity of sewage to be handled by the treatment plants. If plants are designed to handle wastewater *and* runoff, then they must be larger, and they cost more. If designed to handle only the wastewater, then they will overflow each time it rains. Since there is little excitement among tax-payers for first-class sewage-treatment plants, a compromise is usually struck. That compromise allows for a certain amount of rainfall—if there is more, enough to cause an excess of water beyond the planned amount, then untreated sewage overflows or bypasses the treatment plant. In modern New York this occurs whenever rainfall exceeds a quarter of an inch in an hour.

Water enters our houses or places of work rather mysteriously. Most of us are so accustomed to the faucet that some believe that water resides therein. What happens to water, once used, is just as mysterious to most. It makes its way out through drain pipes to the sewers, through the sewer system, to a treatment plant (if any), to a stream, a river, the estuary, but always ending in the ocean. But, by the time water gets to the ocean it has been altered in many ways.

In the late 1800s there were a few small sewage treatment plants operating around the city, the first built in 1884 (82). By the turn of the century, as a result of sewage discharged at the head of the docks and piers, conditions in the harbor were so bad, that the public pressured for construction of modern sewage-treatment plants. Within 25 years treatment of sewage led to a new problem—the disposal of the sludge created in the treatment process.

Sewage sludge is a commodity for which there is low demand. The economics of the situation seemed to suggest that dumping of the sludge at sea was the answer. As the population grew, there was more sewage; as we used more water, the sewage became more dilute, requiring larger sewers and larger sewage treatment plants. The hard reality is that the primary cost of sewage treatment is the separation of water from the solids (83). Hoisted on our own petard by our desire for more water, in the face of stabilizing population growth we cannot escape the need for more expenditures on sewage treatment.

Similar problems surfaced on Long Island and in less populated New Jersey. The porous sands that permit rainfall to enter the soil and collect in the aquifers also permit sewage to penetrate the shallow aquifers. Recently, even deeper wells have been found to be contaminated by industrial wastes injected into the subsoils during the second world war. Most recently even the lightly populated agricultural regions of eastern Long Island have been found to have severe groundwater contamination through the infiltration of the potato nematode-control chemical Temik and to be overrich in nitrates from the heavy use of chemical fertilizers.

We are, unfortunately, more concerned with the front end of this system than the back. We worry more about the quality of the food and water we bring to our homes than about the quality of the sewage we deliver back to the environment. Nor do most people really want to know where their sewage goes. There have been periodic concerns about poor water quality resulting from sewage contamination, but these usually surface when things have very definitely gone awry.

In the early part of this century, problems resulting from lack of sewage treatment became very apparent—noxious odors arising from the rivers surrounding Manhattan. These were sufficiently bad that users of Jacob Reis' play piers in the East River complained loudly (84). And, since the 1920s, there has been a persistent concern for the effects of sewage on the reduction (sometimes elimination) of oxygen from the waters of the harbor (85). Even today, the ubiquitous boring molluscs so destructive to wooden structures all around the world cannot survive in the harbor waters because of the low oxygen levels (86). That depletion is the direct result of the discharge of quantities of treated and untreated sewage into the rivers surrounding the city.

There are 2,600,000,000 gallons of treated and untreated sewage being discharged daily into the Bight from 131 major municipal discharge points (87). With the exception of the northern and western portions of Manhattan, northeastern Staten Island, and a small part of eastern Brooklyn, most of this sewage has had some treatment.

While the sewers of Paris were made famous by the legendary figures who inhabited them, the sewers of New York are less well known, but no less spectacular. Consider the fact that the water supply system for the city alone delivers something on the order of 1.5 billion gallons of water per day. That quantity is not unlike the filling of an Olympic-sized swimming pool every second.

Discharges from southern New Jersey are from small municipalities, and, compared with the major input from the metropolitan region of New York and New Jersey, are relatively insignificant. Most of the industrial waste discharges are from New Jersey's industrialized region. Long Island is constructing its first sewerage system and in the near future will be exporting its groundwater in the form of wastewater to the Bight.

In the next chapter we will be looking more closely at the impacts of these discharges on the Bight. But let us note here that there are many things going on in this business of waste disposal: (1.) the discharge of human, domestic wastes through sewage systems; (2.) the discharge of industrial wastes through the same systems; (3.) the problem of the combined sewers of New York City; (4.) the direct discharge of industrial wastes; and (5.) the runoff of street drainage with its mixture of fecal material from animals, and metals, petrochemicals and asbestos fibers from automobiles.

What Does It All Mean?

At some time in the early nineteenth century, the population of the Bight region passed a critical point. The metropolitan region and its bedroom communities were no longer self-sufficient, particularly with respect to energy and water. This population complex, critically sited on the estuarine terminus, became an importer of these commodities (along with a host of others) and an exporter of the wastes of their use (along with the wastes of all the other imports): a flow-

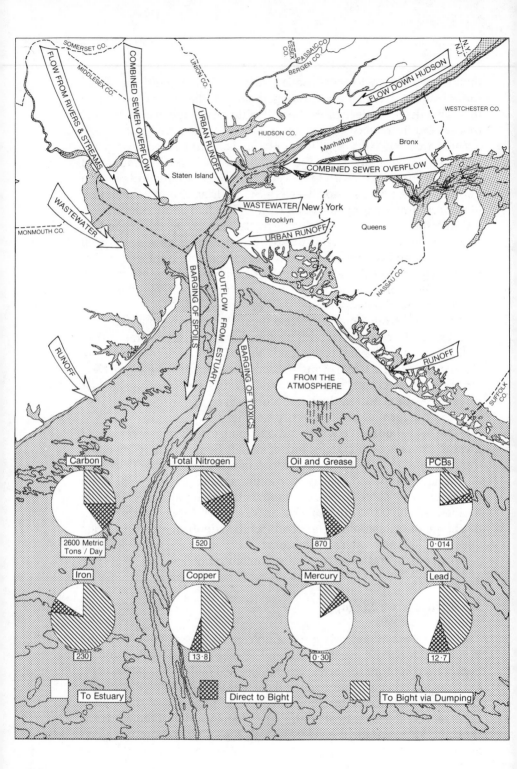

through economy of trade became a flow-through system with its local environmental resources. At first the estuary bore the brunt of the waste-disposal onslaught, but its capacity to absorb the wastes was soon exceeded. The wastes accumulating in the harbor then were transported, by people and by natural processes, to the Bight.

Growth of the region's population to its present size could not have occurred without the Bight. Access to the ocean meant that tremendous quantities of living and then fossil fuels could be cheaply transported to the urban complex. Proximity to the ocean allowed the metropolitan complex to delay, until quite recently, decisions on sewerage and waste treatment forced upon other municipalities by public health concerns. Simple economics dictated that the cheapest means of waste disposal be followed, and that was to dump it in the ocean.

At the same time that we were increasing in numbers, industry was becoming more complicated. Technology improved our lives and made our present society possible, but only at the cost of increasingly sophisticated processes resulting in increasingly sophisticated wastes. And too, many of us didn't use the new products of our "better living through chemistry" very well—we overused, spilled, improperly disposed of and otherwise abused many pesticides, herbicides, and other materials available to us. But always the ocean was there—the ultimate in waste disposal.

We moved our wastes to the ocean and it had no choice but to accept them. But there came a realization that things couldn't continue in this fashion. Something had to change. And, with that realization came a new chapter in the life of the Bight.

Figure 14. Sources of wastes discharged to the New York Bight. Sources, indicated by arrows, are highly generalized. Many wastes are discharged into the estuary—some directly to the Bight. Man contributes to the Bight's pollution by directly discharging wastes by barging them from land, or the estuary. The pie-diagrams show the relative importance of these three means of pollutant additions by shading. The white portion of the circle represents discharges to the estuary; the cross-hatched comes directly to the Bight, mostly from the atmosphere. The diagonally slashed sector represents that portion of wastes carried to the Bight by barging of spoils, sludge or toxic or industrial wastes. (Map by Sharon Ellis; data from MESA New York Bight Project)

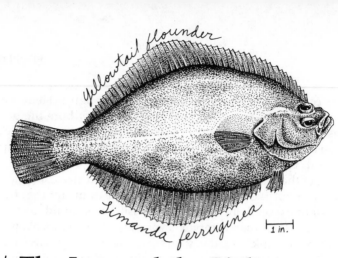

5 / The Law and the Bight

We've looked at the processes of the Bight, its resources and its uses. Again and again we have seen conflicts: conflicts between uses and abuses; short-term gains realized against long-term costs. Above all we have seen a picture of a bit of coastal ocean surrounded by a high density of population and industrial development. From the view point of some, the resources of the Bight are being pillaged by greed and neglect: overharvesting and slow destruction of a quality environment. In the view of others, the Bight is being efficiently and effectively used as a corridor of commerce, a recreational resource for tens of millions, a source of food, and as a repository for wastes produced by our society either too costly or too toxic for other means of disposal. These are conflicts often encountered in a commons situation—each user sees his use as being only an increment of a larger picture and not of consequence to the total. Each user seeks to maximize his use at cost to everyone else.

We can look at this same situation from another viewpoint: the users of the Bight are engaged in a zero-sum game (1). Each user is either a winner or a loser, but the sum of all of the gains and losses is zero. Harvesters of resources work against the biological reproduction rate of the species they catch. Higher harvest rates (a gain) result in depleted stocks and lower catches (a loss). Polluters gain lower costs for waste disposal but recreationists and fishermen lose through habitat deterioration. This is, of course, just another way of saying the same thing: confrontations arise when each of the multiple users of a common resource attempts to maximize their own situation and to not sustain any losses from their present position.

When confronted with these kinds of situations, our society has looked to some relatively uninvolved party to resolve the conflicts, to minimize the loses to any one segment of society. That uninvolved party has often been government and in the last 20 years, specifically the federal government. As people became aware that industry use of air and water resources for waste disposal was a cost that they were bearing without recompense, the environmental movement grew and sharpened. In the early 1970s, as a capstone to environmental understanding, a spate of federal legislation having direct effects upon the coastal waters of the nation was put into place. Included were the Coastal Zone Management Act of 1972 (P.L. 92-583), which encouraged coastal states to plan their use of coastal lands and waters; the Fishery Conservation and Management Act of 1976 (P.L. 94-265), which established the 200-mile exclusive economic zone and regional fishery management councils for the management of fishery resources; the Ocean Dumping Act of 1972 (P.L. 92-532); and the Federal Water Pollution Control Act Amendments of 1972 (P.L. 92-500).

We have encountered the Coastal Zone Management Act in discussing the margins of the Bight and the Fishery Management and Conservation Act with regard to the Bight's resources. Water quality will now be the focus of our attention.

Of all the ways in which we humans use the Bight the most directly destructive is as a dump. For many years those who thought about it at all assumed the ocean to be so vast and not sufficiently important, that we used its capaciousness to dispose of our unwanted and even hazardous chemicals, warfare agents, debris, garbage, and other effluvia. In time we found that this wasn't so. We were poisoning, even though minutely, our coastal waters and some of its uses were foreclosed to us by these actions. Tens of thousands of acres of productive shellfish grounds have been closed to harvesting—some for decades. Visibly diseased fish are caught by commercial and sport fishermen. And, we found that America's number one recreational pastime—being on the beach—wasn't so pleasant when its sands were littered by tar balls, plastic debris clearly emanating from a sewer someplace. Our aesthetic senses were offended if not our well-being.

Just as with other issues of environmental quality, neither the kinds nor the quantities of materials disposed of in the coastal ocean posed a sufficient problem for public action until environmental awareness grew in the late 1950s and early 1960s. While this practice is as old as mankind's habitation in the coastal region, it was a problem which grew in size with our population. In the forty years between 1930 and 1970, the population in the coastal region of the country had doubled and industrial development along the coasts increased (2).

As actions were taken to clean up the air, rivers, streams and lakes, there was a tendency for waste disposal to be transferred to the ocean. As housing was constructed along the coasts, fewer and fewer landfill sites were available. Disposal of solid wastes in the coastal ocean became an increasingly attractive alternative. Volume of wastes discharged at sea increased 335% from the mid-1950s to the mid-1960s (3). In the New York Bight the carrying of wastes to the ocean and dumping them there is utilized more than elsewhere in the country. In 1980 about 100% of municipal wastes (principally sewage sludge) and 87% of the industrial wastes dumped in the nation's coastal ocean occurred at 5 designated sites in the apex of the Bight, and one other just beyond its outer margin (4).

Close in to shore are the designated sites for dumping of sewage sludge, dredge spoils, cellar dirt (or construction materials) and acid wastes. Further out is the wreck dumpsite where abandoned or damaged vessels were sunk, and furthest off shore, and beyond the Bight is the chemical waste dumpsite.

Dredge spoils make up about half the volume of barged waste dumped in the Bight (5). Dumping of spoils at sea is not unique to the Bight region, nor are the amounts dumped particularly significant. But it has been learned that it is the largest transfer mechanism for contaminants such as heavy metals and organic toxics from estuary to the Bight.

At first this was a local problem for dredge spoils were dumped within the harbor. But by the 1880s the New York Harbor Commission was unable to deal with contractors who dredged, moved out of sight, and dumped, with the result that channels were quickly refilled. The only organization of government then able to deal with the situation was the U. S. Army Corps of Engineers. Through the River and Harbor Act of 1888, the corps was given authority to regulate dredging and spoil disposal (6). Between 1890 and 1914, a large number of authorized disposal sites were established in the Bight. But these nearshore sites became navigation hazards themselves as sediments accumulated and a relatively permanent location for spoil disposal was established at the head of the Hudson Shelf Valley (7).

Sewage sludge, often thought of as being solid, is actually about 95% water. A necessary by-product of sewage treatment, sewage sludge contains the organic materials associated with domestic sewage plus a complex array of toxic metals, chlorinated hydrocarbons (such as PCBs), chlorinated pesticides and assorted viral and bacterial pathogens. While many municipalities have used incineration, landfilling, soil conditioning, and other means to dispose of their sludge, New York and New Jersey communities used ocean disposal. The ocean was close by, the costs were low, and there wasn't a perceived effect on the ocean.

Nationally, sewage sludge makes up about 15% of the total of wastes barged to the ocean (8). In the Bight region it constitutes the second largest volume (about 31%) of barged wastes (9). All of it has come from New York and New Jersey communities and, until recently, the City of Philadelphia. Some California cities pipe sewage sludge to the ocean. They can do this because the continental shelf off California is very narrow and pipelines can be constructed which run out to the shelf edge. The Bight's burden of sewage sludge results not from a failure to seek alternative means of disposal but from a combination of historical factors and geography. In simplest terms, in the mid-1800s the most economical, and seemingly effective means of disposal was to dump at sea and nothing much has changed that situation.

Cellar dirt, or the nonfloating rock and soil from excavations for buildings and some brick and mortar debris from their construction and demolition, is dumped in the Bight simply because there is no other place to put it—at comparable costs. Volume of this material dumped, and its nature, varies greatly from year to year but generally increases as large public works are undertaken. During the period of 1965 to 1970, cellar dirt made up only about 5% of the volume of dumped wastes (10). Ships were sunk at the wreck site until 1980 when it was closed. Scuttling of old wooden sailing ships and of barges was an inexpensive disposal technique, but most steel-hulled vessels are salvaged if at all possible.

The industrial wastes site at the margin of the Bight is the most recently established. Its definition resulted from requests from New Jersey manufacturers for a site for disposal of toxic chemical wastes which could not be disposed of on land because of the hazards presented. Its use has been steadily increasing.

Many people only somewhat aware of the practice of dumping of wastes in the Bight firmly believe that garbage is a major component. Perhaps such a perception comes from the visibility of the garbage scows carrying solid wastes from loading points around the harbor to the landfill sites. But dumping of garbage in the Bight has been prohibited for almost 50 years.

Stopping the dumping of wastes in the oceans and the Great Lakes became a part of the environmental movement. On the national scene, the newly formed Council on Environmental Quality was directed by President Richard Nixon to make its first study an evaluation of ocean dumping (11). In its report the Council concluded that "there is a critical need for a national policy on ocean dumping" (12).

But in the New York Bight region, awareness of degradation caused by dumping had come earlier. Studies by the Food and Drug Administration in 1964 and 1968 demonstrated that bottom waters in the vicinity of the sewage sludge dump contained excessive coliform bacteria, indicators of shellfish contamination by human pathogens (13). These investigations resulted in closure to shellfishing of an area of about 160 square miles around the sludge dump in the inner portion of the Bight. Later, in 1974, the closed area was extended to include waters adjacent to New Jersey's northern shore and the Rockaways of Long Island. This was the first time that a part of the ocean floor had been closed to shellfishing by the U. S. Food and Drug Administration. The effect upon the operators of an estimated 101 vessels which had fished for sea clams there was immediate (14).

Two reasonably predictable actions followed growing awareness of the effects of ocean dumping: the Congress of the United States began to take legislative action and there was a call for further research. These two actions are the basis of this chapter.

Legislating Cleaner Water

The Council on Environmental Quality, in its study of ocean dumping, found that ocean dumping could be harmful to the marine environment, that feasible and economic alternative disposal techniques were available, and that a national policy on ocean dumping was critically needed. It recommended that the Congress terminate unregulated dumping, recommendations underscored in legislation passed 23 October 1972, the Marine Protection, Research, and Sanctuaries Act. This legislation adopted a national policy of regulating the dumping of all materials into ocean waters and preventing or strictly limiting the dumping of materials which would "adversely affect human health, welfare, or amenities, or the marine environment, ecological systems, or economic potentialities" (15).

The "Ocean Dumping Act," as it has come to be called, was divided into three sections, or titles:

Title I. Ocean Dumping;

Title II. Comprehensive Research on Ocean Dumping;

Title III. Marine Sanctuaries.
We shall look at Title I in this section and deal with Title II later on. The section on Marine Sanctuaries isn't relevent to this discussion.

Contained in the Ocean Dumping Act is the important conclusion that *unregulated* dumping is a danger and that its regulation should be the policy of the United States. Title I of the legislation provides the tools by which this would occur by prohibiting ocean dumping without a permit. The legislation allows for dumping of wastes (other than dredge spoils) if permits are obtained from the Environmental Protection Agency and provides that permits for dumping of dredge spoils are to be issued by the Army Corps of Engineers. The act specifically bans the dumping of radiological, chemical, or biological warfare agents and high-level radioactive wastes but permits the dumping of other materials if it is determined that "such dumping will not unreasonably degrade or endanger human health, welfare or amenities, or the marine environment, ecological systems, or economic potentialities" (16).

At the same time as the Ocean Dumping Act was being drawn up, the Congress was in the midst of a great struggle to pass sweeping Federal Water Pollution Control Act Amendments. On 18 October 1972, that legislation, passed over President Nixon's veto, became law. This complex legislation contains the declaration of a "national goal that the discharge of pollutants into the navigable waters be eliminated by 1985" and sets the objective of restoring and maintaining the physical, chemical, and biological integrity of the nation's waters (17). While much of this legislation was designed to deal with the inland, fresh, waters of the nation, two sections spoke specifically to ocean discharges: Section 403 regulates the discharge of nondredged materials from onshore outfall pipes, from all single discharge points within the Territorial Sea and from point sources other than vessels or floating craft out to 12 miles; Section 404 regulates discharges of dredged materials into navigable waters (that is, out to the 3-mile Territorial Sea boundary). This section also authorizes the Corps of Engineers to issue permits for the discharge of dredged or fill materials at specified disposal sites in navigable waters.

These two actions by the Congress, while well-meaning, were only a partial improvement on the situation. The confusion by two legislative actions having the same general intent, but approaching the problem very differently, contributed to a lot of discussion and dispute. But at the same time, they did have the effect of reducing the quantities of wastes disposed of in the Bight. The Marine Protection, Research, and Sanctuaries Act responded directly to the issue raised by the Council on Environmental Quality: the need for regulation of dumping to ascertain how much of what was being dumped where.

Further, the Marine Protection, Research, and Sanctuaries Act called for a research program "for the purpose of determining means of minimizing or ending all dumping of materials within five years of the effective date of this Act"—that was, by October 1978 (18). Title I of the legislation did not terminate dumping but rather aimed to regulate all dumping and to "prevent or strictly limit" dumping of substances which would adversely affect man or the environment (19). These two provisions of the legislation have led to conflicting views on the goal of the act. Is that goal to limit dumping and prevent adverse effects or does the implication contained in the title on research suggest that the Congress intended to phase out all ocean dumping (20)?

Amendments to the Water Quality Act, on the other hand, set forth some specific objectives. Under Section 403, the administrator of the Environmental Protection Agency was instructed to set out guidelines by which the degradation of waters in the Territorial Sea, the Contiguous Zone, and the oceans could be determined (21). Those guidelines were published in October 1973 (22).

A result of these approaches was a determination by the Environmental Protection Agency that it would end interim permits for the dumping of industrial wastes by 1978. But because of the varying possible interpretations of the legislation, the Environmental Protection Agency has been attacked by those who feel it is not acting fast or effectively enough to terminate ocean dumping, and by those who feel that it has been too assiduous in terminating dumping as an alternative for waste disposal.

In February 1975, the Environmental Protection Agency issued an interim permit to the City of Philadelphia containing a notice that it was to terminate ocean dumping of sewage sludge before 1982. Administrator Russell Train supported the deadline "not so much on significant evidence of actual harm at the site but on the general concern of the scientific community over continued addition of heavy metals and other pollutants to the ocean" (23).

By June 1976, the Environmental Protection Agency had completed revision of its 1973 guidelines in the form of criteria and regulations for ocean dumping and, following the earlier action of the administrator, stated that no new interim permits would be issued and renewals would be available only to those showing good faith in their efforts to phase out of ocean dumping by 1981.

The final criteria and regulations were issued in January 1977, and they established the 1981 deadline for ending the dumping of materials which could unreasonably degrade or endanger human health or the marine environment (24). In this issuance the Environmental Protection Agency noted that the Congress had "expressed impatience with continued issuance of interim permits and the EPA agrees that five years is sufficient time for dumpers to develop technology to end reliance on ocean dumping which violates environmental criteria" (25). To speed things on their way, the Environmental Protection Agency also provided funds for research on such alternative technologies.

The Environmental Protection Agency's position might, at this time, be summed up as follows:

> What the Agency has attempted to do is to estimate as best it can those levels of pollutants which may be expected to cause environmental harm, to apply a safety factor, and to refuse to sanction dumping of wastes containing pollutants in these amounts unless there is no other environmentally acceptable alternative. EPA has also tried to prepare its regulation in view of criteria established under the Federal Water Pollution Control Act, State laws, and other Federal pollution laws. Obviously it makes little sense to allow discharges of mercury through a pipe into Chesapeake Bay at levels higher than discharges from a barge into the deep ocean waters, for example. The Agency must also consider its credibility as a regulating agency. If it demands that a small community or industry cease dumping within a period of time, it should be confident that there are feasible alternatives which may be implemented within that time period. Increasingly, this is true; and it is the reason all interim permit holders have been given firm phase-out dates . . . Increasingly, EPA has become aware that the alternatives to ocean dumping require careful evaluations; they may not always be better (26).

With the summer of 1976 came an onslaught to the beaches of Long Island and New York City. Large amounts of debris, including materials clearly originating from sewage and other substances presumed by the public to be of similar derivation piled up. While the newspapers howled again at this desecration of the beaches, worried governmental officials closed these same beaches. Congress scheduled oversight hearings on the Ocean Dumping Act, including one on Long Island. These authorization and appropriation hearings gave evidence of the heat being applied to the Congress by coastal constituents. The Merchant Marine and Fisheries Committee of the House of Representatives is described as "losing confidence in EPA's ability to compel municipalities, which now dump their sewage sludge into ocean waters, to adopt environmentally acceptable land-based alternatives. It is therefore, the committee's intent to establish, by statute, the requirement that all ocean dumping of municipal sewage sludge which may be harmful cease on or before December 31, 1981'' (27).

Despite research which showed that the debris washed up on the beaches in the summer of 1976 was not derived from the sewage sludge dumpsite (28), the Congress, particularly Congressman Hughes from New Jersey, was adamant. And in November 1977, President Jimmy Carter signed the amended Ocean Dumping Act into law: the termination of dumping by 31 December 1981 was official.

But matters were still not at rest. The Senate's Committee on Commerce, led by the powerful ocean interests of its chairman, Senator Warren Magnuson, directed the National Ocean Policy Study, Senator Ernest Hollings, chairman, to make a study of ocean dumping (29). This inquiry found that ocean dumping was low on every agency's priority list and that no one was in charge. Further, while

Figure 15. The "sludge monster" as created by John Huehnergarth. (Reproduced from *Audubon*, vol. 76, no. 4, pp. 108–109 with permission of the Audubon Society; and with permission of John Huehnergarth)

earlier legislation had given the National Oceanic and Atmospheric Administration a mandate to sponsor research on land-based alternatives to ocean dumping, the work wasn't being done. Hearings were held in the House of Representatives and it was concluded: "numerous agencies, departments, and instrumentalities of the Federal government sponsor, support, or fund activities relating to ocean pollution research and monitoring. However, such programs are often uncoordinated and can result in unnecessary duplication" (30).

Later, the House of Representatives Committee on Science and Technology defined the problem:

> It is generally conceded that we are on the verge of a major explosion in the utilization of the sea. Many experts believe that man will begin to sharply increase his dependence on fish as a protein source. Many U. S. fisheries are already depleted as a result of years of overfishing. The extension to a 200-mile fishing limit will make fisheries management easier, but research continues to be required to determine the effects of various pollutants in the marine environment (31).

In May 1978, the National Ocean Pollution Research and Development and Monitoring Planning Act of 1978 (P.L. 95–273) became law. Its purposes included: (1) establishing a comprehensive 5-year plan for research and monitoring of ocean pollution; (2) developing the necessary information base for rational, efficient, and equitable utilization, conservation, and development of ocean and coastal resources; (3) directing the National Oceanic and Atmospheric Administration to carry out the program. The Congress wished that a plan be before it in 1979 which would identify the national needs and problems relating to ocean pollution including the "economic, social, and environmental values of ocean and coastal resources" (32). Further, priorities were to be established for meeting the needs and solving the problems.

Included in the first report submitted under the legislation by NOAA were high-priority issues of land-use practices, outfalls of municipal sewage, disposal of industrial waste, and disposal of dredged material. Sewage sludge dumping was given low priority (33).

By 1980 further amendments were made to the Ocean Dumping Act. Public Law 96–381 directed the administrator of the Environmental Protection Agency to conduct research to minimize or end, as soon as possible after the date of the legislation, dumping in ocean waters

(34). The amendment was offered "to balance the impacts of ocean dumping of sewage sludge against those of land disposal and select the least harmful alternative, thus allowing an extension of the 1981 deadline if ocean dumping were found to be the least harmful" (35). Public Law 96-572 amended that section of the Ocean Dumping Act which contained the 1981 deadline for sewage sludge dumping and extends the deadline to include industrial wastes defined as "solid, semisolid, or liquid waste generated by a manufacturing or processing plant the ocean dumping of which may unreasonably degrade or endanger human health, welfare, or amenities, or the marine environment, ecological systems, and economic potentialities" (36). The latter extension was an expression of confidence by the Environmental Protection Agency that industrial dumpers would be out of the ocean by the deadline (37).

But dredge spoils remained a separate issue, complicated by the necessary interplay between the U. S. Army Corps of Engineers, charged with maintaining the nation's waterways, and the Environmental Protection Agency's requirements to prevent dumping of contaminated materials. The corps's authority is an ancient one. The inability of local governments to cope with the problems resulting from illegal spoil disposal caused the Congress in 1886 to give such authority to the corps (38). That authority was strengthened in the River and Harbor Act of 1888 which gave the supervisor of New York Harbor, Corps of Engineers, authority to issue permits for disposal of dredge spoils.

Little attention was paid to the spoil disposal business in the Bight until the mound of spoils actually became a navigational hazard of its own (39). But by the mid-1970s it was becoming abundantly clear that dredge spoils were a contaminants problem in their own right and that through the transport of sediment from the estuary to the Bight, in the form of dredge spoils, man was actually moving massive quantities of pollutants from the harbor to the ocean.

Under the Ocean Dumping Act of 1972, the Corps of Engineers could issue permits under criteria developed by the Environmental Protection Agency, with that agency retaining veto rights over any permit (40). Critics charged that the criteria developed by the Environmental Protection Agency were inadequate, that the Corps of Engineers failed to strictly apply those criteria in granting permits and that the corps didn't follow the criteria for its own dredging projects which do not require permits (41).

Without alternatives available for spoil disposal, the situation in the nation's harbors grew ever more difficult. In some ways the Port of

New York was in a relatively good position—its harbor had been extensively dredged prior to restrictions and compared with, say, the Gulf coast ports, its maintenance dredging problems were relatively minor. In 1970 the corps had initiated a 5-year Dredged Material Research Project, but it looked at a general problem and each harbor presented its own specific sets of situations. So in 1977 the corps commissioned a scientific workshop on alternatives to spoil disposal in the Port of New York (42). Alternatives to ocean dumping emerging from that workshop were:

1. Shallow ocean disposal;
2. Disposal in borrow pits created by sand mining, with the spoil capped with clean sand;
3. Disposal in confined upland sites;
4. Containment in islands constructed for that purpose;
5. Disposal techniques "possible in special cases." Included here was the use of spoils for beach nourishment (placing the sand on the beach to replace that which has been eroded away); use for sanitary landfill cover or caps; selective dredging to reduce contaminants; disposal in abandoned piers; disposal in Long Island Sound; use of spoils for environmental enhancement; and disposal in rivers and/or harbors (43).

Of course, all these alternatives required further study and refinement and so could not be put into place at once. Research is continuing now on these, and other means, of disposing of dredged spoils. In the interim, a number of measures were undertaken. An interagency technical committee was established to review and define revisions to the dredged materials' ocean dumping criteria and a program of interim capping of dredged materials at the Bight dump site was initiated.

But ocean pollution was also of international interest, although here the mechanisms for action are less well defined and the pace more ponderous. In 1954, nations meeting in London formulated the International Convention for the Prevention of Pollution of the Sea by Oil. Taking the force of law in the United States in 1961 with passage of the Oil Pollution Act (P.L. 87–167), this legislation set up penalties for discharge of oil by U. S. registered ships in the Territorial Sea and the 12-mile contiguous zone and for any vessels in territorial waters (44). The 1958 Convention on the High Seas requested participating nations to reduce oil pollution from offshore production and called for prevention of pollution by radioactive wastes. And the Convention on the Territorial Sea and the Contiguous Zone and the Convention on the Continental Shelf urged conservation of resources and their protection from pollution. These conventions were adopted by the United States in 1964 (45).

In the absence of enforcement mechanisms, these measures were not very effective. Increasing development of offshore petroleum resources and use of the ocean for waste disposal led to international conferences in Oslo in 1971 and in London in 1972. The latter resulted in the Convention on the Prevention of Marine Pollution by Dumping of Wastes and other Matter, which pertained to all marine waters, not just those of the nations adopting the convention. Among other items, this convention prohibits the dumping of highly toxic chemicals and metals, petroleum products, high-level radioactive wastes, and biological and chemical warfare agents (46). It permits, under strict regulation, the dumping of less damaging chemicals, metals, biological agents and scrap. The U. S. Senate ratified the Convention in 1973 and it became law in 1974. An amendment to the Marine Pollution, Research, and Sanctuaries Act of that year brought the Ocean Dumping Act and the Convention into agreement (47). This now prohibits the transport from the United States, or in U. S. registered vessels, any materials for dumping into ocean waters without permit. It also prohibits other nations from transporting wastes to the United States for the purpose of dumping.

Research—The MESA New York Bight Project

The call of the waters of the deep ocean and its mysteries had greater challenge for the oceanographic community than did the "brown waters" of the coastal region. Complexities of problems (and research opportunities) presented by burgeoning development of the nation's coasts was only beginning to be noted by the scientific community in the late 1950s and early 1960s. Few federal agencies had mandates for studies in the coastal oceans, for these could be thought of as the purview of the states. Such studies as were done were usually quite narrow, relating to measurements of tides, the plotting of navigational charts, and in some cases measurements of water quality. Thus, as the nation became concerned about the quality of its coastal waters and the effects of the discharge of wastes into those waters, there was limited knowledge to draw upon, and few institutions organized for those kinds of investigations.

Even when funds to support research on ocean dumping became available, the scientific community was ill prepared for the task. This was a new field of investigation. New questions had to be formulated to guide research in the most productive directions. New techniques for measurement of substances not previously encountered by the researchers had to be developed. At least one university faculty committee decided that sewage sludge, as a subject of original research, was not sufficiently intellectual for the promotion of the researcher. In the litigious milieu during implementation of the new piecemeal environmental legislation, scientists had to carry out their research and to transmit sometimes very preliminary findings to public hearings and to courts of law. They began to grapple with the difficult business of translating research results, seldom crisply black and white, for the media—for dumping had become news. This was a new era for environmental science. For the oceanographic community, the issues of ocean dumping became, briefly, paramount. And the stage, for much of the research activity, was the New York Bight.

Studies of the effects of ocean dumping in the New York Bight began unauspiciously. In 1974 the Food and Drug Administration, a unit of the Public Health Service, had undertaken surveys of the sludge dump sites in the New York Bight and off the Delaware River in response to concerns over possible contamination of the surf clam fishery. The result was the closure of extensive areas to shellfishing.

The U. S. Army Corps of Engineers, because of its responsibility for maintaining the navigability of the nation's waters was, in those days, the closest thing in existence to a coastal ocean agency. The Amended Fish and Wildlife Coordination Act and the Federal Water Pollution Control Act required the corps to notify the Department of Interior when it planned to move a disposal site, and the Interior Department in turn to either affirm or object to the action. Recognizing that most dumping had gone on in the Bight and that many sites had never been evaluated, the corps' Coastal Engineering Research Center contracted a 2-year ecological study to the U. S. Fish and Wildlife's laboratory at Sandy Hook, N. J. in September 1968. The corps had requested the Smithsonian Institution to plan such a study and later asked the Smithsonian to evaluate the progress of the research and the final report prepared by the Sandy Hook laboratory (48).

Research became political. On 8 February 1970 Congressman Richard Ottinger issued a statement which accused the Corps of Engineers of creating a "dead sea" about 20 miles in diameter by allowing the dumping of sewage sludge and dredge spoils (49). His statement was based on a draft of the corps study, now called "The Sandy Hook Report" (50), released in preliminary form. But not everyone agreed with the findings. The Corps of Engineers characterized it as "tentative, incomplete and subject to change" (51). Others, including the Smithsonian's oversight committee also questioned the evidence (52). The ensuing public controversy between the corps, Congressman Ottinger, the Sandy Hook laboratory and the panel of Smithsonian Institution scientists was but a precursor of things to come as public debate over ocean dumping research commenced.

Ready as politicians and the public were to take action, particularly in light of an issue as potentially powerful as a "dead sea," none could contribute to the fundamental problem: we didn't know what was being dumped, in what quantities, and what, if any, effects were being caused by dumping. The Sandy Hook study, rather than providing answers to those questions, had the effect of spurring other kinds of actions, including passage of the Ocean Dumping Act of 1972.

Title II of the Marine Pollution, Research, and Sanctuaries Act gave to the National Oceanic and Atmospheric Administration, U. S. Department of Commerce, authority to carry out a comprehensive and continuing program of monitoring and research on the short-term ecological effects of ocean dumping. It also authorized a similar study of the long-range effects of pollution, overfishing, offshore development, and other activities affecting the ocean, and initiated research on techniques of minimizing ocean dumping by October 1978 (53). To meet this requirement a research program called MESA (Marine Ecosystem Analysis), already created by the National Oceanic and Atmospheric Administration, was thrown into the breach. Its broad goals were to:

1. describe, understand, and monitor the physical, chemical, and biological processes of discrete marine environmental systems;

2. provide information and expertise required for effective management of marine areas and the rational use of their associated resources; and

3. analyze impact of natural phenomena or man-made alterations on marine ecosystems (54).

The last-stated objective was to be the jewel in the MESA crown. The difficulty was, however, that it was premature, for we often did not know enough. That was to be demonstrated in the New York Bight Project, the first of four geographic areas selected for the MESA approach.

Origins of the MESA New York Bight Project predate the Ocean Dumping Act, and even the formation of the National Ocean and At-

Figure 16. Captain R. Lawrence Swanson, National Oceanic and Atmospheric Administration. Captain Swanson was head of the MESA New York Bight Project. (Photo courtesy of MESA New York Bight Project, NOAA)

mospheric Administration (55). In light of its eventual success, it has numerous claimant fathers. Certainly one of the front-runners for such recognition is

> Martin Lang, an old-line Democrat from the borough of Queens, [who] entered the city government during the depression and worked his way to the top. A receptivity to new ideas set him apart from the stereotypical career civil servant, as was evident in his attempts to initiate an ambitious study of the entire New York "bight" [*sic*] area, in-

Figure 17. Dr. Joel O'Connor, Senior Scientist, National Oceanic and Atmospheric Administration. Dr. O'Connor played a key role in the development and conduct of the research program of the MESA New York Bight Project. (Photo courtesy of HSC Photography Service, SUNY at Stony Brook)

cluding the continental shelf around New York, all coastal seas and estuaries, and each river up to the point of potable water. Lang had been seeking federal funds for three years [in 1968] (56).

The MESA New York Bight Project began with lofty and comprehensive goals established in interim form by September 1973, and formally incorporated into the Project Development Plan in July 1974.

Goal A: To identify and describe the major existing ecological systems, processes, stresses and responses operating in the Bight and define their relationships and rates of change.
Objectives:
 1. Identify the characteristics and distributions of the New York Bight sediments;

2. Identify any major factors influencing primary productivity and food chains;

3. Identify the major organisms and their distribution in the New York Bight;

4. Characterize the driving forces and responses of the major features of tides, currents and water mass distribution;

5. Determine the ecological effects of organic enrichment and nutrient loading;

6. Identify the cumulative ecological effects of environmental stress.

Goal B: To determine the types, transport rates, fates and impacts of pollutants and other man-related stresses on the New York Bight ecosystem.

Objectives:

7. Identify the pollutants that are most critical to the New York Bight ecosystem;

8. Identify transfer routes and fates of major chemical pollutants;

9. Determine how the alteration of input rates and/or locations of pollutant sources would affect distribution, cycling and fate of contaminants;

10. Define the inputs, concentrations, distributions, pathways and fates of contaminants and pathogens in the New York Bight ecosystem;

11. Determine the requirements for an efficient monitoring program that will detect environmental change (57).

At that time, ocean dumping wasn't clearly identified in our first objective, but it was generally considered to be a task that would be accomplished along with a broader examination of pollution and its relationship to natural and man-induced impacts on the marine ecosystem. Many of us, in fact, probably visualized our involvement with ocean dumping being quite peripheral to what real science needed to be accomplished. Some have indicated that ocean dumping research really was applied research or an engineering problem, and that we as scientists should treat it with a certain aloofness that would not taint our image in the scientific community (58).

Those words, written in April 1976 by R.L. Swanson, then manager of the New York Bight Project, describe most elegantly the MESA project's self-image as it came upon the scene.

In 1973 the MESA New York Bight Project located headquarters on the campus of the State University of New York at Stony Brook. Its small staff (never more than eight or nine professional scientists) supervised the development of specific objectives, coordinated NOAA's many research capabilities such as the National Marine Fisheries Service and National Ocean Survey, awarded grants and contracts to gain the knowledge needed, and attempted to synthesize the results into forms which would be of use to those who were making decisions about the Bight. In the eight years of the project (from 1972 through 1981—field operations began in August 1973 and ended in September 1979) about $24.5 million was expended in research and synthesis acivities— probably more money spent learning how the Bight worked than in all the previous fragmented research ever done on the Bight.

But from the beginning the project was plagued by events outside its control—events which shaped the science sponsored by the project to some considerable degree, which deflected the project's priorities from stated goals, and which detracted from the orderly pursuit of knowledge. On the other hand, in the fullness of hindsight, some feel that these outside forces were a factor in making the New York Bight Project one of the National Oceanic and Atmospheric Administration's more successful endeavors from the view of its impacts on public policy formulation. What were these events?

Commander Swanson described the project's beginning:

> December 1973 changed our attitudes considerably. Suddenly, sewage sludge was page one material . . . We [MESA New York Bight Project office staff] were besieged with requests for data, analysis of the situation, and recommendations. Initially, our comments and suggestions were held in rather low esteem, while an unheard-of assistant professor from Brooklyn College became a national celebrity and a folk hero on Long Island—an individual who single-handedly was taking on the city of New York and the federal government (59).

That event was the rise of the "Sludge Monster," a creation of the media (60). A marine geochemist reported finding in bottom samples off Long Island's south shore, black goo which he interpreted as being a portion of the "main sludge mass" which had "broken off" and was moving toward the beaches (61). In time this observation was conclusively shown to be false, but the spector raised by the Sludge Monster was such that business on Long Island's beaches that summer was poor. The effect of the sludge monster episode was to redirect the MESA New York Bight's resources to the question of sludge dumping and to make the project "be extremely open with data and information; . . . take every opportunity to inform the public, through . . . hearings and lectures, of our understanding of the situation; . . . assist EPA in reaching a reasonable management decision, based on scientific understanding, regarding using the dump site" (62).

This redirection was costly to the original goals of the project, for much staff time was utilized testifying at seemingly endless hearings, and ships and research personnel were diverted to what was a non-problem and a side issue to the major problems of the Bight. But public concern had been raised and questions had to be answered (63). Emerging from the MESA New York Bight's activities on the sewage sludge problem were these achievements:

1. The Environmental Protection Agency was encouraged to pick a firm date for phasing out ocean dumping of sewage sludge;

2. The Environmental Protecton Agency Region II Headquarters was convinced to *not* move the sewage sludge dumpsite;

3. Public standing of the project was greatly enhanced by the openness, frankness, and apparent validity of the project's research results (64).

In June 1976, another "pollution episode" occurred which again diverted the New York Bight Project from its main course. That event, which has now come to be called the "floatables event" was the stranding of tar and grease balls, plastic debris including tampon applicators, decomposed condoms, plastic sheeting from sanitary napkins, and disposable diapers. Associated with this mix were plastic straws, styrofoam cups, plastic bottle caps, cigarette filters and a host of other man-made materials (65). The Sludge Monster was fanned back into life and public outrage was enormous as beach after beach was closed during the hot summer. But the project staff had gained experience from its earlier trials—as well as a now-welcome fund of information about the Bight—and the issue was brought to a reasonably quick solution. Floatables were quickly attributed to overflows associated with the City's combined sewers, pier fires in the harbor, a medium oil spill in the harbor the month before the event, and explosion of two sewage sludge holding tanks on the south shore of Long Island (66). Seven months after the event, a well-documented analysis was available to the public and the decision-making community. But numerous hearings, media interviews, and other less formal mechanisms had already provided project staff with an opportunity to present their findings (67).

Later during that eventful summer of 1976, natural conditions conspired to cause a massive fish kill off the New Jersey coast. Public fears that this, finally, was the result of the dumping of sewage sludge were once more laid to rest (68). But this event had a different kind of impact upon the New York Bight Project, for this depletion of oxygen was fully worthy of study in its own right, being of a magnitude such that distinguishing between man-made and natural

Figure 18. Some of the MESA New York Bight Project staff examining debris from Long Island beaches following the floatables event. On left, facing camera, Charles Parker; kneeling—Stanley Chanesman and R. L. Swanson. (Photo courtesy MESA New York Bight Project, NOAA)

causations was critical and difficult. A fuller discussion of this event will be given in the next chapter.

But the MESA New York Bight Project did more than chase down pollution episodes. It sponsored sound research, made significant contributions to science, and moved our understanding of the New York Bight far ahead. How do those sorts of accomplishments occur? The best answer is that they happen through the processes of science: by enlisting the collaborative efforts of gifted individuals, by providing opportunity and support for their curiosity to be satisfied, by publishing and discussing research as it is being planned, conducted, and upon its conclusion; through meetings, conferences, workshops and symposia at which ideas and conclusions are interchanged among a broad array of interests; and by the translation of science into forms which are of more general interest than to just other scientists. In these the MESA New York Bight Project did well. For example:

1. One hundred and eighteen scientific papers have been published as well as 183 technical reports, annual reports, and other communications (69);

2. The MESA New York Bight Atlas monograph series of 30 volumes was published (70);

3. The 1975 symposium, "Middle Atlantic Continental Shelf and the New York Bight," was attended by over 500 scientists and observers. Its contributions were published as a special symposium volume (71);

4. A 1978 workshop convening over 100 scientists discussed the consequences of urbanization and industrialization, effects of urban discharges, effects of changes proposed in the estuary, impacts of human activities on fish, shellfish, and the foodchain, impacts of development on the shorezone, implications of present and future contaminant levels, and the probability of marine environmental crises. These new ways of looking at the Bight and its problems are leading towards a series of special volumes on those very issues one of which is this book.

5. A symposium in 1979, "Ecological Effects of Environmental Stress," summarized the nature of environmental effects from the loading of pollutants in the Bight and the kinds of decisions and actions required to lessen or eliminate these effects. That symposium's findings are being published as a volume entitled "Ecological Stress and the New York Bight: Science and Management."

6. Sea Grant extension specialists were utilized in New York and New Jersey to assure that the results of the New York Bight Project would find their way into the educational process and into museums and exhibits wherever appropriate.

Contributions of the MESA New York Bight Project to our understanding of the Bight and its processes are also many. Some of them are:

1. Defining the environmental impact of ocean dumping, particularly relative to other sources of contaminants in the Bight.

Prior to MESA studies it was widely assumed that ocean dumping caused greater environmental impacts than other uses and abuses of the Bight. The MESA studies have resulted in an understanding that the transport of contaminants through the estuary and the atmosphere are larger and more significant than had been realized. Probably the most significant research done towards developing this understanding was comprehensively quantifying the kinds and sources of contaminants put into the Bight (72).

2. Determining the principal factors contributing to oxygen depletion in the Bight and the rates and interactions of these causitive factors.

The 1976 fish kill in the Bight was caused by oxygen depletion in the bottom waters of a significant area of the Bight. Because this occurred over such an enormous area, and because its causes were not at all clear, the MESA New York Bight Project and the National Marine Fisheries Service organized extensive investigations. The several factors leading to this environmental event were identified and their relative importance determined. The results of this study, published in a comprehensive report (73), contribute to our understanding of oxygen depletion events elsewhere in the coastal ocean. This study also offered an opportunity for the synthesis of the studies of physical and chemical oceanography, meteorology, and the dynamics of carbon, oxygen, and nitrogen interactions in the Bight which had been sponsored by the project.

3. Identification of the key contaminants in the Bight.

Because the New York Bight receives many more kinds of contaminants than can be detected and measured with any reasonable amount of funding, the MESA New York Bight Project staff assembled, in June 1977, a panel of 37 experts to assist it with the task of determining the contaminants that are, or may become, the most serious problems in the Bight. In their deliberations, the panel was aided by the existence of a number of listings of priority pollutant lists prepared elsewhere. Although the initial hope had been to obtain a ranked listing of the ''20 or so'' most serious contaminants, the panel found that there was little basis for such a determination. Instead, three catagories were determined: (a.) major perceived threats that require continued study; (b.) potentially significant threats for which data must be collected and evaluated; (c.) no threat at present, on the basis of existing information.

In addition the panel made some broad recommendations:

(1) Regulatory programs to characterize potentially dangerous discharges must be improved to provide reliable, comprehensive information for many major pollutants.

(2) A wide variety of chemicals should be measured in the sludges or effluents of sewage treatment plants, and in dredged material.

(3) Statistics on hazardous cargoes should be broken down to identify the amounts of particular chemicals in the New York harbor cargoes.

(4) Determination of the extent to which coarse and fine sediments are resuspended by wave action with the apex of the Bight (74).

Figure 19. The National Oceanic and Atmospheric Administration (NOAA) research vessel *George B. Kelez*. This vessel was the primary "platform" for New York Bight research conducted by the MESA New York Bight Project. (Photo courtesy of MESA New York Bight Project, NOAA).

Near the estuary and off Long Island, fine grained sediments do not accumulate on the bottom, but are stirred up during periods of storm and are, while resuspended, transported around within and out of the Bight. The techniques developed in this study are now widely used elsewhere in the world for determining sediment resuspension. But, perhaps most important for us, it was learned that the sewage sludge not decomposed at the dumpsite does not stay there but is widely dispersed through the Bight, finally making its way into the coastal marshes or out of the Bight (75).

(5) Finding the causes of diseases and abnormalities which occur in fishes in the Bight.

Fin rot is a condition in which the fins of the winter flounder are partially or completely destroyed. Extensive studies of fin rot in the Bight, and elsewhere, have shown that this disease is a response to stress in the fish by a series of contaminants and not the result of any one and that it is not a specific response to contaminants in sludge.

While fin rot indicates that conditions in some portions of the Bight are not what they should be, it clarifies an issue which has been widely expressed as a specific result of sludge dumping.

Mackerel eggs in the surface waters of the Bight were found to show genetic abnormalities which prevent their development. These abnormalities have now been found to result from toxic substances present in the Bight's surface waters, present in concentrations sufficiently great to affect the sensitive eggs of these fish. These abnormalities occur over half the spawning area of mackerel in the Bight, so impacts upon the stocks of this species are plausible, if not yet demonstrated (76).

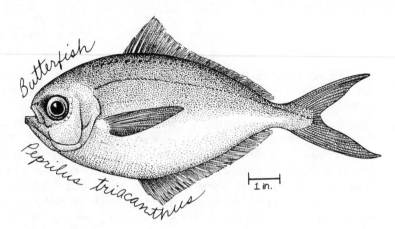

Butterfish

Peprilus triacanthus

1 in.

6 / The Bight As a Dump

> New York City was born of the sea, and after a century and a half it re-
> mained a community dependent upon the sea for its livelihood and for
> the promise of future greatness. Founded as a trading post, it had never
> [by 1775] outgrown its original function (1).

New York remains a city of commerce today, living by trading with
others. Trade is the lifeblood of a megalopolis, for population density
is such that it is no longer possible to produce locally the resources for
self-sufficiency. A modern city such as New York grows almost none
of its food, makes none of the fibre for its clothing, imports its
building materials, energy, and even "imports" much of its population in the form of commuters. Population density of residents and of
workers in the metropolitan center is such that land values are high
enough to make construction of skyscrapers economically feasible:
land of that value cannot be used for mere raising of food. Also, our
cities were built when cheap energy made it possible to import needed
resources over vast distances at low cost.

As the megalopolis imports the food, water, and materials for life
and commerce, so too must it export finished products to balance the
trade. And, as the megalopolis imports raw materials to sustain itself,
it must also rid itself of its wastes. Because these wastes may have no
present economic value they must be disposed of in the most efficient
and least costly fashion. For a city on the sea, such as New York,
where better to place this waste than in that great ocean which lies at
its doorstep.

We have recently come to learn that our own ingeniousness has
made it possible for us to create a simmering broth of toxic chemicals

that threaten our environment and our lives. These toxic materials, and other wastes, seem to be a cost we are willing to pay for the life we wish to live, for they are by-products of our technology-oriented society. The problem has thus become: how can we economically re-use these wastes, or failing this, how and where do we safely dispose of them? The ocean, because it is so vast, and because we don't really see it or use it as we do the land, can become our dump. The capacity of the oceans to accept our wastes, assimilative capacity, is studied in the hope that we shall not have to change our ways of doing things. The hope is that the ocean is sufficiently commodious to continue to safely accept these wastes. If this is indeed true and the ocean is suffi-ciently vast to accept all, or some of our wastes, then money to be spent on making things will not have to be lessened by being spent on cleaning up afterwards. But this is the subject of current research— it really isn't known.

Our wastes are enormous in quantity and in diversity. Cataloguing them is a long and frightening task. Lists of toxic chemicals run into the tens of thousands. There are other kinds of wastes less life threatening, and less dramatic, but which are just as difficult to dispose of—and sometimes as troublesome in their effects on us and on the environment. These are the wastes which occur in very large volumes and are only moderately harmful. These wastes are expen-sive to treat because of their volume; it is cheaper and easier to dump.

Some broad categories of wastes disposed of in the Bight are as follows: (1) Domestic wastewater—Sewage is the name of the game here. The outflow of water and the substances we have added to that water from our homes; runoff: the washings of our streets and from our lawns and farms with their fertilizers, pesticides, herbicides, and fungicides. (2) Industrial wastes—A by-product of the industrial revolution and better living through chemistry, these wastes have become more difficult, more frightening because they have become increasingly toxic as our manufacturing has become more sophisticated. Here are the chlorinated hydrocarbons, the organophosphates, and a host of other polysyllabic descriptors of the chemist's art. And, the toxic metals. (3) Spoils—The substances removed from excavations, be they from building sites, subway tun-nels, or dug from the bottom of the harbor in the process of dredging channels. The major portion of spoils are sand and muds which have accumulated in the estuary. But some of the harbor's sediments, par-ticularly the finer materials, have been contaminated by petroleum hydrocarbons, heavy metals, and a wide variety of other substances spilled or discharged into the harbor. (4) Refuse—The things we don't want any more that we can't get down the toilet or leave by the side of the road. This ranges from paper and plastic wrappings to discarded automobiles; dead pets to construction debris.

There are other kinds of wastes disposed of in and around the Bight region in many ways—a diversity of ways that increases as the alternatives for disposal are narrowed. The diversity of kinds of wastes which must be disposed of is increasing. The rate almost exceeds our ability to devise techniques to find them again when they have become a part of our chemical environment. This is a particular problem in the oceans. Their fluid properties and complex chemistry may frustrate the search for minute quantities of toxics. Small additions of some substances by man may be overwhelmed by massive transfers of those same substances within the ocean itself.

We put wastes into the ocean in a number of ways. The simplest is dumping at the shoreline. As we have seen, this process was barely able to keep pace with increasing numbers of people in the city and people became tired of mucking about in their own debris and sewage. Waste disposal was then moved offshore into the estuary and still later into the Bight itself, as the harbor became so highly polluted our forefathers couldn't stand it. We now carry our wastes into the coastal ocean directly, through dumping, or indirectly through discharge of solid or liquid materials at or near the shore. Future plans usually call for disposal still farther off shore.

We use the ocean as a dump because it is a simple and cheap way to dispose of wastes. When we do this, we are using a heritage which belongs to all of us and potentially affecting other things which are common resource. This is the same concept as the pollution of rivers and atmosphere by a few which affected us all. We became concerned only when the level of pollution of air and fresh water resources was such that they were degraded to a point no longer acceptable to us. In thinking of the ocean as dump, we must determine how much degradation is occurring and how much we will accept.

Dumping in Perspective

The New York Bight is an indentation in the eastern coast of the United States, not a more isolated body of water such as a lake. It is a part of the global ocean and through the Bight move waters of the North Atlantic Ocean. Estimates are that about every nine months its waters are exchanged with those of the ocean. This exchange is more rapid near the estuary where it takes only several weeks. The oceans of the world have been sufficiently polluted that, to the degree that the ocean contains contaminants, these will move through the Bight with the water. We know all too little about the kinds and amounts of those contaminants, but one can think of it as being a sort of a background level of oceanic pollution against which we measure those specifically added in the Bight region. This is an important concept, for the volumes of water (and everything that the water contains) moving through the Bight by natural circulation are so vast that though dilution is great, the total quantities of contaminants so moved can dwarf those amounts added by man locally around the Bight. These already contaminated waters also lessen the capacity of the Bight's waters to absorb additional wastes.

There are other sources of contaminants which must be examined for us to appreciate how our use of the Bight as a dump affects its waters. For example, we are sometimes keenly aware that we have grossly polluted the atmosphere. We know that contaminants in the atmosphere may be carried far away from the place where they were added before falling out as particles or being washed out in rainfall. Atmospheric fallout provides a steady rain of contaminants back onto the land and into the ocean, particularly the coastal oceans.

Over 20,000 tons of particulate and gaseous substances are added each day to the atmosphere in the counties surrounding the Bight (2). While we know little of the fate of the over 500 tons of particulates, 1,400 tons of sulphur oxides, 1,500 tons of nitrous oxides, 3,000 tons of hydrocarbons and 12,000 tons of carbon monoxide injected into the air around the Bight, over 100 tons of heavy metals may fall back from the atmosphere to the Bight daily (3), of these, lead is the most abundant. A major source of that lead, of course, is from automobile exhausts and the combustion of leaded gasolines.

But the major contribution from the atmosphere to the Bight is freshwater. More than half (59%) of the freshwater entering the Bight comes from rainfall (4). But as rain falls on the Bight, it also falls on the lands surrounding the Bight. Once on land, water moves downslope back to the ocean by several pathways. That portion of rainfall which runs off the land is called, naturally enough, runoff. Other rainfall sinks into the earth and becomes a part of the groundwater. Some groundwater may be taken up in wells and piped into homes or industries and then becomes a part of the wastewater stream; other portions seep into the bays, rivers, and streams and become a part of their flow into the Bight. Runoff is the second largest source of freshwater to the Bight (5). Freshwater flow from the Hudson River makes up about 31% of the runoff into the Bight, with the Raritan and

Passaic rivers contributing about 4% each. New Jersey's coastal region in its entirety (except for the watersheds of the Raritan and Passaic rivers) adds very little runoff while Long Island's porous sands absorb most of the rain that falls (6).

Contaminants contained in runoff waters contribute significantly to the pollutant load of the Bight. Although only about 35% of the freshwater reaching the Bight comes as runoff, 39% of the oil and grease, and 43% of the zinc added to the Bight are carried from this source. Chromium, copper, mercury, lead, and other heavy metals are added in significant quantities (7). Runoff is also a means by which pesticides, herbicides, and other chemicals used in agriculture, as well as industrial halogenated hydrocarbons such as PCBs, are transported to the Bight.

There are several different runoff situations, however. In urban areas the prevalence of paved surfaces causes much of the rainfall to find its way to the streets and thence to storm sewers. This runoff is higher in oils, grease, and metals derived from automobiles and trucks than that from other areas. From agricultural and suburban areas, runoff is apt to be higher in nitrogen and phosphorus (perhaps from fertilizers) and in some organic contaminants. Because of pets and the overflow effects of combined sewers, fecal coliform additions from urban runoff are usually higher than those of less densely settled areas.

One vexing runoff problem that we will examine later is that of the PCB contamination of the Hudson River. PCBs dumped into the River from General Electric plants at Hudson Falls and Fort Edwards has been extensively documented (8). Those PCB contaminants are now a part of the bottom sediments of the Hudson River and are carried, in part, slowly southward. The remainder is buried in river deposits. If these PCB-rich sediments reach the estuary, and perhaps the Bight, they could pose an enormous problem in the future.

Compared with the quantities of freshwaters contributed to the Bight by rainfall and runoff, the total wastewater flow, including both municipal and industrial sources, is small, amounting to only about 6% of the total freshwater flowing into the Bight. Why then are the wastewaters of importance? The answer lies in the kinds and amounts of foreign substances that have been added.

Municipal and industrial wastewater contributes half of those materials which, through their decomposition, remove oxygen from the waters of the estuary and Bight, and are the largest source of nitrogen (42%), second largest source of phosphorus (36%), and the principal source of fecal bacteria (9). Municipal and industrial wastewaters are also important sources for copper, zinc, lead, and chromium among the heavy metals. These suggest that wastewater warrants a closer look.

Wastewater

Today with our knowledge of scientific methods of sewage disposal, the system followed in the eighteenth century seems startlingly primitive; yet as late as 1936 the mayor of New York pointed out that the city's method of sewage disposal was precisely the same in principle as when the Dutch ruled the town (10).

That statement is still true today. Part of the reason is that we deal with *water supply* as a system separate and different from *water disposal*, and we always have. Charles Gunnerson has made the point:

The common characteristic of both the municipal and industrial approaches [to waste treatment] is that water supplies have been developed and rate structures set with no regard for the costs of getting rid of the water while sewerage systems are designed and optimized with no regard for the cost of flushing water'' (11).

Water presents an excellent case study of the problems of importing and exporting large quantities of raw materials to an urban region. Each day metropolitan New York brings in a stupendous 1.5 billion gallons of water, degrades it, and disposes of it as a waste. Areas surrounding the metropolis don't import water from the same distance. For smaller, less densely settled areas, groundwater or local streams or reservoirs serve as domestic and industrial water supplies. These communities often discharge wastewater in such a fashion that the sources are increasingly contaminated by the degraded water. New York City residents, however, enjoy some of the highest quality water in the country, at low cost, because the source and discharge areas are separated by hundreds of miles (12). The metropolitan region has never invested enough to treat its wastewater adequately to prevent pollution: it has been able to get away with this and avoid serious consequences to the health of its residents and commuting workers only by discharging wastewater to coastal waters and allowing them to be seriously degraded.

Through the nineteenth and early twentieth centuries, wastewater disposal techniques failed to keep pace with water importation. Population growth and greatly increased per capita water consumption made late nineteenth century conditions deplorable. As urban areas became mired in the mud created by their own wastewater, public opinion forced the development of sewerage systems.

Through the sewers built by towns and cities around the Bight flows nearly 2,500 million gallons of wastewater each day (13). Of that quantity, two-thirds is from Manhattan, Brooklyn, the Bronx, Queens, and Staten Island. Less densely populated, and sewered, Nassau and Suffolk Counties on Long Island contribute only about 4%, and the coastal New Jersey counties about 30%, most of that from Bergen County in the north. New Jersey's coastal region and Long Island contribute relatively insignificant amounts of wastewater because of their lesser populations and the use of cesspools. In contrast, the core of the metropolitan region discharges 95% of its wastewater directly into coastal waterways, 20% of it as raw sewage. Today two municipal sources contribute over half of the organic load to New York Harbor, and to the Bight. These are the primary treatment facility of the Passaic Valley Sewerage Commission and the raw sewage discharged from New York City (14).

But such disposal, while inexpensive and easy, is not without cost, and the cost is a degraded environment. As early as 1866, a citizens' association was formed in New York City to create a Metropolitan Sanitation District and a Board of Health in a vain attempt to solve the problem of harbor waters, seriously polluted by sewage and deficient in oxygen (15).

The amount of dissolved oxygen present in water is used as a measure of the degree of pollution, particularly by sewage which is high in organic content. That organic matter oxidizes in the water, removing the dissolved oxygen. In New York Harbor the first measurements of dissolved oxygen were made in 1909 (16), when a respectable 65% (of saturation or maximum oxygen content) was measured in the lower East River and 55% in the Harlem River. Within four years these levels had declined to 43% and 20% respectively. The decomposition of sewage in some places in the harbor was such that "gases were given off which were most offensive and a bubbling effervescence could be observed" (17). Oxygen content of harbor water continued to decline, and by 1927 levels of 21% were found at the lower East River, and 17% in the Harlem River (18). Oxygen content of these and other waters around the city continues to be low today (19).

The estuary and, to a lesser extent, the Bight are the recipients of the domestic, industrial, and agricultural wastes of a population of about 17 million people. These same waters provide shellfish and finfish as foods for this population and are a source of enjoyment for boaters, swimmers, and other recreationists. We've known for a long time that the mix of human wastes and water is a potent combination for the quick spread of disease. Centuries ago our ancestors experienced massive plagues unknowingly spread by contaminated drinking water (20). While now almost everyone knows that sewage and drinking water must be kept separate, we have not yet fully admitted the possible linkage between our sewage and the salt water in which we swim and boat and from which we take food.

We hope that this linkage is broken by treatment of sewage. New York City began building sewage-treatment plants back in 1884, and by 1927 the largest and most modern in the nation were in the City. But, other kinds of expenditures came to have a higher priority and the quality of wastewater treatment slowly worsened. Some, but all too few, municipalities around the Bight also built sewage-treatment plants as their population grew and funds permitted. Today, there are 75 treatment plants discharging treated wastewater into the estuary, 47 along the New Jersey coast and 6 on Long Island (21).

The first step in the treatment of sewage is called primary. It differs from raw sewage discharge only in that some screening and settling may be done to reduce floating and suspended solids. Only those nutrient materials and heavy metals which are settled out are removed: the effectiveness of treatment is largely aesthetic. A goal for wastewater treatment in the metropolitan region is to achieve secondary treatment. In this, the biologically degradable portions of the wastewater are reduced by microorganisms, resulting in the removal of most of the suspended solids and the organic matter and some of the nutrients, nitrogen, and phosphorus. But the remaining nitrogen, largely in the form of ammonia, reaching the estuary and the Bight, has the ultimate effect of reducing the oxygen level in the waters. Pollutants such as dissolved toxic substances also pass through sewage treatment.

Current federal regulations call for the improvement of wastewater treatment to still higher levels. Some informed observers feel that the enormous expenditures that would be required for the construction and operation of such plants would be prohibitively expensive, or unwarranted. Others feel that such advanced secondary or tertiary treatment should be required of all wastewater treatment.

Industrial wastes are often discharged into sewerage systems, posing new problems because they may contain substances toxic to the microorganisms involved in the treatment of sewage, with the result that the system fails. Industrial wastes often require special treatment for the removal of oils, metals, and toxic organic chemicals, treatments which are highly specialized and too expensive for the huge volumes of domestic wastewater. Separation of industrial and domestic wastes at source is best, but is impractical in an urban area in which many small businesses and industries find it cheaper, and expedient, to discharge their wastes into the municipal system rather than pay the additional costs of separate collection systems.

Sewage, even when treated, is a source of nitrogen and phosphorus, elements which act as fertilizers to plant growth. Nitrogen is often in short supply in the ocean and can be a limiting factor in the growth of phytoplankton. Often the development of phytoplankton blooms is limited by the availability of nitrogen. But as we have seen, we put a lot of sewage into the Bight, and hence a lot of nitrogen. When a body of water is overfertilized, there is an excessive growth of plants, particularly the phytoplankton, and a condition known as eutrophication develops. This situation can have profound impacts upon an environment: it is the reason, for example, that Lake Erie was called "dead" some years ago. Lake Erie had, then, as much life in it as ever, but it was dominated by more unpleasant forms and ones whose excesses in growth could result in noxious masses on the beaches. In the Bight, we have experienced, as we shall learn in the next chapter, far-reaching effects from eutrophication.

Wastewaters are often disinfected by the addition of chlorine, which kills many of the pathogens contained in sewage. While this process is one of many years standing, there is some evidence that it has detrimental effects on the environment through the accumulation of chlorinated hydrocarbons. New York City disinfects its wastewater outflow only during summer months for both practical and economic reasons (22).

The Sewage Sludge Problem

Sewage treatment removes solids from the wastewater. This residue is called sludge. Sludge really isn't a solid, but rather is pretty wet, being about 95% water. What to do with the sludge has always been a problem. Drying it is expensive; composting is useful but made difficult to impossible for sludge from industrial or urban areas because of the heavy metals or other toxic substances which can contaminate soils or groundwater; incineration is costly (because of the water) and may contribute to air pollution problems. For some cities, ocean dumping of sewage sludge was an obvious answer. About 15% of the sludge generated by municipal sewage-treatment plants nationally is discharged into the sea (23). Boston and Los Angeles discharge their sludge through pipes into the sea. New York City, Newark, and Yonkers cart theirs by barge to sea and dump it. Philadelphia has stopped dumping its sludge in the Bight and started composting in only the last year (24). But, with attention being focused on ocean dumping, all have been encouraged to seek alternatives, and research on those alternatives has been funded.

Sludge has been dumped at the sludge dumpsite in the New York Bight since 1924 (25), but wasn't really noticed until 1970 when Congressman Ottinger ran on the "dead sea" platform and 1974 when the "Sludge Monster" appeared. The dumping of sewage sludge has had clear local effects upon the environment. In an area of about 5 square miles immediately to the west of the dumpsite, in the Christiaensen Basin, there are essentially no bottom living organisms except for one species of polychaete worm (26). Many other animals either cannot survive in the vicinity of the dump or, if they do, are so severely stressed that they are subject to diseases such as fin rot, degeneration of their shell (lobsters), gill fouling, and parasitism. There is also evidence at times of temporarily depressed bottom oxygen levels in the vicinity of the dump, and it is clear that the dumping of sewage sludge does contribute significantly to the toxic contaminant load of the Bight (27).

But it is not so clear that sewage sludge is the major source of the contaminants found in the Bight. Despite the over 150 barge loads of sludge dumped each month, totalling over half a million cubic yards of digested and raw sludge from 12 New Jersey plants, 11 New York City, and 3 Nassau County sewage treatment facilities (28), the effects of sludge dumping are not as profound as is other waste disposal into the Bight. Sludge is a major source of oil and grease and of heavy metals, for these are only partially removed from the wastewater stream by treatment and are concentrated in the sludge, but these contributions are overshadowed by the quantities added from other sources (29).

What is of concern is that as sewage and industrial waste treatment improves around the estuary, the quantities and toxicity of sludge produced by the plants will also increase, and disposal will become a larger and larger problem. If ocean dumping of sewage sludge continues and sewage treatment is improved, then the sewage problem is merely being moved from the harbor to the Bight. Ocean dumping is a means by which our society exports a nearshore problem further offshore. No problem is really solved or resolved: resolution is deferred until the volume increases to intolerable levels. Solution really rests with dealing with the problem at its source by segregation of domestic and industrial wastes and isolation of large volume low-toxicity wastes from low volume, high-toxicity materials. Each waste may then be treated by an appropriate technology at an appropriate cost.

Industrial Wastes

Almost 80% of the industrial wastes dumped into United States coastal waters in 1977 were placed at two sites in the New York Bight (30). One, the Acid Waste dump is in the inner part of the Bight about 17 miles from the Statue of Liberty. It was established by the Corps of Engineers in 1948 (31). The second dump is 106 miles east of Ambrose Light, off the edge of the continental shelf. Its name is the Industrial Waste site, but it is often referred to as the 106-mile dumpsite or the "DWD one-oh-six" (for deep water dump site) (32). It has been in use since 1965.

In the spring of 1973, the Environmental Protection Agency began terminating dumping by about 150 industrial waste generators or industries which had been using the Acid Waste site. By 1979 only 13 industries were still dumping at the site, with ten of them on schedule to stop dumping by the end of 1981. Two, Allied Chemical and NL Industries, have been told that their wastes are not harmful and that they may continue to dump there (33).

Dumping at the 106-mile Industrial Waste site in 1979 were American Cyanamic Co. of Linden, New Jersey; E.I. duPont de Nemours & Co. of Grasselli, New Jersey and Edge Moor, Delaware, and Merck & Co. of Rahway, New Jersey. All are scheduled to stop dumping by the end of 1981 (50).

Chemical wastes are as old as the Industrial Revolution. As our society has increased its use of chemicals to sustain our standard of living, the quantities of wastes produced have also increased. But, it has been only in the last 10 years that the effects of improper disposal have become apparent to the public. Two factors have contributed to the increasingly important industrial waste-disposal problem: increasingly sophisticated and complex chemical technology and increasing numbers of people.

Northern New Jersey was the locus of many innovations in the refining of petroleum during the last decades of the 1800s (35). The wastes from the early refineries which sprang up around Raritan Bay have for centuries had an impact on it and on the estuary and the Bight. J. W. Mersereau, New York State Oyster Protector at that time, worked closely with oil refiners on the shore of Kill van Kull and Staten Island Sound to reduce the "volume of obnoxious effluents" entering the waters there and affecting the production of the shellfishery (36). But these refineries were only the forerunners of the complex of petrochemical industries which sprang up wherever there was access to refined petroleum and the task of coping with industrial wastes became more than one man could handle.

New York and New Jersey's industrial complex is an aging one—its plants not as efficient as modern ones. They are more "leaky" of pollutants and more costly to modernize in order to reduce the quantities of wastes produced in the manufacturing process. But it is still an important base of industry, having almost 8% of the nation's industrial capacity (37). Important segments of that industrial base are chemicals, printing and publishing, apparel and textiles, and electrical manufacturing (38). Most of this industry is concentrated in the core counties of the Bight region all around the estuary: Manhattan, Brooklyn, Queens, Essex Bergen, Union, Hudson, and Passaic counties (39).

Most of these industries clustered around the estuary are not ocean dumpers as we have identified them and many would deny that their wastes went into the estuary. These industries either use industrial waste-disposal firms who may, or may not, dispose of the materials properly or simply discharge their wastes into the municipal wastewater stream. In 1972, 88 industries were discharging about 4,250 million gallons a day of industrial wastewater into the estuary (40). Unknown quantities of unknown substances seep into the Bight from landfills (some of which contain industrial wastes) and from toxic chemical-disposal sites both legal and illegal.

Movement of enormous quantities of petroleum products and petrochemicals into, out of, and all around the harbor results in spills. In 1978, 21,281 barrels of crude oil, 45,897 barrels of gasoline, 75,707 barrels of petroleum distillates, 31,257 barrels of diesel oil, and 228,821 barrels of residual fuel oil were spilled in New York Harbor (41).

Increasing amounts of toxic materials appearing in sewage presents a new and important problem. Many of these chemicals cannot be effectively treated by state-of-the-art sewage treatment plants. Those

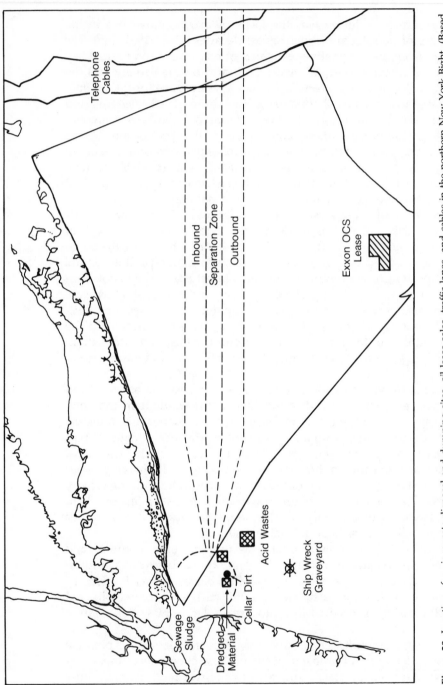

Figure 20. Location of major waste disposal and dumping sites, oil lease sales, traffic lanes, and cables in the northern New York Bight. (Based on Davies *et al*, in Squires and McKay, 1982)

chemicals that cannot be legally disposed of through the municipal wastewater system are often turned over to disposal firms which may treat the wastes or dispose of them in other ways. The experience of Love Canal, near Niagara Falls, N.Y., showed us how ineffective, and potentially hazardous, careless disposal procedures are. A final option, particularly for the most hazardous of chemical wastes, is ocean dumping.

In the New York Bight sails a fleet of vessels characterized by their rubber-lined hulls and called by names such as "Sparkling Waters," "Lisa," "Maria," "Forest," and the "Liquid Waste 1." Their task is to carry industrial wastes to the ocean sites and to discharge them there. What are these wastes? At the Acid Waste site is discharged byproduct hydrochloric acid from Allied Chemical and by-product sulfuric acid-iron wastes from the manufacture of titanium dioxide by NL Industries (42).

A more complex suite of chemicals is disposed of at the 106-mile site. This is to be expected, for the spot was created at the request of New Jersey industries who wished to dump toxic wastes for which inland disposal permits, or practices, were not acceptable because of the potential for pollution of water supplies. Hydrochloric acid-iron wastes resulting from titanium dioxide pigment manufacture are dumped by duPont's Edge Moor plant. DuPont's Grasselli plant dumps a sodium sulfate solution "generally containing less than one percent of soluble, low molecular weight organic compounds, such as methanol, methylamines, and phenol" (43). Merck's wastes are intermediate products from the manufacture of thiabendazole (44). The most toxic wastes dumped are those resulting from Allied Chemical's manufacturing processes for "rubber chemicals, paper chemicals, water treating chemicals, non-persistent organophosphate insecticides, mining chemicals, intermediates and surfactants" (45).

Toxic Substances

Toxic substances in the waters and sediments of the Bight come from a variety of sources, many of them from industrial wastes. But domestic sewage adds many and runoff from agricultural lands often contains complex organic pesticides, herbicides, or nutrients. The array of these chemicals is staggering, and only a very few have been studied in respect to the effect they may have on human health or on the environment. Included here are, for example, synthetic organics (solvents, chlorinated hydrocarbons, pesticides, fungicides and herbicides, and plastics), metals, acids, petrochemicals, alkalies, and petroleum combustion products.

Some of these substances are designed to be lethal to one or more organisms. Others are toxic to some or many organisms quite accidentally. But either way, their misuse can lead to severe harm to other than targeted creatures or plants. As agriculture became more sophisticated and as chemistry is used to make life more livable through drugs and plastics, the wastes and residues of the chemicals used have become more deleterious.

As an example, insect control was, by modern standards, a primitive business before the 1940s. But chemistry was adding new weapons to the persistent struggle against agricultural pests: chlorinated hydrocarbons and organo-phosphorus insecticides. Perhaps the most widely known example of the former group is DDT, first synthesized in the laboratory in 1874 (46), used during the second world war as a medical insecticide, and by the middle of the twentieth century was in widespread use as an agricultural and horticultural insecticide (47). Parathion, Malathion, and Lindane are some of the better-known organo-phosphates which also came into widespread use after the war. By the early 1960s, warning signals of the effects of overuse and misuse of these potent weapons was appearing. Rachael Carson's "The Silent Spring," which appeared in excerpts in the *New Yorker* in 1962, caught the attention of the world and a great controversy raged for almost a decade, within and outside of the scientific community about the impact of DDT on the environment (48).

Scientists noticed that bird eggs were thinning, and in some cases had become so thin that the eggs couldn't hatch. Eagles, falcons, and hawks were put into a well-publicized fight for survival. Finally, public opinion was sufficiently aroused that a ban on DDT use, in most circumstances, was made the law of the land. Slowly the environment recovered from that threat; and so too did the threatened animals. DDT is now something most don't remember.

Since DDT and Rachel Carson's *The Silent Spring* we have been besieged by a seemingly never-ending, life-threatening series of chemical crises: the cranberry scare, mercury in swordfish, fluorocarbons and the ozone shield—all have been played out in the media to the exhaustion of the public (49). But again, high levels of anxiety arose in use with the disclosure that the industrial waste dumps in the vicinity of the Hooker Chemical works in Niagara Falls, N.Y., posed threats to the health of the people living in and around them. Love Canal, the most notorious of those Hooker Chemical dumps, became a household word spelling out the hazards of life in a chemical society. It was no longer something exotic such as Agent Orange, a defoliant used in Viet Nam; now it was toxic chemicals all around *us*.

Another class of chemicals that has gotten a lot of attention in New York State is polychlorinated biphenyls or PCBs. This chemical, sometimes in combination with other chemicals, has been the cause of closures of sport and commercial fisheries in Lake Ontario, the Hudson River, other smaller lakes around the state.

PCBs were first manufactured in 1929 and were quickly found to be highly useful for a wide range of industrial purposes. In the United States they have been widely used in electrical equipment as an insulator and as a heat transfer fluid. But the very attributes that make this chemical useful for industrial purposes pose some very real biological hazards. It accumulates in fatty tissues and persist in the body long after they have been removed from the diet and may cause a variety of diseases. In 1968 the Japanese Yusho incident, in which rice oil contaminated by PCB during its manufacture severely affected large numbers of people, brought this chemical to international attention.

The problem in the Hudson River was caused by over 25 years of dumping of waste PCB in the river above the Fort Edward Dam by the General Electric Company (50). In that period over 500,000 pounds were disposed of in the River (51) although disposal rates had decreased from over 30 pounds per day to ounces per day from 1966 onward. Samples of fish and other organisms from the river revealed high levels of PCB as early as 1969, but the importance of the finding was not recognized until 1975. In 1976 a ban was placed on the commercial fishery for all species except Atlantic sturgeon, American shad, goldfish, and baitfish. From Fort Edward to Troy, all commercial and recreational fishing has been closed, but from the Troy Dam to the estuary sportfishing is permitted, although fishermen are advised to limit consumption.

In 1976 a final agreement between the State of New York and General Electric was reached in which disposal was to be severely curtailed, alternatives to PCB in their manufacturing processes sought, and an extensive research program seeking a solution to the problem initiated.

The dimensions of the PCB problem are quite clear. There are an estimated 640,000 pounds of it in the sediments of the Hudson River. Some appreciable quantity of that is potentially deliverable to the estuary. In 1977, for example, the Upper Hudson Basin delivered approximately 6,000 pounds of PCB to the estuary (52). A study of the possible transfer suggests that in the next 20 years as much as 120,000 pounds of PCB could be transferred from the River Basin to the estuary.

One of the things we found out about DDT, PCB, and other toxic chemicals is that suddenly they seem to be everywhere. General Electric's contributions of PCBs weren't the only sources of that contaminant to the Hudson River. Landfills which drained into the river were found to be adding PCB: electric apparatus, carbon paper, and a host of other materials containing PCB provide a continual source leaching slowly into the environment. And, even the atmosphere is a significant source, for emissions from manufacturing plants have put tons and tons of PCB into the air, where it provides a steady rain all over the world.

And all of this is finding its way to the ocean. Today sediments from the estuary contain 100 times as much PCB as do sediments from farther out in the Bight. Most of the PCB, as with other toxic materials, are associated with fine sediments. If these fine sediments become buried by the processes of sedimentation, then the PCB is probably "locked" up and may not reenter the system; but if these fine sediments are rolled up by waves during storms, then they move, sometimes hundreds of miles, before settling to the bottom again. And, during the period when they are suspended in the water column, the fine sediment particles and the PCB molecules are "available" to organisms and assimilated, so that the PCB molecule can begin to move slowly through the food chain as one organism eats another. Perhaps more important, when the sediments are stirred up, the PCBs are released to the atmosphere in considerable quantities.

Because there are so many chemicals in our environment and because we know so little about most of them, attacking the question, do they pose a hazard, is almost impossible. As most contaminants added to land, or freshwater, find their way to the ocean, identifying which of the multitude ought to be examined is a special problem for science. One way of getting at the solution is for a group of experts to collectively produce such a list. One such workshop identified as major threats requiring continued study: chlorinated pesticides (including Aldrin/Dieldrin, Chlordane, DDT, Endosulfan, Endrin, Heptachlor, Hexachlorocyclohexane and Toxaphene, and many of their decay products), polynuclear aromatic hydrocarbons, polychlorinated biphenyls (PCBs) and the metals lead, mercury, and plutonium. An additional 11 were thought to be potentially significant but more information about them was required for a definitive assessment. That listing included benzidenes, chlorobenzidenes, chlorophenols, diphenylhydrazine, halogenated diphenyl ethers, isophorene, low-molecular-weight halogenated hydrocarbons, petroleum hydrocarbons, and the metals arsenic, cadmium, and thallium (53). Perhaps the most worrisome thing about that listing is how little we know about any of these chemicals now widespread in our environment.

It has been said that if one added up the weight of all the contaminants being put into the estuary, including such things as suspended particulate matter, lead, zinc, mercury, copper, and cadmium, and spread it evenly around the estuary, the loading would be one ton of contaminant material for each and every acre of estuarine bottom each week (54). Obviously the heavy metals must be a part of that load.

Some metals are clearly contributed from industrial processes. Others come from ubiquitous sources, such as copper, which leaches continuously from all of the pipes in all of the homes in the Bight region. The magnitude of the problem of metals can be illustrated by the story of lead (55). It was one of the first metals used by man, found in pottery glaze as far back as 7,000–5,000 B.C. (56). The ease with which it could be obtained, smelted, and manipulated soon made it a highly used and prized metal. The Romans used lead extensively for ornamentation and for construction. By the birth of Christ, the output of lead had increased 1,000 fold. With the decline of the Roman Empire, lead production fell, but again reached the peak levels by the beginning of the Industrial Revolution. In the 250 years since then, production of lead has increased 100 fold. With the development of tetra-ethyl lead, the "no-knock" additive for gasoline, lead was being dispersed into the environment not only through its smelting and the disposal of it and its wastes into the aquatic environment, but by its dispersion into the atmosphere by millions upon millions of automobiles. Lead is now everywhere in our environment and in our bodies.

Mercury and cadmium are both considered to be highly toxic and both have been implicated in marine accidents affecting human health (57). In 1953, the first documented case of mercury poisoning from marine sources appeared among Japanese who had eaten shellfish contaminated with mercury from a plastics plant. By 1971 121 cases had been reported, with 43 deaths. The poisoning reached epidemic proportions when in January of 1975 there were 798 verified cases. This "Minimata event" attracted a great deal of attention because of the extreme effects upon human fetuses. Again, in 1965, in the Agano River Estuary of Japan, 49 people were affected by the contamination of fish from mercury discharged by an industrial operation and 6 died (58). Mercury suddenly became implicated in poisonings in many places: birds in Sweden; fish in Lake St. Clair, Canada; and, fish in Ohio's Lake Erie waters. In 1970 a serious turn was taken when high mercury levels were found in canned tuna on U.S. supermarket shelves. The Food and Drug Administration then took a stand and set a standard for the amount of mercury to be permitted in food (59). The controversy surrounding the setting of such standards is great and the problem of doing so is complicated.

The stakes are high when a safe level for a contaminant is set—food producers and processors (let alone cosmetic manufacturers and other industries affected by such standards) can stand to loose millions of dollars. Establishing a safe level is affected by the degree of risk individuals are willing to accept, variations in the tolerances individuals have to the various contaminants, dietary and other differences in habits which individualize the intake of the contaminant, the naturally occurring levels of contaminants in the environment and a host of other factors. It is little wonder then that each action by the Food and Drug Administration is fought over, usually with excellent coverage of the controversy by the media. There is little better agreement on such standards within the scientific community—even on mercury (60, 61). In large part the controversy results from the subjective nature of the final decision.

Cadmium occurs in high concentrations in some parts of the estuary, principally at Foundary Cove, opposite West Point on the Hudson River. A former nickel-cadmium battery factory located there had disposed of cadmium at the site which is now finding its way, through sediment transport, to the Bight (62). Blue crabs taken from the area have high concentrations of cadmium in their flesh (63). The New York State Department of Environmental Conservation has now issued a health advisory on the consumption of those crabs in the lower estuary.

Most metals stay within the harbor system, which, because of its action as a sediment trap, captures most of the particulate material, and hence most of the contaminants. But man has intervened and the estuary exports contaminants to the Bight in the form of transported, or barged, materials. The biggest culprit is dredge spoils.

Spoils of Dredging

Ever since Europeans settled on Manhattan Island, there has been a steady alteration of the shoreline of the estuary: filling and dumping to fill low or wetlands, bulkheading and rip-rapping, dockbuilding, converting streams to channels, and digging channels and then dredging them to still deeper depths. As machinery was built and engines increased our capability to do more work, the magnitude of the changes grew. One such achievement was the construction, in 1887 to 1891, of the channels (first the Gedney and later the Ambrose) across the bars of the harbor—among the first channels to be constructed and maintained by dredging (64). But no sooner were they built than more deepening was required, because ships were growing larger as steel plates replaced wooden timbers in ship's hulls. With longer, wider, and deeper ships, the channels and anchorages of the harbor had to become deeper for the port to remain operative and competitive.

Over 240 miles of channels dredged to a maximum depth of 48 feet define the network of possible vessel movements in the Port of New York and New Jersey today. There are more than 300 miles of channels in other Bight ports. But even the "modern depth" is not enough for the newer generations of supertankers and giant container ships. And, besides the need for dredging created by the increasing size of ships, there is a continual influx of sediment being deposited in the estuary. This has to be removed in a program of maintenance dredging just to keep the channels open.

When the Gedney channel was constructed, 4.3 million cubic yards of coarse sand and gravel were removed; later, when the Ambrose Channel was dredged, over 50 million cubic yards were dug out (65). By the 1970s an average of 8 million cubic yards of spoils were being removed yearly in maintaining channels and anchorages (66). Today's harbor has about 26 square miles of its 387 square miles, or about 7% of its area, regularly dredged (67).

Dredging is the means by which we maintain the lifeline of maritime commerce our nation, and our lifestyle, depends upon. Dredging is a destructive process, for in the removal of harbor bottom we destroy marine organisms and affect the life cycles of others. It alters the configuration of the bottom, thereby changing current patterns, shore erosion, and a host of other factors. But dredging is a requirement to maintain commerce and we must accept the negative effects in order to have the benefits. Dredging is only a part of the story though, for while "dig we must", there is also the need to put what we have dug up some place.

Disposal of the spoils from dredging should be a simple problem. It is really only moving the bottom of the ocean around from one point to another. And, indeed, for many years disposal of dredge spoils was a relatively simple practice—they were dumped near where they

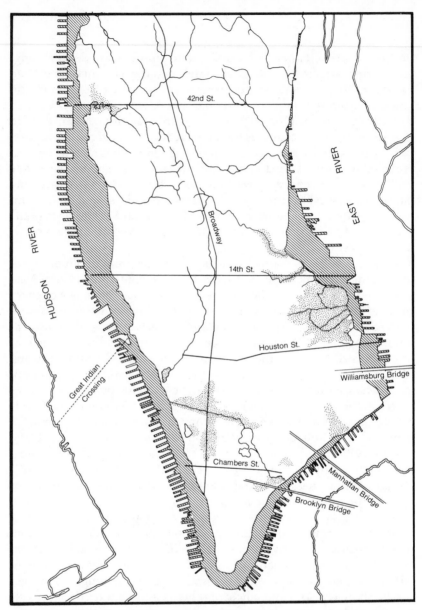

Figure 21. Landfill along Manhattan Island. This drawing of the southern portion of Manhattan Island is taken from a larger map compiled by Townsend MacCoun from earlier surveys of Manhattan Island. It shows the shoreline and drainage as it existed in 1609. Growth of the Island by filling, principally to the pierheads, is shown up to 1909. At present the coast of Manhattan along the Hudson River is undergoing another cycle of pierhead filling. If Westway, a replacement for the Westside Elevated Highway is built, most of the Hudson River shoreline will have been moved towards the River by man's activity. (Drawing by Sharon Ellis from photostats of the MacCoun Map, New York Historical Society)

were dredged. At first this was in the harbor, but as the spoils often quickly washed back into the channels from which they were dug, the practice was stopped. Some spoils were then taken outside the bars and dumped at sea, others were used to fill wetlands, but those accessible were soon filled. Through the years a number of sites have been utilized for ocean dumping of spoils, but from about the turn of the century, the current location, the Mud Dump Site, has been used (68). Such enormous quantities of spoils have been dumped there that the mound created is now, itself, a hazard to navigation.

That the dredge spoils have made a mountain really isn't a significant problem, however. All that would be needed to rectify that would be to change the site of the dumping. But all those spoils we've been moving are more than just sands and muds from the bottom of the harbor. They include all the pollutants settled to the bottom from our sewage, from industrial wastes, from spills of oils and other chemicals, and from the runoff of our streets. All in all, it is a powerful and potent combination of contaminants. In the complex chemistry of the waters of the estuary, petroleum hydrocarbons and other spilled and dumped substances react and alter in the sunlight, forming complicated organic substances about which we know little aside from their sometimes powerful toxicity. Heavy metals from wastewaters; chlorinated hydrocarbons from industrial wastes; asbestos fibers worn from brake linings and washed from city streets; these and a brew of other substances accumulating at the bottom of the harbor are carried from the estuary to the Bight with the spoils.

While clean, or relatively uncontaminated sediments make up the bulk of the spoils, as much as 75% of the spoils taken in the harbor (69), the remainder is pretty bad. Those are the finer sediments with lots of clay and organic particles. These have the property of absorbing or attracting metals and many of the organic contaminants to their surface. While the process removes pollutants from the water and traps them in sediments where they may be buried and locked up for long periods of time, it presents a problem in spoil disposal. These finer-grained sediments are usually found in dead-end channels, such as the Gowanus Canal in Brooklyn or other places where the slow water motion allows them to settle. These dead-end channels are among the most highly polluted places in the harbor.

In this story of the dredge spoils we see the true nature of ocean dumping: moving the problem further away from where we are. We started dumping our wastes in the harbor but were forced to move further away because of pollution and shoaling. Now, as we move the bottom of the harbor, we are also moving those earlier pollutants along with the sediments. Dredge spoils are now the largest source of copper, cadmium, lead, and chromium in the Bight (70). They may well be one of the largest sources of chlorinated hydrocarbons such as PCB (71).

Because of the contaminants contained in dredge spoils, there has been a tendency to accuse them of being the bad actors in the ocean dumping story. But this charge is undeserved, for the spoils are derived from the contaminated harbor bottom and some of that harbor bottom might find its way out of the harbor to the Bight by natural processes. The easy answer, of course, is that the harbor bottom shouldn't have been contaminated in the first place. In dumping the spoils at sea, the Corps of Engineers is not "a dumper" disposing of unwanted materials. Some spoils are sand, and sand has a very high value in the metropolitan area, but spoils are not usually something which can be beneficially used. Those which are coarser sands are cleanest of contaminants and might be used for fill, for construction aggregate, or for other purposes. But usually they are taken in the wrong place at the wrong time and trying to make use of them becomes an economic nightmare.

To find a solution for the contaminated spoil problem the Corps of Engineers has begun a program of research to find acceptable means of placing the spoils somewhere where the pollution can be contained or reduced. This is a necessity, for if the channels of the harbor aren't maintained, they will silt up and the harbor will be useless for commerce. An early warning was sounded in 1980 when it was found that the Passenger Ship Terminal berths had silted, so that the *Queen Elizabeth II*, the *Leonardo DaVinci*, and other large cruise ships were unable to dock (72). New York Harbor requires less dredging than many of its competitors because it is closer to the sea (Philadelphia and Baltimore are far up the estuary) and the Hudson River carries relatively little load compared with the Mississippi (the site of the port of New Orleans). But there has been a bias towards the southern ports in the development of dredging programs (73), a bias which might be ended by having the costs of dredging borne by the local ports and taxpayers rather than by the nation as a whole.

Refuse

Every day New York City produces over 20,000 tons of refuse (74). And each and every ton must be put somewhere. In 1979 an average of 10,200 tons of garbage per day were carried from the city by marine barges to the Fresh Kills landfill on Staten Island (75). That amount is further increased by the 1,400 tons each day of "wet residue and fly ash" from the city's six incinerators, which each day burn 3,800 tons of refuse, and by 7,500 tons dumped daily in the three truck-filled landfills remaining in operation (76). And that is only New York City. Each and every community around the Bight is equally busy creating its own garbage problem.

No one denies that there is value in garbage. It's just that there are vested interests in not using the garbage effectively. Over half a million bottles represent over 5% of the weight of refuse collected (77) each day in New York City, but bottle manufacturers and others have lobbied effectively against a bottle law that would encourage recycling. Aluminum is about 1% of the weight of the city's garbage, an amount that would make a roll of aluminum foil 7,500 miles long (78). Paper contained in garbage, making up over 50% of its weight (79), comes from the equivalent of 100,000 trees consumed each day. Some years ago it was estimated that the Sunday *New York Times*, which cost (then) 75 cents, cost an additional 10 cents to dispose of (80). Sixty-five thousand abandoned cars sold as scrap yielded $650,000 income to the city (81). Recovery of some of the materials in garbage would reduce the costs of its collection and, perhaps more important, would reduce the volume that ultimately needs disposal.

Today there is growing interest in garbage as a source for recoverable and reusable materials. This is a new technology and municipalities are concerned about the investments they will have to make in adopting it and fear the possibility that they may guess wrong and prematurely select the wrong process. Taxpayers, while always vocal about their tax burden, are not so uniformly opposed to the existing disposal option—landfills (82). There are also questions about the burning of refuse to produce energy. Will this create new air pollution hazards? Will the clean air technologies really work? Among the issues involved in the dispute are the compatibility of the existing collection system with the requirements of recycling; how recycling will interact with economic development; and, how resource recovery will affect other disposal-related problems such as the co-disposal of garbage and other wastes like sewage sludge (83).

Refuse includes a multitude of wastes other than those from our homes. One example is the debris from the continual renewal of the city—the tearing down and building up. Construction and demolition wastes, quaintly called "cellar dirt," can be substantial in amount. From 1965 to 1970 the average quantity of cellar dirt to be disposed of was over 1 million tons per year (84). Where does one put the rock from the excavation for buildings, for subways and water tunnels? Construction of the City's subways between 1900 and 1950 created over 31 million cubic yards of rock which had to go somewhere (85). Refuse of all kinds other than garbage amounts to almost 500,000 tons per year (86).

Cellar dirt, less floatable, could be used either in the construction of new lands or be carried out to a dump site established at the head of the Hudson Canyon in the Bight (87). Rock from the construction of the City's subways was used to restore about 100 acres to the badly eroded Governors, Rikers, and Ellis islands. But still, nearly 1 million tons per year are dumped at the cellar dirt site in the Bight (88).

Through the city's development, refuse disposal followed a simple progression: remove it to a site some distance from its source. When that site becomes a problem, remove it a further distance. Thus, garbage was progressively moved from the house to the street, from the street to the piers along the coast, from the coast to the estuary, and finally out to Long Island Sound and the Bight where it was dumped. Although for many years garbage was dumped at sea, it tended to float around for a while and then come back to the beaches. The U.S. Army Corps of Engineers, given the problem of regulating this disposal business, developed an elaborate system of sites that varied by tide and season to reduce the incidence of garbage floating onto the beaches. The system was fundamentally unworkable (89). Litigation resulted and finally, in 1934, garbage was legally dumped at sea for the last time (90).

The problem remained. What to do with the garbage? Unwanted land which could be used as a dump became scarcer. Unorganized dumping is frowned on because of problems with disease, odors, and rodents. Official dumps became landfills or better, sanitary landfills in which the refuse is accumulated, compacted, and buried beneath some clean soil. The problems of the dump are solved, in part. But what does one do when there is no vacant or unwanted land? Wetlands, then (the 1930s) called marshes and swamps and unappreciated for their value in the coastal ecosystem, became a prime target. If filled in, new land for housing and industry was created. And so was introduced the great era of the sanitary landfill.

By 1966, 20% of Manhattan, Brooklyn, the Bronx, and Queens was built on filled lands; about half was former garbage dumps or other waste-disposal sites (91). Since the early 1930s New York City has completed filling 38 landfills, a total of 5,438 acres. Six sites now active have an additional area of 3,104 acres (92). Fresh Kills, the largest

Figure 22. Garbage scows being filled at New York City Department of Sanitation stations on Manhattan for hauling to the Fresh Kills, Staten Island landfill. (© 1973 Wave Hill Incorporated, photo by Wendy Holmes, courtesy of Wave Hill Incorporated)

of these, is a 2,900 acre landfill on Staten Island which is scheduled to be filled by 1985 (93). A 20,000 acre tract in the Hackensack Meadowlands, once renowned as the breeding grounds of New Jersey's famed man-eating mosquitoes, was turned into landfill for 125 towns in 6 counties of New Jersey in the 1960s (94). Small municipalities of New York also contributed their garbage to New Jersey—some from as far away as the City of Glen Cove on Long Island's north shore. About 515 acres of it were rapidly filled (95). Where possible, the new lands were used for recreation or parks: the New Jersey Sports Complex and Shea Stadium stand atop such landfills. Flushing Meadow Park (site of the 1964 World's Fair), Orchard Beach; and Great Kills Park (96) are also on filled land.

As we learned more about them, sanitary landfills were found to be somewhat unsanitary. While the process of capping the refuse cut back on vermin and odor, slow compaction of the garbage squeezed out liquids, a liquor found to contain many of the toxins of the stuff in the landfill. For example, PCBs in some manufactured products have been moved from the landfill to the surrounding environment by this process. And in the environmentally sensitive period of the late

1960s, concern over the great loss of wetlands brought their use as landfill sites to an end. Both New York and New Jersey enacted stiff wetlands preservation legislation.

An alternative to the filling of wetlands with garbage is creation of islands. In 1956 a scheme to create a new island of 350 acres by connecting Hoffman and Swinburne Islands with dikes and filling it with garbage was proposed (97). Although the proposal never got off the ground it has never been abandoned and is resurrected with each new landfill crisis.

What are the options to landfills? Incineration of garbage is a declining alternative for metropolitan areas. Air pollution problems have closed many incinerators—some permanently, others while they are being improved to meet requirements. But incineration only reduces the volume of the refuse. The toxic materials and the valuable materials remain. Can systems be worked out by which the paper and other combustible products can be incinerated while other constituents are reclaimed and recovered? This is the hope of the evolving technologies. Being considered today by the Port Authority of New York and New Jersey are a series of industrial sites, each having as an energy source such an incinerator system.

Decomposition of organic material in the absence of air, and its oxygen, leads to the production of methane gas: methane, the major constituent of natural gas, is a wonderfully clean source of energy. Recoverable methane from New York City landfills has been estimated to be as much as 7 trillion BTU per year—a figure that represents something like 0.2% of the energy needs of the entire city (98). Leases for production have been issued on a 400-acre tract of Fresh Kills. Brooklyn Union Gas has stated that it would like to develop the Fountain Avenue, Brooklyn, landfill for methane production for use in the Starrett City housing complex a short distance away. Half the annual production of the landfill could provide the energy needs of that housing complex for heat and hot water. The Pelham Bay landfill, some 80 acres piled to an average height of 150 feet, could provide 90 million recoverable BTU per hour for 10 years, about equal to the needs of nearby Co-op City (99). New Jersey Public Service Electric and Gas, the State's largest utility, has announced plans to extract methane from the 656 acres of garbage dumps in the Hackensack Meadows (100). That company estimates 100 billion BTU production each year—a value of $200,000 annually.

No one denies the cost of current disposal techniques of garbage and refuse. New York City alone spends over $100,000,000 each year on its garbage: more than the total expenditures of 10 states. But only changing economics will make recycling and recovery possible, for when prices of metals and other recoverables become high enough, development will occur. An example of such a change in the value of the landfill is that of their coming use as a source of energy. No other society generates as much refuse through its use of multitudinous layers of food wrappings, through manufacture of inexpensive throwaway items. Refuse and the Bight are linked because the Bight has been seen, fleetingly, as society's answer to the garbage problem. While the dumping of garbage in the ocean is not now practiced, we have used the Bight's margins intensively for that purpose. We may be sure that, as disposal alternatives tighten in the future, many will see the ocean as the great-granddaddy landfill of them all.

atlantic mackerel

Scomber scombrus

1 in.

7 / The Costs of Dumping

A major use of the New York Bight is as a dump for those wastes which we don't want to treat because of expense or difficulties in disposing of them in other ways (we lack entrepreneurial initiative in the field of recycling). Does this dumping affect *us*? Does it make any difference that we do it? Answering these questions is difficult because there are so many ways of looking at them. One way would be to ask how dumping in the Bight affects our health—are we in danger of disease or death? Another way of looking at it is to ask how dumping affects our perception of the Bight. Do we think of the Bight's waters as being "dirty," unclean, and not so satisfactory for swimming or fishing?

There are other ways to look at the effects of dumping of wastes on the Bight which don't spring so readily to mind. For example, does dumping foreclose or limit other uses of the Bight or its resources either now or in the future? Will we, by dumping, limit the potential for beneficial use of the Bight by our children? Are we, by disposing of toxic wastes which are hazardous to us affecting the lives or life cycles of other creatures which live in the Bight? In other words, is the Bight's ecosystem being affected? And, finally, in that measurement most used by our society, what are the economics of dumping? Obviously some taxpayers are not having to build sewage-treatment plants when raw sewage is disposed of in the Bight's tributary waterways. But are others paying a cost for that dumping of sewage? Who are they and what are those costs? Building a treatment plant helps, but sewage sludge is produced and, when it is ocean dumped, are others paying? Are we solving a problem or just moving it around?

Others have asked these same questions. For example, in 1972, in response to a rising tide of concern for the effects of waste discharge into the ocean (among other issues), Congress enacted two important pieces of legislation: the Federal Water Pollution Control Act Amendments (the Clean Waters Act) and the Marine Protection, Research, and Sanctuaries Act, better known as the Ocean Dumping Act. The latter states that permits for dumping should be issued upon determination that "such dumping will not unreasonably degrade or endanger human health, welfare or amenities, or the marine environment, ecological systems, or economic potentialities" (1). Have we reached these points? Have we degraded the environment? Or, is ocean disposal of wastes still an option available to us?

The answers are complicated, not straightforward. Many scientists feel that the capacity of the ocean to absorb wastes has not yet been exceeded, except locally. Some feel that if waste disposal in the ocean were undertaken properly, the ocean could be an effective means of discarding many substances which otherwise pose severe problems for mankind. Others feel that any disposal in the ocean is inappropriate and that we have already done too much damage to coastal waters. Because the New York Bight is one of the most dumped in areas of the nation's coastal waters, getting over 70% of the sewage sludge, a little less than 14% of the dredge spoils, and over 80% of the industrial wastes, it is a good place to look for answers (2).

What we should be looking for as we try to answer these questions about ocean dumping is how dumping relates to our health, well-being, and environment, and how the quality of our life is altered. Pathogenic viruses or bacteria or toxic substances are present in the waters of the Bight and may cause disease. This is a very direct relationship between dumping and our well-being. It can be easily assessed. Aesthetically offensive effects, such as flotsam and jetsam on the waters or oil on the beaches, outrage or annoy us but don't threaten our health. These effects are those most frequently argued in economic terms. Still other and more subtle, but unseen, things may be occurring to the creatures of the sea. Their death or disruption affects us, if at all, only through the pocketbook in what we pay for food and taxes for public works such as sewage-treatment plants. But others, such as fishermen, are vitally concerned, for their livelihood is at stake.

Human Health

The best-known way for a person to be affected by the marine environment is from infectious diseases contacted in the water. The infective agents may be bacteria, viruses, fungi, or protozoan or metazoan parasites which get into marine waters from human and animal fecal material. Classic waterborne diseases which have plagued mankind include cholera, typhoid fever, bacillary and amoebic dysentery, and infectious hepatitis. Ascarid worms and other parasites and a variety of enteroviruses also cause enteric or internally induced illnesses known to be transmissable in salt waters. Less well-known are agenst such as the bacterium *Vibrio parahaemoliticus*, which can cause "food poisoning" and wound infections and the phytoplankton dinoflagellates (such as *Gonyaulax* and *Prorocentrum*), which can cause paralytic shellfish poisoning and upper-respiratory complaints through the toxins they form.

Despite the number of infectious agents present in fecal wastes and therefore in waters into which sewage is dumped, the number of outbreaks of disease from contact with salt water is relatively small. Environmental health scientists record such outbreaks as "events" and epidemiologists collect all the records they can of such events. When one looks at a catalogue of health events related to the marine environment, one is struck by the large number resulting from the eating of shellfish relative to those from, say, swimming. There are, of course, other ways in which we come in contact with the marine environment, but these seldom, if ever, result in disease outbreaks.

Behind this interesting relationship of shellfish to human disease is the important biological process called bioconcentration. Bioconcentration is the process by which shellfish accumulate viruses and bacteria in up to five times the concentrations found in the water (3). Shellfish use the fine filaments of their gills to strain the seawater to capture plankton, bacteria, and other organisms on which they feed. Being an efficient means of capturing food, it is also an effective means to capture and accumulate pathogenic bacteria and viruses. While the shellfish themselves are not affected by these pathogens, the very high concentrations in which they can occur means that eating raw shellfish taken from polluted waters can be an effective way of getting many diseases. Hepatitis is such a disease commonly associated with shellfish.

Contamination of nearshore waters of the Bight, particularly in the region of sewage outfalls, has resulted in the closure of many beaches and of many acres of shellfishing grounds in the Upper and Lower New York Harbors, Raritan Bay, portions of Great South Bay, Moriches Bay and Long Island Sound, as well as a great area of the Bight in the region of the sewage sludge dump. In every case the area closed to shellfishing greatly exceeds that actually polluted, that extra area being a safety zone established to provide an additional margin of protection. Harvesters of shellfish, faced with declining supplies, will often agitate for more stringent application of closures, restricting the size of the buffer zone. Or they will argue that a new and better standard is required for measuring pollution. And in the extreme they will point out that they, or someone they know, regularly eats shellfish from closed beds and "doesn't get sick."

Closed shellfishing areas are established by health officials when the numbers of coliform bacteria present in the waters exceeds 70 MPN per milliliter (70 most probable number of bacteria, as measured in repetitive tests in about 1/500th of a pint of water). Coliform bacteria are those normally inhabiting the intestinal tract of mammals—ourselves, our pets, wild and domesticated animals. The principle is that the presence of coliform bacteria indicates the possibility of sewage contamination of the water. While the coliform bacteria themselves are not harmful, their presence indicates the potential presence of disease-causing bacteria or viruses. Many of those are difficult to isolate and count in seawater; coliform bacteria, on the other hand, are relatively easy to identify and culture, making the task of measuring pollution easier.

Many users of the marine environment, particularly shellfishermen, feel that the standards of water quality which have been drawn are too strict, that a better measure of pollution should be found. But there is compelling evidence that the use of coliform bacteria as indicators of possible contamination has served us well. Since 1900 there have been over 7,000 recorded cases of shellfish-borne disease in the United States and Canada, over half of which have been in New Jersey and New York (4). This geographic concentration of disease reports results, in part, from the enormous numbers of shellfish harvested in these two states, by the high concentration of people living there, and because there are excellent newspapers which report outbreaks of disease.

Nonetheless, there are some interesting patterns to be found. Typhoid, once the scourge of the shellfish industry, has almost disappeared. The last outbreak was in Denmark from the consumption of French oysters and occurred in 1972, but the last occurrence in the Bight region was in 1954 (5). Infectious hepatitis is of more recent concern. Large outbreaks in 1961 and 1964 caused renewed concern for shellfish sanitation and resulted in stricter surveillance of the closed beds. But poaching remains a problem and one which will increase as the price of clams rises. Some estimates place the proportion of the catch of hard clam taken from closed beds of Long Island as high as 35% (6). In 1980 the New York State Department of Environmental

Conservation was warned that the treatment of poachers by judges was insufficiently severe to deter poaching (the average fine for poaching was then about $30 (7)). The department was also informed that four New Jersey consumers who contracted hepatitis in 1979 were infected by a shipment of clams from Great South Bay (8). The implication that the clams were poached from closed waters is clear.

Closure of shellfish beds because of pollution by human sewage is not restricted to the nearshore region. In 1970 and 1974 the Food and Drug Administration closed enormous areas of surf clam grounds because of sludge dumping and outflow of waters with high coliform counts from the estuary. In addition, because the harbor sediments are rich in sewage-derived materials, spoils carried from the harbor to the Mud Dump Site also carry enormous numbers of human-derived viruses and bacteria. While we can feel somewhat detached from the problem of high coliform levels in the Bight, protected as we are by the closed shellfishing areas and the fact that most of us seldom see the real Bight, there are some implications for us.

These implications first became apparent in 1972, when it was noticed that some of the coliform bacteria from the site had characteristics which made them resistant to antibiotics (9). These bacteria obtained their resistance through the transfer of genetic materials from other bacteria living in the sludge dump area. Those bacteria presumably developed the antibiotic resistance as a result of their living in an environment heavily contaminated by metals and other toxic substances (10). This finding posed some immediate concerns, and newspapers reported the presence of a "superbug" spawned by the Sludge Monster (11). Further examination of the disease-resistant strain suggests that no immediate public health threat is posed (12).

Fewer people become ill from swimming than from eating shellfish because to take in the number of bacteria or viruses required to get sick requires swallowing a lot of water. Drowning may occur first. Another factor is that the bacteria and viruses tend to become associated with fine-grained particles in the water. As these settle to the bottom of the bay or harbor, these particles with their bacteria may become food for the shellfish and are effectively removed from the water in which we usually swim.

While it is probable that typhoid and dysentery resulted from swimming in the polluted waters of New York harbor at the turn of the century, there have been no cases of these diseases since 1920 clearly associated with swimming. Upper-respiratory complaints among bathers in the mid-1970s were found to have resulted from the presence of dinoflagellate blooms in Bight waters (13). Dino-flagellates, like some other phytoplankton, produce toxins as a part of their metabolic processes and these toxins can cause respiratory symptoms.

But there is always a possibility of serious disease resulting from swimming in polluted waters. A classic study done of New York City beaches in the summers of 1973 through 1975 showed that swimmers in polluted, although not closed, waters incurred higher rates of gastrointestinal symptoms (vomiting, diarrhea, nausea, or stomach aches) (14). The symptoms were more common on those beaches closest to the mouth of the estuary which also had the highest numbers of coliform bacteria in their waters. While more serious enteric disease outbreaks have not been noticed, the hazard remains.

Many nonswimmers enjoy the salt air as they sit on the beach. That salt air results from minute droplets of seawater carried by the on-shore breeze usually found during the day. Is there a possibility that bacteria and viruses which might be in the seawater could be carried by these aerosolized droplets? It has been investigated and is a possi-ble, though improbable, means of disease transmission (15). The den-sities of bacteria and viruses in the droplets are simply not high enough for the level of exposure to be sufficient.

Reduction of the pathogenic bacteria present in seawater, and of the indicator coliform bacteria, can be accomplished by treatment or elimination of the discharge of sewage into coastal waters. Primary and secondary treatment alone do little to kill bacteria and viruses. Chlorination of the sewage does have the effect of reducing their numbers. But recently this process of chlorination has come under question because of the effects of chlorine on other marine organisms and because of the possible formation of chlorinated organic molecules which are highly toxic. Other methodologies include treating the sewage with ozone or with radiation.

But there are other hazards to mankind from contaminated waters. Growing in importance are the chemicals in the environment: syn-thetic organic molecules from solvents, pesticides, insecticides, petrochemicals, plastics, and the products from combustion of oil, coal, and even wood; metals acids, alkalies, and others. As we have seen, these are added to the Bight from the atmosphere, from municipal and industrial waste water, from runoff and other sources including spills. It is fortunate for us that most of these chemicals have an affinity for particulate material in the water and that, with the particles, they settle to the bottom. If not resuspended, these can become buried and are gradually removed from our part of the biosphere. Unfortunately, storms resuspend fine sediments settling in the Bight, so it is only when these particles are trapped in wetlands or washed off the shelf that we see no more of them locally.

For these kinds of contaminants, the way from the environment to us, and sickness, is through our food. In the case of the Bight, the pathway is through shellfish or finfish. While in Japan transmission of both mercury and PCBs through environmental pathways have been implicated in severe human tragedy, we have not had, in this country, a similar situation. In part this is because of actions by government to prevent commercial exploitation of contaminated seafoods and by educational programs to reduce consumption of contaminated fish by sportsmen. Unfortunately sportsmen tend to have short memories or feel that what they consume can't do too much harm, for the health advisories seem to have only a slight effect. In New York State, as a result of PCB pollution of the Hudson River and both PCB and Mirex contamination in Lake Ontario, health advisories have been issued. People are encouraged to limit consumption of fish caught in these waters and, through cooperation with educational programs such as Sea Grant, have been taught means by which intake of contaminant may be limited.

A number of chemicals have been identified as being of critical importance in the Bight region. At this time PCBs and dioxin are close to posing a hazard sufficient to warrant a health advisory. It is conjectural, but it may be that if sufficient PCBs are carried down the Hudson River to the Bight, that there may be cause for a health advisory in those animals caught in the Bight which concentrate it. At this time, however, fish from the estuary, including those which move in to spawn and then move out (like the striped bass) have higher levels of PCBs in their tissues than those same species taken from the waters of the Bight.

Bioaccumulation is the mechanism which brings contaminants such as chemicals and metals to higher levels in fish and shellfish. It works this way. Organisms at the bottom of the food chain pick up some of the contaminant and it assimilates in one of their organs. Many of those creatures are filter or suspension feeders, organisms which pick up particulate matter to which metals and other chemicals have an affinity. While these animals may have substantial amounts of contaminants in their bodies, the amount may not be harmful to them because they have found ways to inactivate these chemically. These contaminants are passed along from prey to predator, and as each predator eats its prey, the body burden, or amount incorporated in the tissues of the organism, increases at each step. Highest concentrations of contaminants are found in those organisms at the top of the food chain: salmonid fishes and striped bass are examples. Each is known to have the highest levels of PCB in their bodies of all organisms in New York waters. It is an unfortunate fact of life that highest level predators are also the most prized sportfish, a prize fishermen are unwilling to go without.

Disposal of wastes in the Bight is polluting its waters. But as yet effects upon human health are absent or difficult to determine. Disease occurrences have been found along the margins of the Bight where polluted waters are closed to shellfishing and bathing. The presence of various pathogenic bacteria and viruses in coastal water, particularly, results in an incidence of subclinical gasteroenteritis, eye, ear, nose and throat infections, but not ones of such significance to be regarded as other than a nuisance among the population. Increasing amounts of metals and some organic chemicals pose a future health hazard, particularly if the amounts increase.

But if the picture of the Bight, as it relates to human health, is acceptable, what of some of the other measures of its condition?

Aesthetics—The Floatable Crisis

What we see greatly affects the value we place on places or objects. A littered park is less used and less well thought of than one which is clean. Beaches which are cleaned regularly are more popular than those which aren't, even though they may be in highly polluted areas (16). Perception of water pollution is often measured more by the flotsam and jetsam we see floating on the surface or stranded on the beach than by the unseen bacteria, viruses, and chemicals. Aesthetics, or our visual perception, of the Bight can be extremely important in determining the value we place upon it.

But measuring aesthetic values is very difficult indeed, for people react differently to a given scene, painting, or pollution episode. Environmental degradation, however, often results in a broad public outcry. One well-documented aesthetic insult resulting from our use of the Bight as a dump will illustrate this: Long Island Beach pollution in 1976 (17). By examining this happening, which has come to be called the "floatables event," we can see how the public reacts when confronted by "aesthetic" pollution they believe may also be health threatening.

On May 8, 1976, a fuel barge went aground in the upper Bay of New York Harbor, releasing 700 gallons of No. 6 oil. This wasn't the first spill of the year, but it did mark the start of the highly unusual juxtaposition of happenings that constitute the floatables event. On June 2, two sewage sludge storage tanks on Pearsall's Hassock in Great South Bay, Long Island, exploded. Although about 1.6 million gallons of sludge were kept on the island, about 1 million gallons got into surrounding waters. Despite containment efforts, the sludge was seen passing through the East Rockaway Inlet into the Bight the next day. That same day, June 3, three piers burned in Weehawken, New Jersey, and eight days later, two others in Manhattan were destroyed by fire. Pier fires are not unusual in New York Harbor because there are so many abandoned and partially collapsed structures. The Corps of Engineers vessel *Driftmaster* collects, by skimming, debris from the harbor and especially, debris resulting from a pier fire. Although she collected many tons on this occasion, much fine charred wood escaped clean-up (18).

Mother Nature was also conspiring to make this event notable. Rainfall in the Hudson River Basin had been heavy and the flow of the Hudson River was especially high. On June 9 the winds swung around from the north to the south, and a persistent and unusual southerly flow was established that would continue for almost two weeks. Both of these situations—high river flow through the estuary into the Bight and a subsequent persistent flow of southerly winds—established conditions which resulted in the "floatables event" (19).

On June 14 a mass of floating debris was reported washing up on Long Island's south shore beaches. Tar and grease balls up to 4 inches in diameter, which had a striking resemblance to human feces, were found on Fire Island. The following days saw increasing amounts of debris reported all along the beaches from Jacob Riis Park in the west to the Hamptons on the east. Plastic objects, charred wood, grease and tar balls dominated the "normal" flotsam and jetsam of garbage and trash from ships and boats as well. Both dominated the usual plant materials drifting out from the bays. Some beaches were closed on June 16, but when a new "wave" of floating debris hit the beaches on June 19, almost all were closed to bathing. On June 23 New York's Governor Hugh Carey declared the south shores of Nassau and Suffolk Counties disaster areas (20).

Certainly the situation was serious. Hundreds of thousands of summer bathers and beach-goers were turned away. Businesses dependent upon that flow of people suffered substantial economic loss as the public went away unhappy. Attendance levels remained low, even after the beaches were reopened, with some 30% fewer than usual visitors (21). The cost to the island's economy as a result of the closures of the beaches has been estimated at between $25 and $30 million (22).

Important as the immediate effects on beach use were, the perception of many people was that the Sludge Monster had returned. More informed citizens came to the conclusion that some threshold of environmental degradation had been reached and that the Bight had been "ruined." People stayed away from the beaches all summer in droves because of the perception of polluted waters and possible health hazards, and because of the appearance of the beaches. And well they might have. What was the material which floated up on the beaches? It was a mix of natural and waste materials: seaweed, eelgrass and reedy materials; burned wood fragments; plastic debris including fragments of styrofoam cups, plastic bottles and beverage containers, tampon inserters, plastic sheeting fragments, straws, bottle caps, sanitary napkin liners, toys, cigarette filters and cigar tips, and so forth; condom rings and fragments; grease and tar balls of various sizes and appearances; cardboard materials, particularly food packaging; food materials including chicken heads and entrails; and other materials (23).

Among the many questions posed by this event were: What caused it? Was there a health hazard? What can we do to prevent a recurrence? These questions need to be answered, for they are reasonable questions and, happily, there is an equally reasonable body of information with which to respond.

What caused the event seems to be answerable in terms of two special factors operating together: high flow out of the estuary, caused by the unusual rainfall, carried much debris from the harbor. Northerly winds widely dispersed the floating debris in the Bight, but the later, persistent, southerly winds caused it to collect and move northward toward Long Island's beaches.

No immediate or long-term health hazard was presented by this event. Measurement of the numbers of coliform bacteria present in the waters showed levels no higher than would be expected and not high enough to warrant closure of the beaches. Coliform bacteria were present in some of the grease balls in very high numbers, but this is thought to be only because the bacteria thrived on the grease ball itself. But the question persisted—is this material sewage-derived? Does it come from the sludge dump? If not, where?

There are, as we know, many sources of contaminants in the Bight. But this was a special kind of material, floating debris. The sources were:

Oil spills—The Coast Guard was able to trace the source of the tar balls back to the oil spill which occurred on May 8. But while that was a source of tar balls for this episode, oil pollution on the beaches is a persistent problem. For the first 6 months of 1976, Coast Guard records show a 315% increase in volume of oil spilled over the same period of the previous year (24).

Explosion of the sewage sludge storage tanks. The contribution of this explosion to the beach pollution is not precisely known. It is clear that efforts to contain the sludge released by the explosion were ineffective (25).

Pier fires—It seems pretty certain that some of the charred wood from the New York Harbor pier fires did find its way to the Bight and then to the beaches (25). In 1976, the Corps of Engineers removed over 500,000 cubic feet of drift material from the harbor. They estimate that pier fires contribute significantly to that amount (27).

Municipal wastewaters—In the last chapter we learned that these are the primary source of contaminants in the Bight. But secondary sewage-treatment facilities are supposed to remove most of the floatables from the wastewater. But do they? During May and June of 1976, western Manhattan discharged 200 million gallons of raw sewage per day into the Hudson River and the Red Hook area of Brooklyn contributed another 50 million gallons a day. Raw sewage contains all those things we flush down the toilets whether they sink or float. In addition, because of plant failure or because of construction, an additional 178 million gallons of raw sewage, which should have been treated, were discharged by New York City in that period (28). The Passaic Valley treatment plant handles volumes of sewage well in excess of design standards and, as a result, doesn't do it well (29). Because the quantity of floatables screened out by sewage-treatment plants is known in relation to the volume treated, we can estimate what might have been put into the estuary in May and June 1976 from raw sewage. That quantity is a staggering 2,000–13,000 cubic feet of floatable materials each day (30).

Combined sewers—Because storm and sewage drains are combined in much of the metropolitan region, excess rainfall causes sewage-treatment plants to overflow and discharge raw sewage and floatables. In May and June 1976, that occurred on 19 days during the critical period (31).

Trash tossed overboard from ships—It is clear from the kinds of items found on the beaches that ships' garbage did contribute to the "floatables event." Although vessels are not supposed to discharge their bilge water or dump garbage over the side of the ship while they are within three miles of the shore, it is done. Crews are eager to clean the vessel from its port stay. Estimates are that a 40-person crew of a ship generates 140 pounds of wet garbage a day, 28 pounds of domestic-type trash a day, and 10–15 pounds of nondomestic trash, such as oily rags, timbers, cans and bottles (32). Each year over 7000 ships pass through the Bight: that could mean over 7000 tons of trash and garbage dumped.

Trash discarded by boaters—Recreational boaters are litterers of the first order. Coast Guard estimates are that each boater tosses 1 pound of paper, plastic or metal cans over the side of his boat each day and as much as one-half pound of garbage a day (33). Given the number of boaters using the Bight, this is a source of 2500 tons of litter each year (34).

Dumping in the Bight—While floatable materials are transported to the Bight in sewage sludge and, to a lesser extent, in dredge spoils, dumping was not a significant contributor to the beach pollution. For example, it is believed that few of the 30,000 tampon applicators estimated to have landed on the beaches came from the sludge dump-site; only minor quantities of the oil and grease could have come from that source (35).

Solid waste disposal around the margin of the Bight—A frequent sight in New York harbor are the barges of garbage being transported to the landfill sites. Despite loading practices designed to minimize "blow-off" and a vessel skimming floating debris from waters near landfills, some unknown quantity does get into harbor waters and then to the Bight.

Again we have seen that the sources of pollution of the Bight are many. The tragedy of the floatables episode seems to be that some of the problem results from littering, one of the most easily avoided sources of pollution. Another major kind of floating debris results from the ubiquitous use of plastics which neither degrade naturally or disappear by other means. Plastics have become dominant elements of our beach debris from the Antarctic to the Arctic. Many of the items which contributed to the debris in the beach pollution could have been made from materials other than plastics, materials which would biodegrade and not persist upon our beaches.

What are the chances for other floatable episodes? First of all, they aren't new. Concern for the occurrence of debris upon the beaches of Long Island has been noted for over half a century (36). The special circumstances of events surrounding this particular episode are not that unusual:

1. The flow rate of the Hudson, and the resulting flushing of floating materials from the harbor, is periodic. The flow rate for 1976 was high only as measured in spans of decades.

2. Persistent southerly winds, which resulted in debris being blown ashore, can occur each spring or summer.

3. There are more than enough sources of debris so that special events such as sludge tank explosions aren't required.

We are fortunate that circumstances of winds and currents are such that the floatables go out to the ocean and not to our beaches more frequently than not.

Ecosystem Effects

In 1957 the Dutch scientist Brongersma-Sanders published a study of the mass mortalities then known to have occurred in the seas of the world (37). In these events large numbers of marine organisms die over large extents of seafloor. The reasons for such mass mortalities are various, ranging from traumatic events such as earthquakes and landslides, to biological causes such epidemics of disease, to environmental alterations such as sudden changes in temperature. The summer of 1976 in the New York Bight produced another mass mortality, one which will be recorded in any future summary of such events, and one which was well studied as a part of the MESA New York Bight Project and by the National Marine Fisheries Service (38). This mortality occurred principally among the shellfish populations along the New Jersey coast and resulted in the death of about half of the surf clam populations, with lesser but extensive kills of the sea scallops, ocean quahogs, and lobsters. In all an area of about 3,320 square miles was affected, an area a little less than half that of the State of New Jersey (39).

The cause of the mortality was the almost total depletion of oxygen from the bottom waters over this extensive area. While fish could swim away and survive, and most did, sedentary shellfish could not escape. What depleted the oxygen from the bottom waters? Many people were quick to accuse that old nemesis the Sludge Monster. Others blamed the always convenient villain, New York City. The surf clammers brought suit against the federal government and local governments in New York and New Jersey, claiming that the dumping of sewage sludge was the culprit: that suit has since been terminated on other grounds (40). The true causes are suspected but probably will never be fully understood. But there is enough evidence to charge the principal culprit, Mother Nature.

A number of environmental conditions were unusual in 1976. River flow, particularly that of the Hudson, was greater than usual and in February and March, air temperatures were higher than they had been for a quarter of a century. In June and July, persistent winds from the south and southwest, coupled with a dearth of the usual storms which pass through the Bight, resulted in some very special oceanographic conditions. A very strong salinity gradient (a pycnocline) was established which effectively divided the waters of the Bight into upper and lower layers. Usual transfers of oxygen between layers which occurs by vertical mixing of the water column in times of storm didn't occur. This same wind pattern resulted, it is thought, in an unusual water circulation pattern which concentrated particulate organic matter from the estuary and from plankton blooms, particularly just off the New Jersey coast (41). This loading of organic material beneath the pycnocline began to decay, causing depletion of oxygen. Absence of mixing between upper and lower waters to renew the oxygen caused its level to fall to nearly zero.

Mass mortalities of this sort have occurred in the Bight region before, although never over such an extensive area, and they have never been so intensively studied. In 1951 there was a fishkill off Jones Beach, Long Island (42), and in 1968, 1971, and 1974 there were recorded instances of large numbers of fish and shellfish being found dead in and around the wrecks which are favorite diving spots of New Jersey sport fishermen (43). In every case, the cause is thought to be the same, large quantities of decaying organic matter diminishing the oxygen content of the water to levels below which the organisms cannot survive. Special atmospheric or oceanic circulation conditions lead to the concentration of organic materials and the absence of normal mixing which keeps oxygen levels from going so low.

An important question is: To what degree do human activities, specifically the use of the Bight as a dump, contribute to the development of these conditions? That answer, unfortunately, is not as clear as one would like. At the time of the 1976-mass mortality, there was an extensive bloom of the dinoflagellate *Ceratium tripos*, a normal constituent of the phytoplankton flora of the Bight. But where concentrated by physical conditions, its numbers were extraordinary—some described it as a "red tide." This bloom began in January and rapidly built up in numbers suggesting that local enrichment of the nutrient supply was a factor (44). The cells of *Ceratium* moved towards the Jersey shore and were aggregated below the thermocline in April and May. The population of *Ceratium* declined rapidly after July (45).

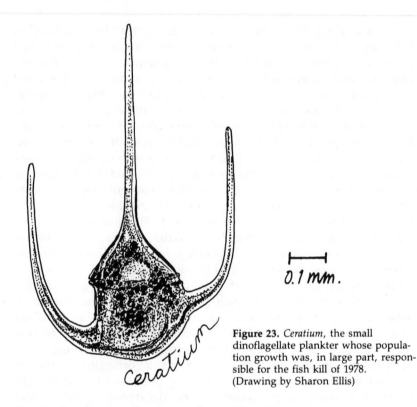

0.1 mm.

Figure 23. *Ceratium*, the small dinoflagellate plankter whose population growth was, in large part, responsible for the fish kill of 1978. (Drawing by Sharon Ellis)

Respiration by the *Ceratium* cells and benthic organisms and oxidation of organic material occurring below the pycnocline was a major factor in the oxygen depletion.

Atmospheric conditions leading to both the floatables event and to the anoxic event of 1976 seem to be the major culprit in causing both. In the anoxic event, the winds and the circulation they established resulted in greater than usual nutrient-rich waters moving onto the continental shelf from the ocean (46). These nutrients, together with sewage transported to the Bight from the estuary, stimulated the bloom. The unusual addition of the oceanic nutrients and the fact that unlike other phytoplankters, *Ceratium* is apparently not consumed by grazers, led to the heavy drain on bottom oxygen (47).

The conclusion reached by those who studied the anoxic event in greatest detail was that while human activities add greatly to the nutrient and carbon load of the waters of the Bight, these in themselves do not apparently result in anoxic conditions. But given some unusual circumstance in which some external force is involved, as, in this instance, the on-welling of ocean waters onto the continental shelf, the system is overloaded and disaster results. The only conclusion which can be reached from this observation is that our own activities are adding to the pollutant load of the Bight, particularly near the mouth of the estuary, to an extent approaching a maximum. Much more and we might be *causing*, not just contributing to, anoxic events (48).

But one might say that the anoxic event was an extreme situation, an "act of God." Can we plan our lives around such events? Or, should we adopt a more normative position and accept our losses from such disasters? If so, we must ask if there are other, more persistent effects from our waste-disposal practices upon the ecosystem of the Bight.

We have seen that disposal of our wastes in the Bight affects it in ways that are subtle and difficult to assess. The pathways between what actually happens and what is important to us are tortuous. While measurement of effects on our own health or well-being is straightforward once we know the transfer mechanism, effects on the rest of our environment are not as easy to see or measure. What we must look at now are how wastes in the Bight affect other organisms, the rest of the biological ecosystem. Because our science of the marine ecosystems is rudimentary, we can look at the complex of life in the Bight only from the most primitive reckoning. It is rather like trying to understand a large corporation by looking at a part of the financial data in its annual report. It is difficult to determine from these numbers what the corporation does, how well it is doing it, and how, as a stockholder, we should feel about it.

Given enough time, plants and animals will change and adapt in many ways so that every way of "making a living" is adopted. Earning a living, in this sense, means ways in which to obtain food, shelter, and suitable conditions for reproduction. The Bight provides more ways of earning a living or "niches," as biologists call it, than one can enumerate. From sandy beaches thrashed by surf to the cyclical rhythms of the tidal marshes, from the vertically structured life of the wharf piling to the relatively flat, cool, dark expanses of the floor of the continental shelf, every place which can be inhabited is and many ways of making a living are tried. The organisms inhabiting the Bight range in size from single-celled phytoplankton to whales; in complexity, from bacteria to mammals. Each of these organisms has a particular set of physical and chemical requirements for its existence: Each has things which it cannot tolerate either for its own well-being or for its reproduction.

Adapting to Man

The kinds of creatures living in the Bight have been moving into it over the last 15,000 years or so. As the glacial ice melted and the ocean waters began to creep back up over the continental shelf and into the embayment we call the Bight, a new world was being colonized. Not all the animals came at once, for in the way of the world, some organisms are more adventurous than others and these colonizers prepare the way for the rest. Still others moved into the Bight, lived there for a while, and left as conditions changed.

About 200 years ago, one of the late arriving animals, the European variant of *Homo sapiens* appeared in this new world and displaced the indigenous variant around the margin of the Bight. This invader increased in numbers and as it did, profound changes began to occur: The shape of the estuary was altered, wetlands were filled in, rocks were piled up where rocks hadn't been before, and peculiar and strange substances began to find their way into the waters of the harbor and the Bight. The pace of change increased and many of the earlier arrivals couldn't adapt to what was happening. They gave up. Oysters in the harbor and the lower Hudson were smothered by sediments eroded from depleted lands stirred up by dredging and filling; spawning grounds of the commercially important smelt were destroyed by digging and filling; others such as the sturgeon were hunted almost into extinction. In the last several decades something even newer has been introduced by *Homo sapiens*: toxic chemicals. These are so new that most organisms simply can't adapt to them. Those which can move do so, the ones which can't suffer.

How does environmental change affect the organisms of the Bight? We sometimes hear people say, "It can't be too bad because the fish aren't dying." But there is more to life than death. One of the most important parts of life is reproduction, for if a species doesn't successfully reproduce, it "dies," or more properly, becomes extinct. For successful reproduction a minimum of two environmental conditions must be satisfied. The environment within the organism and that outside it must be satisfactory. Generally speaking, if the external environment is right, the internal one usually will be too. But drugs and toxic substances can alter the internal environment, sometimes without affecting the external. For example, marijuana, if used frequently and long enough, can inhibit sexual activity in humans. This disruption of the internal environment doesn't necessarily affect the mature organism sufficiently to cause death, but could result in unsuccessful reproduction. Among simpler marine organisms, a range of things from temperature to chemicals can affect success of reproduction.

Other effects may be more subtle. If we drink too much coffee, the caffeine causes a "stress" response—we are irritable. In the same way, marine organisms can be irritated and show stress. During the anoxic event, divers reported that lobsters were observed in the highest parts of wrecked ships. They were presumably climbing upwards seeking oxygen to limit the stress they were feeling (49). Toxic substances in the environment cause stress responses in organisms. If enough of the toxics are present, the response will be death; at lesser levels a toll is being taken in lesser success of reproduction and in outward migration of the species. When people comment that "the fish aren't being killed," what they mean is that corpses are not visible. But what is not said is that the invisible effects on the population may be as severe as their death.

Toxic substances aren't the only factors which stress organisms. We have learned that many foods, taken in moderation, are all right but in excess can cause disease. In the Bight, nutrients such as nitrogen and carbon are good in reasonable quantities, but in excess they can lead to consequences such as the anoxic event. Unfortunately, the Bight is now the scene of many excesses. Some of the consequences are:

Fin rot—Many fishes caught in the inner portion of the Bight, and particularly from around the sludge dumping area, have their fins badly mutilated or eroded away. The condition is particularly common in the winter flounder (as many as 4% of the specimens from the inner Bight showed the disease), but occurs in other species as well (50). Fin rot, as it has been called, is not unique to the Bight but occurs in other places where coastal waters have been badly polluted. The causes of fin rot are not completely understood but appear to be related to contaminated sediments. It occurs in fishes which have been stressed by chemicals in the environment. While the condition is not fatal for the affected fish, there is a widespread popular impression that such diseased fish indicate that the waters are severely polluted (51).

Black gill—Rock crabs live on the bottom and walk around on it. Because they are so close to the bottom, they come in contact with the fine sediments and particulate matter which accumulates on their gill filaments. It is this fouling of the gills which gives the disease its name. Again, the condition is most common in the inner Bight, particularly where bottom sediments have been altered by the accumulation of sewage sludge, where as many as 6% of the rock crabs may be affected (52). Again, the condition is not apparently fatal among the crabs, but does indicate that they are stressed in much the same way a person suffering from emphysema is stressed.

Mutagenicity of mackerel eggs—In 1974 it was reported that developing eggs of the Atlantic mackerel collected from the Bight showed irregularities (53). These ranged from death of the developing cells, arrest of the development at an early stage, and irregularities of division of the genetic material in the developing embryos. Continued study of these mutated embryos has sought to link their presence with surface and near-surface chemicals. The evidence suggests that eggs of the Atlantic mackerel are being killed by pollution of surface waters, although a direct link with particular chemicals is not yet known. But there is evidence that mortality of mackerel eggs may be as high as 98.8% compared with estimations of mortalities of 60% made in the 1930s (54). No other species are yet known to be similarly affected.

Degradation of communities of bottom organisms—The different kinds of organisms living together in one environment is called a community. Communities are remarkably similar in diversity and relative numbers of each kind of organism from place to place in the ocean. This is because, through time, such assemblages have evolved in a balance between prey and predator and among the different ecological niches present in any environment. Stress such as that induced by pollution will not necessarily result in the death of all organisms in an area. More usually, the most sensitive will be killed first and depending upon the degree of pollution, the structure of the community will be affected to a greater or lesser extent. Rather than the ''dead sea'' proclaimed to exist in the Bight, scientists have known for a relatively long time that community structure among the bottom-living (benthic) creatures in the vicinity of the sludge dump had been greatly altered. Further study has shown that the entire area of the inner Bight, that most greatly affected by all pollution, has an abnormal assemblage of benthic organisms characterized by lack of diversity and low abundances of all organisms (55). Ecologists who studied the ''dying'' Lake Erie have noted similar changes.

But all of these effects are subtle. Some will say that we should, at most, consider them as warning signs, and be concerned only with those aspects of waste disposal which affect us economically—for this is the way some in our society have chosen to measure our well-being.

The Economic Impact

There are some direct measures of the costs of waste disposal in the Bight and the benefits accruing from dumping can be calculated. But measuring the economic impact of waste disposal in the New York Bight region in some sort of cost-benefit ratio comes up against a series of imponderables. How may we calculate the effect of waste disposal in the Bight on our perception of it and our future needs for it? We do not know how to reckon this sort of an account as yet. So, we shall retreat to some firmer ground.

During the anoxic event, when there was a great disruption of the fishery, it was possible to count the dollars lost. During the "floatables" episode, it was also possible to estimate losses directly sustained by local businesses. What were these?

Depletion of bottom oxygen off the New Jersey coast in 1976 affected few of the fish directly. Most simply swam away from the area in which oxygen was depleted. Of course, for the commercial and sport fishermen who had expected to catch them in that huge area of low oxygen, the cost of their absence was considerable. Fishermen had to steam further to find the fish, or they didn't try to catch them at all because of their bitterness towards dumping. For some, there were benefits. The summer flounder were concentrated into a narrow area between the anoxic zone and the beach, making them easier to catch (56). But on the basis of interviews with captains of commercial fishing boats, it has been estimated that there was a loss to New Jersey's coastal fishermen of as much as $20 million. The fish not caught by the commercial fishermen were not processed or marketed, causing a further loss of about $50 million (57).

But the fishery most affected was that of the surf clam and the ocean quahog. These large clams are dredged at depth and the meat of the foot minced for use in clam products and to be eaten as minced, fried clam. It has been estimated that 69% of the offshore stock and a lesser portion of the nearshore resource was destroyed by the depletion of oxygen. The value of the surf clams killed is estimated to have been about $123 million (58). Taken all together then, losses to the harvesters, processors, and marketers of the clam resource is estimated to have been about $430 million (59).

This direct loss of a harvest is only a part of the story. Because the surf clam takes seven years to grow to market size, the destruction of the progeny of those clams which might have reproduced means that there will be a continuing loss to the industry until the stock is built up again. To offset that reduced crop, increased harvest of the ocean quahog is expected (60).

Ocean quahogs themselves did not escape destruction, 6% of the standing crop is estimated to have been killed. Losses in this fishery were estimated to have been about $34,000 at dockside (61). The sea scallop and lobsters were affected to a lesser extent. Sea scallops sustained somewhere between 8 and 12% mortalities and a crop value loss of $72,000. Lobster harvest was reduced by about 30%, with a value of the loss being estimated at $410,000. Again, in each of these fisheries, there will be a long period of recovery of the stock during which reduced catches will be expected. For the ocean scallop the recovery period is thought to be about 5 years and for the lobster, it is about 4 years (62).

Recreational fishermen were also losers. Fish were not caught, but then more fish are not caught than are, so that is not a good measure. But one can find out how some of the support industries were affected. For example, many charter and party boat captains were reported to have not fished because of rumors about pollution from Kepone and PCBs having caused the fish kill. Others simply had to go further out, and often with fewer customers. These captains reported losses of an estimated $1.7 million during July to September 1976 (63).

In summary, the anoxic event is estimated to have caused losses to: Harvesters of shellfish and finfish off New Jersey, about $20.1 million; processors and marketers, $50.2 million; commercial-recreational sector, $1.7 million. But we can't stop there. Because those shellfish which were killed did not reproduce, there is a gap in the continuity of the species which will continue until that age class would have been harvested. Put another way, until the stock is re-established, there is a continuing loss of catch to the fishermen. Estimated value of future stock component is about $499 million. The grand total, then, is about $573 million (64).

Recall that in that same summer of 1976, Long Islander's were having their own set of problems as debris piled up on their beaches. Losses there are less tangible, for they are reckoned in the consequences of a 30–50% reduction in beach attendance that July. Some businesses were questioned about the consequences of the nonattendance. Pier fishing was reduced by about 30%, restaurants on beaches had their incomes reduced by about 20%, and bait and tackle shops reported up to 30% less business (65). The total loss to business resulting from the floatables event has been estimated at $30 million (66).

The events of the summer of 1976, then, seem to have cost the New York Bight region about $600 million. This is a large figure taken by itself, but it is small in comparison to some others. For example, the 78,000 tons of imported shoes carried into the Port of New York by cargo ships that same year had a total of about $600 million (67). But it is about 5 times more than what New York City spends annually on environmental protection (68).

We are now squarely up against the decision of what we wish to do.

8 / The Bight in Our Future

We have looked at the New York Bight in some detail. We have seen a rich and powerful society grow up along its borders—a society which once derived its living and then major revenues from the creatures of the Bight. In time, as society changed, values shifted and the Bight's fish and shellfish became less important than the tall ships laden with goods which sailed its waters. Shipping and commerce came to dominate the region's sense of self-importance. The network of waterways connecting the Great Port with the hinterland of the nation made traders and shippers and all those who dealt with maritime commerce, wealthy. It was the Golden Age of the Bight.

Manufacturing grew and prospered as raw materials were brought by ship and the new iron-horse of the railroads. The network of waterways which made the port prosper became useful for disposal of industry's wastes and the sewage and garbage of a burgeoning population. As the waterways became polluted and malodorous, they were no longer pleasant; they were bulkheaded and filled. Marginal swamps and wetlands were converted to valuable land for factories and for housing.

But the nation was growing even as the Bight region was. The Great Port was no longer in the center of things and other ports in other parts of the country were developing and taking its trade. The wealthy and powerful of the City on the Sea were not concerned: there were new things to do. The industry of the region had changed from the making of things to the making of money. New technologies like automobiles and airplanes fascinated all and made a revolution of travel. The port was forgotten. Its once busy wharves grew dilapidated and its waters more fetid with the ever-increasing amounts of sewage and industrial wastes dumped into them.

People turned their backs to the waters which had once made them wealthy and powerful. Buildings and highways were constructed which isolated the people from that which surrounded the islands called Manhattan, Long and Staten. Because the harbor, the estuary, and the Bight were no longer on people's minds, their use as a dump, if known about, could be condoned, accepted. Rather than being an asset, these waters became the giant flush toilet of the growing metropolis. The amounts, kinds, and toxicity of materials piped and dumped into the waters of the Bight and its environs increased.

Society continued to change. The money industry which dominates the metropolitan region is high on the economic food chain—it pays well. Increasing numbers of people had increasing money and time to spend in play. Although the automobile and the airplane offered the world, great numbers of people, autos, and airplanes staying at home made for congestion—speed of movement of the human body dropped to about that of the era of the horse. "Getting out of the city" was a preoccupation in the hot summers. But the "Joisey shore"; Fire Island; the Hamptons (for the rich); Robert Moses' great invention, Jones Beach (for the middle class); and Coney Island (for the rest) were far enough. Play meant the sandy beaches of the margin of the Bight.

And a new ethic was upon the land. Earth Day, brought on by a sudden awareness that our water and air were being befouled by utter disregard for waste disposal, stimulated a revolution. Society began to place a high value on clean air and pure water. Swift reaction from the body politic eventually resulted in new laws and new practices. That which had been exhausted into the atmosphere or pumped into the nearest waterbody was now put into containers and buried on land or carried out to sea in pipes or barges. We had succeeded in cleaning up the waters of the land and the air, but we had done it by merely changing the place where we put our wastes. Love Canal. The searing awareness that we couldn't escape the toxicity of careless chemical disposal brought us down from the euphoria of the environmental decade.

But what of the Bight? It had burped. Indigestion brought on by decades of waste disposal and dumping, first in the estuary and then in the Bight, had finally taken their toll. "Sludge monsters" and the spectre of a "dead sea," were upon the land and in the headlines. Laws were passed and reluctantly things were done—"But the sea is vast and the wastes we dump so small," it was argued. Finally the Bight bit back. In 1976 the combination of a mass of disgusting debris on the beaches of Long Island and a massive kill of creatures of the Bight off New Jersey got our attention. Reappraisal was in order.

Studies were undertaken, reports written, alternatives evaluated, technologies assessed. An end to much ocean dumping was proclaimed: 3 December 1981 was identified as the deadline. Legal actions were initiated to postpone that deadline and the decision for ending of dumping. The economy soured, making interest rates high and a new conservative mood suggested that lower taxes would be in order. A new administration in Washington signalled its lesser concern for environmental enhancement and an absence of interest in the oceans. It became known that ocean dumping wasn't all bad and that the deadline probably wouldn't be enforced. Had we returned full circle to the beginning?

Or, have we learned enough about the New York Bight and what makes it work to decide what we want to do? Is what we have learned important to others? Have we a story to tell—or a lesson to learn?

As Others See Us and We See Them

Half of the 50 largest cities in the world are on the coast of the oceans and the Big Apple is one of them. Although New Yorkers like to think of themselves as being different—and they are—how different are they in the way they treat their coastal ocean? Surprisingly enough, this is an answerable question, and the answer is that the Bight is polluted to about the same degree as the coastal waters near other well-populated, industrialized societies.

Comparison between the Bight and other coastal waters involves four factors: population, industrialization, volume of the coastal water body, and the degree to which its waters are mixed and exchanged with the ocean. Population and industrialization define, in large part, the quantity and character of wastes going into the ocean. In general, the more industrialized the society, the more toxic its wastes will be and the more waste will be generated per capita. The last two factors, volume and mixing, define the degree to which the wastes will be concentrated. If quickly diluted, their impact will be less than if not dispersed. Volume of water in which wastes are discharged alone may define dilution, but if those waters are mixed with those of a still larger volume, further dilution results. Thus pollution in a partially enclosed bay, such as New York Harbor, has a greater effect

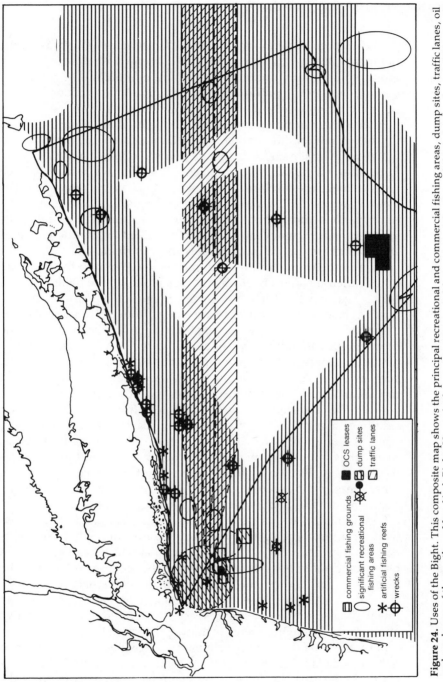

Figure 24. Uses of the Bight. This composite map shows the principal recreational and commercial fishing areas, dump sites, traffic lanes, oil and gas leases of the northern New York Bight. Unmarked areas are not unused for commercial or sport fishing, but are less well known as primary fishing areas. (Adapted from Davis *et al*, in Squires and McKay, 1982)

than discharge into, say, the Bight itself. Because the Bight is larger, but mostly because its waters freely interchange with the ocean, enormous pollution must occur for comparable effects. At even this larger volume, however, combinations of natural events and our own actions can cause severe effects, as in the summer of 1976.

Finally, there is the factor of time. Different kinds of contaminants will be with us for different periods of time. Most of the heavy metals will remain, unaltered for such long periods as to be forever. In some forms they will remain toxic: in others, they will have been complexed so as to make them relatively harmless. Some of the new molecules we have learned to build will persist and persist until caught up on some particle and buried. Other chemicals, such as the nutrients nitrogen and phosphorus, are quickly utilized by marine creatures and their presence is a problem only in their abundance.

Parts of the world ocean which may be compared to the Bight are the Mediterranean, the Seto Inland Sea of Japan, the Baltic Sea, the North Sea and the Irish Sea. When these are examined, the differences among them appear to arise more from the concentrated, or dispersed, nature of the population, and the character of the oceanography than from the thoughtful care given the waterbody by humankind. Areas with concentrated populations around estuaries, such as New York Harbor, have localized high concentrations of metals and chlorinated hydrocarbons and other pollutants. Those which have well-mixed waters suffer less from oxygen depletion resulting from discharge of sewage into coastal waters. In general, while the quantities of wastes discharged into the Bight are enormous, they are not significantly greater, or less, than those of comparable areas. The "condition" of the Bight, when compared with other areas of the ocean, seems no better nor no worse (1). It is not clear whether this finding should cause joy or grief.

It may come as a shock to denizens of New York and New Jersey, who are used to being looked upon askance, that what they have done to their coastal ocean is not unlike that which has happened in other comparable areas. But this seems to be the case. We are not the exception but rather the rule. Human industrialized society, associated with great density population and having a relatively unenlightened environmental respect, has a profound and negative effect upon the environment, including the coastal ocean.

In recent years the scientific community, having found that we had not succeeded in "destroying" the coastal ocean, and that disposal of wastes in the ocean could be undertaken, has been working toward a new concept. That idea is grounded on the finding that strictures against disposing of wastes in the ocean, while instigated for good and proper reasons, have been too narrowly defined. Called assimilative capacity, this concept states that use of the ocean for disposal of wastes may be undertaken, with thought and care, without permanent damage to the ocean, its inhabitants, or to us (2).

Assimilative capacity is hard to define, but has been stated as "the amount of material that could be contained within a body of seawater without producing an unacceptable biological impact" (3). In a recent workshop on the subject, a number of scientists concluded that generally "the waste capacity of U.S. coastal waters is not now fully used," but that in at least the instances of New York Bight and Puget Sound, Washington, "there is evidence that the assimilative capacity for some substances or in some areas has been reached or exceeded" (4).

Another concept, suggested by Professor Karl Turekian of Yale, is that of accomodative capacity. The difference between "assimilative" and "accomodative" may seem small, but it is conceptually important, particularly in the coastal areas where volumes of water are less and interchange may be smaller. Coastal ecosystems do not assimilate many wastes: they accomodate them to some limit and then they are altered.

How do these concepts work? One example might be that under the definition given, the assimilative capacity of New York Harbor for rock and dirt taken from excavations or dredged from the harbor floor was exceeded in the late 1800s. The evidence for this is that the dumping resulted in new shoals which obstructed shipping and which disrupted the rich oyster beds of the estuary. We might even argue that the assimilative capacity for dredge spoils has again been reached at the current Mud Dump site, for it too has become an obstruction for navigation. But this is a very simplistic view of a complex concept.

Concepts such as assimilative or accomodative capacity are very difficult to define, principally because we cannot agree upon the units of measurement. While some scientists would say that the Bight has not been "destroyed," many beach-goers would argue that sullied beaches have a "destroying" effect upon the pleasurability of their experience; fishermen catching visibly diseased fish would feel that things had gone too far. The values each of us use in measuring what is appropriate, enough, too much, are all so different that reaching a consensus is nearly impossible.

Further, assimilative capacity is terribly difficult to define technically in terms of how much, say cadmium, should be permitted to be discharged into the Bight's waters. How much where? When? In the harbor or in the Bight as a whole? What are the safe limits for the accumulation of cadmium in the tissues of organisms? Of man? How does cadmium behave in the ocean? In what chemical form does it move about and become incorporated into organisms? In what form does it become immobilized and subject to burial in the sediments at the bottom on the Bight? These questions and many more like them have only tantalizingly tentative answers. But answers are required before assimilative capacity can be a functioning regulatory tool. When one reviews the discussions of scientists upon the concept of assimilative capacity, one finds, as in so many scientific matters, the arguments are long, detailed, often irrelevant and almost always end with the statement that "more research is needed." And this is true here.

Results of current discussions of assimilative capacity will not be known for many years. The general concept that given enough dilution many wastes can be safely disposed of in the ocean is important and timely. It permits us to continue to do most of what we have been doing with the comforting feeling that, given enough time, many of the contaminants will be lost in the ocean without harm. But the lack, at this time, of definite answers and specifications and given the reduction of budgets for research by which such information could be obtained, it is reasonable to suggest that assimilative capacity is not yet grist for the regulatory mill. As that needed information is slowly accumulated, we will continue to apply the subjective notions of assimilative capacity that really form the basis for the regulations we now have.

Where Are We And Where Are We Going?

Now that it has become clear that some of the spectres of ocean dumping can be safely buried, we must look about us and chart a new course of action less dependent upon hysteria and more on reason and foresight. The Sludge Monster now exists only as an aestheic concept—a hazard he is not. Whether the dumping of sludge in that great swimming pool called the Bight affects one's attitude towards bathing there is a matter of personal values. The "dead sea" has been shown to be, more properly, a depauperate sea. Fish kills of staggering magnitude are a hazard we may have to face somewhat less frequently than hurricanes, but it is also true that they would occur even without our help.

It is also true that some of the problems faced in the New York Bight

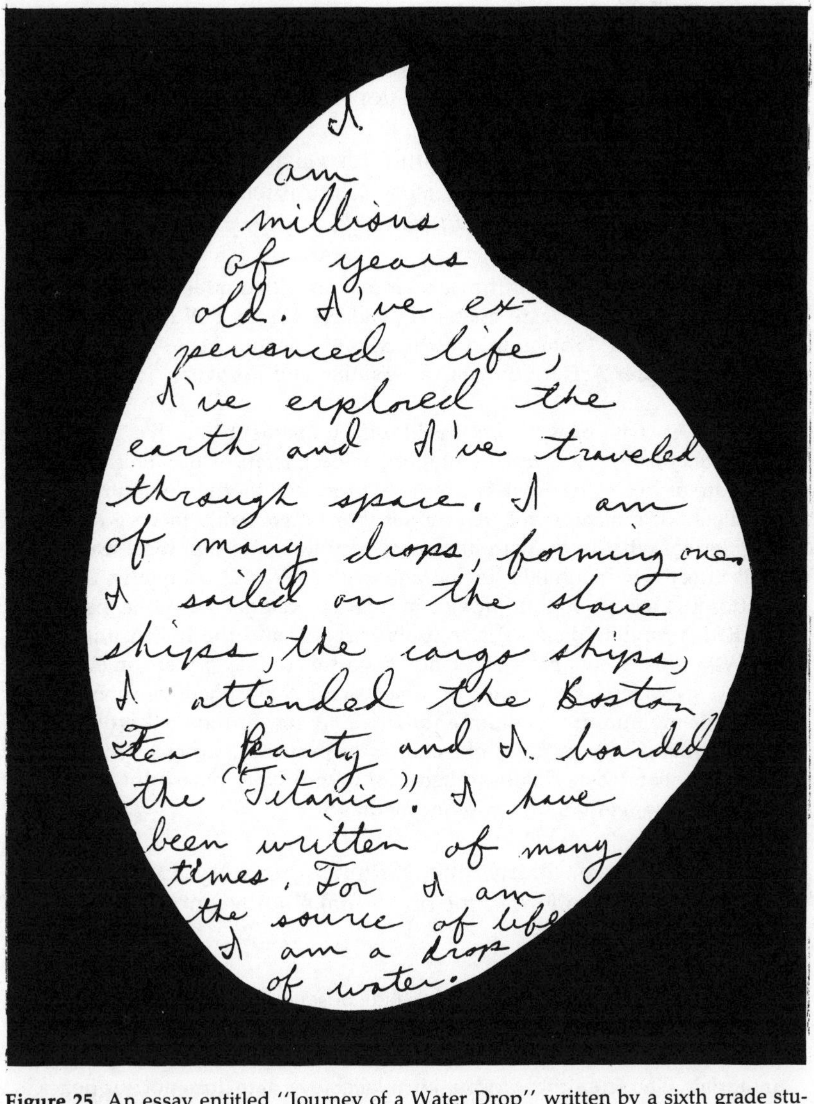

Figure 25. An essay entitled "Journey of a Water Drop" written by a sixth grade student in Public School 63, New York City. (Reprinted from *The Second Wave and Other Tales*, New York Sea Grant Institute, Albany, New York)

are the result of well-meaning and well-intentioned actions. In the environmentally conscious decade of the 70s many laws were passed with the intent of halting the spread of pollution. These attacked one problem, then another, but often in an uncoordinated fashion. Rather than seeking to eliminate wastes as a source of pollution, the site of waste disposal was shifted from air to water, water to land and land to the oceans. Having gotten that far some think that we have nowhere else to put that which we don't want except, possibly, outer space.

This shifting of the target medium for waste disposal was the central theme of the National Advisory Committee on Oceans and Atmosphere report on ocean dumping:

> The Panel then reviewed the substantive laws that affect the management of society's waste material: Federal Water Pollution Control Act . . .; Marine Protection, Research, and Sanctuaries Act . . . ; Safe Drinking Water Act; Resource Conservation and Recovery Act; and the Clean Air Act.
> Because it has proved impossible to implement all five statutes simultaneously, the implementation of each statute has shifted the burden of receiving society's waste products to the medium least regulated at that moment. An industry or municipality faced with the problem of what to do with its wastes may well find that the Clean Air Act effectively prohibits incineration; the FWPCA similarly limits disposal at sea through a pipe or in internal waters by any means; the MPRSA prohibits disposal at sea via barging; and the RCRA and the SDWA effectively prohibit land disposal or deep-well injection. NACOA [National Committee on Oceans and Atmosphere] is concerned that this medium-by-medium approach may have produced groups of regulations whose primary objective is to protect a particular medium from use as a waste disposal medium, without any regard for the impact of these regulations on other media (5).

With these observations, the National Advisory Committee on Oceans and Atmosphere went on to make some findings on ocean dumping (6):

> The laws governing dredged-material disposal in the ocean and in internal waters do not require, nor does scientific evidence call for, stricter regulation of ocean disposal than of internal water disposal of dredged materials. The scientific information available to date does not support a ban on ocean disposal of either all sewage sludge after December 31, 1981, or of all industrial wastes. . . . Ocean waste disposal must remain a viable option.

And, the Committee recommended reversal of the Environmental Protection Agency's policy to not issue ocean dumping permits when any land-based alternative exists (7).

And, further delaying implementation of the December 31, 1981, ban on sewage sludge dumping, New York City's suit against the Environmental Protection Agency's threatened revocation of its dumping permit was settled in the City's favor. New York City had argued that their dumping of sewage sludge did not "unreasonably degrade" the marine environment—the key phrase in the Ocean Dumping Act. Judge Abraham Sofaer, in a lengthy opinion, concluded that the Environmental Protection Agency had not adequately considered the City's argument that land-based disposal was potentially dangerous and that it had failed to prove that sludge dumping was "unreasonably" degrading the environment (8).

In formulating his opinion, Judge Sofaer utilized testimony by Commander R. L. Swanson, now director of the Office of Marine Pollution Assessment of the National Oceanic and Atmospheric Administration:

> [Swanson] . . . noted that the sludge contains several types of potentially harmful material . . . Swanson's catalogue is disturbing. One instinctively recoils from the mention of "fecal coliform," "pathogens," "viral particles," "fungi," "fin rot," "shell disease," and "bioaccumulation" of toxic substances. The City's sludge no doubt contains unpleasant and dangerous substances. Nevertheless, EPA must not be permitted to distort Swanson's careful statements . . . Although Swanson recommended that "the 1981 deadline be adhered to," he based that conclusion upon the desirability—not on any imminent necessity—of an end to dumping. His only definitive conclusion was that "the ocean dumping of municipal sewage sludge is not viewed as an environmentally viable disposal alternative over the long run, meaning over twenty, thirty, or fifty years" (9).

This statement seems to sum up a number of points: (1) many are repelled by the thought of the very ocean waters we so love for sunning, swimming and surfing, being used for the dumping of sewage sludge; (2) because there are no simple, economically acceptable, environmentally compatible alternatives to ocean dumping of sewage sludge *immediately* available, we must not be too hasty in closing out options. The alternatives are not the horns of a dilemma. Affronts to our aesthetic senses are not unalterable: we can view ocean dumping of sludge as a short-term alternative and continue to press for development of alternatives. We can see an end to ocean dumping of almost all wastes if we continue to keep that as a social goal.

Not all agree with these conclusions, of course. Kenneth Kamlet, a long-standing, outspoken critic of ocean dumping, found a number of "errors" in the Sofaer decision, but concluded, "It now seems a foregone conclusion that ocean dumping of sludge will remain with us well beyond the end of this year [1981]" (10).

Part of the difficulty lies in the interrelationship of the Congress and the administrative branch of the federal government. Congressional wording is sometimes difficult to interpret in hard-and-fast regulations susceptible to legal actions. What constitutes the "unreasonable degradation" cited in the Ocean Dumping Act, and how do you measure it? The Clean Water Act requires a "balanced, indigenous population" around an outfall pipe. What is it and how do you recognize it when you see it? These criteria are difficult to implement in precise definitional ways.

But there are other ways of looking at the problem of waste disposal. As a very wise man, Athelstan Spilhaus, once put it, "There are no wastes—just unused resources." Once we have learned to utilize all but those wastes which are just plain intractable, we shall have eliminated many of our problems.

We know that one of the largest sources of pollution of the coastal ocean is ourselves and our own bodily wastes. It is our cities and our municipalities which are the major pollution culprits. Yet railing at local government gets us not very far, for in the end it comes down to the fact that we are often unwilling to spend our own dollars for the treatment and safe disposal of our sewage. Throughout the late 1970s many municipalities and areas surrounding the Bight, as elsewhere in the nation, were carrying out "section 208" water quality management planning operations authorized under the Clean Water Act. These "208 plans" were undertaken with considerable public involvement and became, therefore, statements of the public's expectation for improved environmental quality in return for investment in pollution abatement. In the case of the 208 plans prepared around the margin of the Bight, one reads of anticipation of the return of clean, swimmable, fishable waters. These anticipations must now be placed against costs of achieving the goal, and the willingness of the public to pay.

As long as we continue to dump our wastes, we must be conscious of the effects and of the costs. A return to unregulated dumping is unthinkable. There is no easy solution in the disposal of wastes. No matter where they are put, we shall have to deal with the consequences of their disposal at that point, in that medium, and in that time and thereafter.

It now seems probable that ocean dumping will continue. People are beginning to moderate their positions as easy solutions to the difficult problem of waste disposal evaporate. Even a staunch defender of the ocean, Jacques Yves Cousteau, urged that "we be prudent but realistic in approaching the problem of ocean dumping" (11). While there is active investigation of alternatives to spoil disposal by ocean dumping, the relief from the year-end ban on sewage sludge dumping has recharged interest in this option. The Environmental Protection Agency had, by the spring of 1982, received "inquiries" from Philadelphia, Baltimore, and Washington, D.C. about ocean disposal of sludge (12). Most observers concur that expanded sewage sludge dumping will take place at the Deepwater Dumpsite 106.

The rationale for moving the dump site for sewage sludge is several: (1) there is some indication that the level of contaminant input into the New York Bight may have leveled off. Whether this is a corallary of the so-called steady state of industrial development and population growth is not known, but it suggests that with removal of the dumping from the less-freely exchanged waters of the inner Bight, some improvement in water quality might occur; (2) there is a trade-off between the dumping of sludge and the dumping of partially treated sewage. As the volume of the latter is reduced through improved operations and new treatment facilities, the volume of sludge to be disposed of increases. It can be argued that the sewage is disposed of in the inner Bight, or the estuary, where its impact is greatest, while sludge can be disposed of far out in the ocean where dilution will be greater.

Other factors than the science of measuring the effects of dumping are changing the situation around the Bight. After three centuries and more of unbridled growth of human population and industrialization, the region seems to have reached a plateau of growth. The Sunbelt with its allure of economic expansion and the sunset country of California's cultural mystique are the growth areas of the nation. A leveling off of growth in the Bight region could lessen the pollution load on the Bight even if nothing much more is done to control or treat the existing discharges. While that assertion has merit, it carries with it the caveat that what we are dumping is becoming increasingly toxic both to ourselves and to the organisms of the Bight. But it is equally possible that the urgency for economic redevelopment and the creation of jobs for a growing population of inner-city unemployed will cause political pressures for the relaxing of environmentally directed codes and laws.

To Whom Does the Bight Belong?

And so we have come full circle. There are no easy answers. If we wish to have a quality environment in the ocean off our shores, we must take care of it and not use it as a dump—at least not excessively. Who is to make that decision? The government? As this book was being completed, the revolution in our federal government that came from the installation of a conservative regime following decades of liberalism was being completed. President Reagan meant what he said about "getting government off the backs of the people." And part of the load being removed includes governmental restrictions on environmental degradation.

Should industry or local municipalities make the decision about what should and shouldn't be dumped in the Bight? Which industry and which municipalities? Those which generate wastes difficult or expensive to treat might well respond that they would like to continue to dump. That answer is straightforward economics—it is the cheapest solution to the problem of disposal. But other industries and businesses dependent on a quality environment for their well-being would probably say no. Commercial fishermen harvesting the resources of the Bight must have high quality water to produce high quality fish. Contaminated fish or shellfish can't be sold, or don't sell well. Those who operate businesses dependent upon recreation and tourism would also look askance upon activities which will keep people from the beaches. Sport fishermen, who in some areas seem to simply ignore contamination, could well become an important force in reducing unwanted pollution.

Who then is to take charge? To whom does the Bight belong? The answer, of course, is to everyone, for it is a commons. And, as a commons, the open accessibility of the resources, at no charge to the user, leads to abuses. No one user has an incentive to protect or to conserve the resources. Fishermen have harvested, and overharvested, various of the resources; govenment has made some, largely ineffectual, efforts to regulate the use of the fishery resource. Shippers have continued to ply their trade routes but have been increasingly subjected to regulations on vessel safety and pollution elimination. Governmental agencies have had to carry out extensive studies of the possible impacts of oil drilling on the outer continental shelf before leases could be let. Other potential users, particularly of the Bight, such as sand and gravel miners and aquaculturists find that just-getting-started in the business is highly regulated and fraught with costs and delays.

Perhaps those municipalities and industries that wish to dump wastes should be charged a fee for the privilege. This is hardly a new idea, and it is one which hasn't been readily adopted with regard to air, water, or land disposal. But, if there is one thing we have learned about ocean dumping, it is that it can preclude other uses of the ocean area. Those precluding should ideally reimburse those precluded. More pragmatically, however, increasing the cost of ocean dumping would serve to make other disposal options, including recycling and reuse, more attractive. Perhaps moving the sewage sludge dumpsite to the deepwater dumpsite 106 will, by simply increasing the costs of transportation, have that effect.

The decades of the 1960s and 70s were more than just the environmental era. It was a period of awakening of the public's interest in the sea. A president, John F. Kennedy, who loved the ocean made us nationally conscious of its values and opportunities. Jacques Cousteau's film "The Silent World" burst upon our sensibilities as a chrysanthemum rocket. Television brought "Flipper" to millions of dinnertimes. And for the adventurous, cheap scuba gear made it possible for us to be a part of that watery world we knew so little of. Later, a busy Congress took cognizance of both our growing interest and concern for the oceans and of the enormous value of their resources in the many actions taken: a federal agency concerned with the oceans—the National Oceanic and Atmospheric Administration (NOAA)—was created and a plethora of laws was enacted—most of them good. The Clean Water Act, the Ocean Dumping Act, the Coastal Management Program, the Marine Mammal Protection Act, the Fisheries Conservation and Management Act (which established a 200-mile fishery zone), the Outer Continental Shelf Land Act amendments, the Ocean Thermal Energy Conversion Act, the Deep Seabed Hard Minerals Act, the Deepwater Port Act, and others all date from this creative and vigorous ocean-oriented period.

But more important than the laws was the sense of opportunity prevailing then, and which still persists. We human beings have long stood at the shores of the great ocean and stared out at its mysteries. Even as our ships of space cruise through the limits of our galaxy, and beyond, we find the ocean's enchantment strong, persistent, compelling. Many see opportunities yet unsought, challenges yet unmet. As our planet swells with the numbers of us, and as our resources of food and water are strained, the sea may offer important solutions. Aquaculture, the farming of the sea, is a means by which the ocean's food potential may be increased. The reaping of crops of seaweeds might become an important means for converting solar energy to methane and alcohols. And even as petroleum becomes increasingly expensive, the potential for using marine crops as the feedstock for the chemical industry has an allure that has many scientists working away.

And the kids love the sea. Perhaps they find in its seemingly limitless horizons adventures impossible when bounded by adult constraints and constructions. As a teaching tool, the oceans are unparalleled, for they fascinate while they educate. "Marine youth education" became a bureaucratic way of saying that we had forgotten to include the "World of Water" in our teaching agenda. Children exposed are children caught. As one wrote: "I enjoyed the science program . . . what I liked best was the life in the ocean . . . . Before the science program I wanted to be in the army. Ever since the science program I want to be a marine biologist" (13).

As children grow to become adults, they may carry their interest in the watery world with them. In this way, education may be the ultimate weapon in preserving the ocean. Joel O'Connor has observed: "One could argue convincingly, that only if more of us appreciate the oceans more can we be expected to preserve its aesthetic features. We have evidence, on scientific grounds alone, that "unreasonable degradation" will permit much more degradation. (What we call "scientific grounds" are really rigorous documentation of economically significant impacts. We have all sorts of scientifically documented impacts, they are just not economically important.) . . . So, unless more people come to a reverence for the ocean . . . we will continue to discount the aesthetic losses as relatively insignificant" (14).

In our urban societies we live in a world apart from nature. So divorced, we easily loose our respect for and our understanding of the natural world. And that becomes an artificial condition. Left unattended, that condition leads to our own destruction, for we cannot survive upon the planet alone.

The ocean and the atmosphere are the last of the commons, for in truth, they belong to none of us. Yet with each year growing awareness of the future potential of the oceans for food, for minerals, for energy brings new actions by nations to control those resources further and further from shore. But even when lines are drawn on maps, the ocean does not really belong to anyone. We know that the tragedy of the commons is that no one person sees her or his action as being the one which affects the rights of others. The ocean is so vast, so huge a commons, that it becomes incomprehensible that we, as individuals or small groups, could possibly have any effect. But it is the multiplicative, cumulative force of 17 million decisions of that sort which does.

After ten years in a quandary over what the dumping and discharge of wastes into the Bight was doing to it; after living with threats of natural disaster by exploiters of the media; after reluctantly having taken some actions to lessen the amounts of wastes we dump into the Bight, we have learned that all is not lost. What has been done can be undone. The natural system, stressed and strained as it is, will recover, given the opportunity. We can still make of our piece of coastal ocean, the New York Bight, what we wish. The decision is ours to make.

Winter squid

Illex illecebrosus 1 in.

References

Preface (Pages ix–xiii)

(1) Hardin, G. "The tragedy of the commons." *Science* 162. 3859, 13 (Dec. 1968): 1243–48.

Chapter 1. Perspectives of the Bight *(Pages 1–18)*

(1) Tarrow, S. "Translation of the Cellere Codex." In Wroth, L. C. 1970. *The voyages of Giovanni da Verrazzano 1524–1528.* New Haven: Yale University press, p. 137. See also Lipinsky, L. S. 1958. *Giovanni da Verrazzano, the discoverer of New York Bay.* New York: Published under the auspices of the Museum of the City of New York and the Instituto Italiano di Cultura in New York City on the occasion of the inauguration of the Verrazanno Narrows Bridge on November 21, 1964, p. 9. See also Morrison, S. E. 1971. *The European discovery of America—the northern voyages.* New York: Oxford University Press, p. 317.

(2) Juet, R. 1959. *Juet's journal, the voyage of the Half-Moon from 4 April to 7 November 1609.* Newark, N. J.: New Jersey Historical Society, p. 28.

(3) Carls, E. G. 1978. *Recreation.* MESA New York Bight Atlas Monograph 19. Albany, N. Y.: New York Sea Grant Institute, p. 16.

(4) Memorandum from Michael Kawka to J. S. O'Connor, both of MESA New York Bight Project, U.S. National Oceanic and Atmospheric Administration, Stony Brook, N. Y., dated 7 December 1981.

(5) United States, National Oceanic and Atmospheric Administration, Environmental Research Laboratories. *MESA New York Bight Project: technical development plan for fiscal year 1979.* Boulder, Colo.: Marine Ecosystems Analysis Program, pp. 3–4.

REFERENCES

(6) McCay, F. J. "Human ecology of fishing in the New York Bight. Part two: contemporary New York Bight fisheries." MESA New York Bight Workshop, Williamsburg, Va., 1978. [Summary report] Stony Brook, N. Y.: MESA New York Bight Project, U.S. National Oceanic and Atmospheric Administration, p. 23.

(7) McHugh, J. L. 1977. *Fisheries and fishery resources of New York Bight.* NOAA Technical Report NMFS Circular 40. Washington, D.C.: Government Printing Office, p. 1.

(8) Sovas, G. and Harmon, J. 1977. *New York State and outer continental shelf development—an assessment of implementation.* Albany, N. Y.: New York State Department of Environmental Conservation, p. 11.

(9) Personal communication between Peter Anderson, Region II, Environmental Protection Agency, and Merton Ingham, Office of Marine Pollution Assessment, National Oceanic and Atmospheric Administration, dated 15 June 1981.

(10) Mueller, J. and Anderson, A. 1978. *Industrial wastes.* MESA New York Bight Atlas Monograph 30. Albany, N. Y.: New York Sea Grant Institute, p. 13.

(11) Fuller, R. B. 1969. *Operating manual for spaceship earth.* Carbondale, Ill.: Southern Illinois University.

(12) Freeland, G. and Swift, D. 1978. *Surficial sediments.* MESA New York Bight Atlas Monograph 10. Albany, N. Y.: New York Sea Grant Institute, p. 9.

(13) Edwards, R. L. and Merrill, A. S. "A reconstruction of the continental shelf areas of eastern North America for the times 9,500 B.P. and 12,500 B.P." *Archaeology of Eastern North America* 5 (fall 1977): 2.

(14) Freeland and Swift, p. 63.

(15) Ibid., p. 11.

(16) Ibid., p. 13. See also Swift, D. J. P., Young, R. A., Clark, T., Harvey, G. and Betzer, P. [In preparation] *Shelf sediment transport and waste disposal: experience in the New York Bight.*

(17) Lettau, B., Brower, W. Jr., and Quayle, R. 1976. *Marine climatology.* MESA New York Bight Atlas Monograph 7. Albany, N. Y.: New York Sea Grant Institute, p. 19.

(18) Hansen, D. 1977. *Circulation.* MESA New York Bight Atlas Monograph 3. Albany, N. Y.: New York Sea Grant Institute, p. 13.

(19) Ibid.

(20) Bowman, M. 1977. *Hydrographic properties.* With cartographic assistance by Lewis D. Wunderlich. MESA New York Bight Atlas Monograph 1. Albany, N. Y.: New York Sea Grant Institute, p. 14.

(21) Ibid., pp. 16–19.

(22) Bigelow, H. B. and Schroeder, W. C. "Fishes of the Gulf of Maine." *Fishery Bulletin of the Fish and Wildlife Service* 53 (1953): 429 (also issued separately as United States, Fish and Wildlife Service, Fishery Bulletin 74).

(23) Bowman, p. 37.

(24) Yentsch, C. S. 1977. *Plankton production.* MESA New York Bight Atlas Monograph 12. Albany, N. Y.: New York Sea Grant Institute.

(25) Malone, T. C. 1977. *Plankton systematics and distribution*. MESA New York Bight Atlas Monograph 13. Albany, N. Y.: New York Sea Grant Institute, p. 7.

(26) Ryther, J. and Dunstan, W. M. "Nitrogen, phosphorus, and eutrophication in the coastal marine environment." *Science* 171. 3975, 12 March 1971, pp. 1008–1013.

(27) Judkins, D. C., Wirick, C. D., and Esaias, W. E. "Composition, abundance, and distribution of zooplankton in New York Bight, September 1974–September 1975." *Fisheries Bulletin* 77. 3 (1980): 669–683.

(28) Malone, pp. 22, 23.

(29) Ibid., p. 41.

(30) Pearce, J. B., Radosh, D. J., Caracciolo, J. V., and Steimle, F. W. Jr. 1981. *Benthic fauna*. MESA New York Bight Atlas Monograph 14. Albany, N. Y.: New York Sea Grant Institute, p. 12.

(31) Ibid., p. 15.

(32) Boesch, D. F. "Ecosystem consequences of alterations of benthic community structure and function in the New York Bight region." In Mayer, G. S., ed. 1982. *Ecological stress and the New York Bight: science and management*. Columbia, S. C.: Estuarine Research Foundation, p. 6.

(33) Briggs, J. C. 1974. *Marine Zoogeography*. McGraw-Hill Series in Population Biology. New York: McGraw Hill.

(34) Grosslein M. D. and Azarovitz, T. [In press]. *Fish distribution*. MESA New York Bight Atlas Monograph 15. Albany, N. Y.: New York Sea Grant Institute, p. 15.

(35) Based on data from Grosslein and Azarovitz, 1981, table 1.

(36) Ibid., p. 17.

(37) McHugh, J. L. and Ginter, J. J. C. 1978, *Fisheries*. New York Bight Atlas Monograph 16. Albany, N. Y.: New York Sea Grant Institute, p. 10. See also McHugh, 1977, p. 46.

(38) McHugh and Ginter, p. 42.

(39) United States, National Oceanic and Atmospheric Administration. 1975. *Ocean dumping in the New York Bight*. NOAA Technical Report ERL 321-MESA 2. Boulder, Colo.: Environmental Research Laboratories, p. 56.

(40) Sindermann, C. J. "Effects of coastal pollution on fish and fisheries—with particular reference to the Middle Atlantic Bight." In Gross, M. G., ed. 1976. *Middle Atlantic Continental Shelf and the New York Bight*. Special Symposia, vol. 2. Lawrence, Kans.: American Society of Limnology and Oceanography, pp. 281–301.

(41) Howe, M. A., Clapp, R. B. and Weske, J. S. 1978. *Marine and coastal birds*. MESA New York Bight Atlas Monograph 31. Albany, N. Y.: New York Sea Grant Institute, p. 7.

(42) National Academy of Sciences, National Academy of Engineering, Environmental Studies Board, 1971. *Jamaica Bay and Kennedy Airport, a multidisciplinary study*. Volume II, *A report of the Jamaica Bay environmental study group. Washington, D.C.*, p. 49.

(43) Howe, Clapp, and Weske, p. 74.

(44) Goldfield, M. and Sussman, O. "The 1959 outbreak of Eastern Encephalitis in New Jersey. 1. Introduction and description of the outbreak." *Journal of Epidemiology* 87 (1968): 4.

(45) Howe, Clapp, and Weske, p. 48.

(46) Pilson, M. E. Q. and Goldstein, E. "Marine mammals in Rhode Island." For the University Marine Experiment Station, Graduate School of Oceanography. In *Coastal and offshore environmental inventory, Cape Hatteras to Nantucket Shoals*. 1973. Marine Publications Series No. 2. Kingston, R. I.: University of Rhode Island, pp. 7.1–7.48.

Chapter 2. The Margins of the Bight *(Pages 19–50)*

(1) United States, Army Corps of Engineers. 1973. *National shoreline study*, vol. 2, *Regional inventory report, North Atlantic Region*. Washington, D.C.: Government Printing Office, p. 102 (hereafter cited as *National Shoreline Study*).

(2) Koebel, C. T. And Krueckeberg, D. A. 1975. *Demographic patterns*. MESA New York Bight Atlas Monograph 23. Albany, N. Y.: New York Sea Grant Institute, p. 36.

(3) Milliman, J. D. and Emery, K. O. "Sea levels during the past 35,000 years." *Science* 162. 3858, 6 December 1968, pp. 1121–23.

(4) Taney, N. E. 1961. *Geomorphology of the south shore of Long Island, New York*. U. S. Army Corps of Engineers, Technical memorandum no. 128. Washington, D.C.: Beach Erosion Board, p. 46.

(5) Nordstrom, K. F. 1977. *Coastal geomorphology of New Jersey*. Center for Coastal and Environmental Studies, Technical report #77–1. New Brunswick, N. J.: Rutgers University. See also Nordstrom, K. F. 1975. *Beach response rates to cyclic wave regimes at Sandy Hook, New Jersey*. Marine Sciences Center, Technical report no. 79–3. Rutgers University. See also Nordstrom, K. F., Psuty, N. P., and Allen, J. R. "Beach dynamics and sediment mobility at Sandy Hook, New Jersey." In Proceedings, Columbia University Seminar on Pollution and Water Resources, 1975 (Special problems in ocean engineering). New York: Columbia University Press, vol. 8, pp. 55–86.

(6) Allen, J. R. 1979. "Beach erosion as a function of variations in the sediment budget." Unpublished paper presented at the annual meeting of the Association of American Geographers, Philadelphia, Pa., 22–25 April 1979.

(7) Psuty, N. P. et al. "The New York Bight shore area: a guide for decision-making about the built and natural environment." In MESA/New York Bight Workshop, Williamsburg, Va., 1978. [Background paper] Stony Brook, N. Y.: U. S. National Oceanic and Atmospheric Administration, MESA New York Bight Project, p. 33.

(8) Taney, p. 33.

(9) Ibid., p. 36.

(10) Yasso, W. E. and Hartman, E. M. Jr. 1975. *Beach forms and coastal processes*. MESA New York Bight Atlas Monograph 11. Albany, N. Y.: New York Sea Grant Institute, p. 27.

(11) Wicker, C. G. "History of the New Jersey coastline." In Proceedings, First Conference on Coastal Engineering, 1951, ed. J. W. Johnston. Richmond, Calif.: Council on Wave Research, pp. 316–319.

(12) Heikoff, J. M. 1976. *Politics of shore erosion: Westhampton Beach*. Ann Arbor, Mich.: Ann Arbor Science Publication, p. 69.

(13) Heikoff, J. M. 1979. *Management of the ocean shore of New York State, Rockaway Point to Montauk Point*. Albany, N. Y.: New York Sea Grant Institute, pp. 13–14.

(14) Calculated from data provided by Tom Vernam, Bureau of Shellfish Control, New Jersey State Department of Environmental Protection, Trenton, N. J., and by Bruce MacMillan, New York State Department of Environmental Conservation, Stony Brook, N. Y.

(15) O'Connor, J. S. and Terry, O. W. 1972. *The marine wetlands of Nassau and Suffolk Counties, New York*. Prepared in cooperation with the Nassau-Suffolk Regional Planning Board. Stony Brook, N. Y.: Marine Sciences Research Center, State University of New York at Stony Brook, p. 5.

(16) Based on information provided by John Weingart, Bureau of Coastal Planning, New Jersey Department of Environmental Protection, 23 January 1980.

(17) Wapora, Inc. 1979. *The estuarine study, vol. 1, Impact and management report*. Trenton, N. J.: New Jersey Department of Environmental Protection, Division of Coastal Resources, Bureau of Coastal Planning and Development, p. 27.

(18) Porter, R. "Storm hits coast 2d day; 27 dead, damage heavy." *New York Times*, 8 March 1962, sect. 1, p. 14.

(19) Calculated from data in *National shoreline study*, pp. 101–102.

(20) Ibid., pp. 14–20.

(21) Morris, J. 1969. *The great port—a passage through New York*. New York: Harcourt, Brace & World, pp. 11–12.

(22) Schubel, J. R. et al. "Effects of the Hudson-Raritan estuarine system on the Bight." In MESA New York Bight Workshop, Williamsburg, Va., 1979. [Summary report] Stony Brook, N. Y.: U.S. National Oceanic and Atmospheric Administration, MESA New York Bight Project, p. 21 (unpubl.).

(23) Swanson, R. L. 1976. *Tides*. MESA New York Bight Atlas Monograph 4. Albany, N. Y.: New York Sea Grant Institute.

(24) Schubel et al., p. 13.

(25) Swanson, *op. cit.*

(26) Mueller, J. A. and Anderson, A. R. 1978. *Industrial wastes*. MESA New York Bight Atlas Monograph 30. Albany, N. Y.: New York Sea Grant Institute, p. 14.

(27) Calculated from table of water discharge in Gross, M. G. "Sediment and waste deposition in New York Harbor." *Annals of the New York Academy of Sciences* 250 (1974): 120 (hereafter cited as Gross, "Sediment").

(28) Schubel et al., p. 29.

(29) Wilson, J. G. 1892. *The memorial history of the City of New York*. New York: New York History Co., vol. 4, pp. 503–504.

(30) Albion, R. G. 1939. *The rise of New York port 1815–1860*. New York: Charles Scribner's Sons, p. 3.

(31) Maritime Association of the Port of New York. 1980. *Statistical review of the number of vessels calling at the eleven major ports of the continental U.S. during the calender year 1979*. New York, p. 2 (press release).

(32) Albion, p. 221.

(33) Ibid., p. 95.

(34) Ibid., p. 1.

(35) Ballabon, M. B. and Boddewyn, J. J. "The economic development of the New York Bight coastal zone." In MESA New York Bight Workshop, Williamsburg, Va., 1981 [Summary report]. Stony Brook, N. Y.: U.S. National Oceanic and Atmospheric Administration, MESA New York Bight Project, p. 16 (unpubl.).

(36) Personal communication with Alfred Hammon, supervisor of Port Development, the Port Authority of New York and New Jersey, on 2 July 1979.

(37) Moss, M. L. 1978. "The management of the New York City waterfront." In MESA New York Bight Workshop on the New York Bight, Williamsburg, Va. [Background paper] Stony Brook, N. Y.: U.S. National Oceanic and Atmospheric Administration, MESA New York Bight Project, p. 9 (unpubl.).

(38) Hammon, A. 1976. *Port facilities and commerce*. MESA New York Bight Atlas Monograph 20. Albany, N. Y.: New York Sea Grant Institute, pp. 21, 33.

(39) Moss, M. L. "Staging a renaissance on the waterfront." *New York Affairs* 6. 2 (1980): 9.

(40) Moss, M. L. and Drennan, M. 1978. *The maturation of the urban waterfront*. Paper presented to the joint national meeting of the Institute of Management Sciences and Operations Research Society of America. Albany, N. Y.: New York Sea Grant Institute, p. 5. See also, Moss, M. L. and Drennan, M. 1980. *The New York City waterfront: an analysis of municipal ownership and leasing of public land*. Albany, N. Y.: New York Sea Grant Institute, report series.

(41) Hammon, p. 35.

(42) United States, Army Corps of Engineers. 1971. *New York Harbor—collection and removal of drift project*. New York: New York District, Corps of Engineers, p. "syllabus."

(43) Port Authority of New York and New Jersey. *Facts and Figures 1977*. New York: Port Authority of New York and New Jersey.

(44) O'Callaghan, E. B., ed. 1850. *The documentary history of the State of New York*. Albany, N. Y.: Weed, Parsons & Co., vol. 1, p. 103.

(45) New York (City), Department of Environmental Protection. 1979. *Section 208 areawide waste treatment management planning program.* New York, N. Y., pp. 1-3 (hereafter cited as New York (City), *Section 208 . . . program*).

(46) Squires, D. F. 1981. *The Bight of the Big Apple.* Albany, N. Y.: New York Sea Grant Institute, p. 61.

(47) Gross, "Sediment," p. 112.

(48) Gross, M. G. 1976. *Waste disposal.* MESA New York Bight Atlas Monograph 26. Albany, N. Y.: New York Sea Grant Institute, p. 10.

(49) Gross, "Sediment," p. 115.

(50) Herzlinger, R. "Costs, benefits, and the West Side Highway." *The Public Interest* 55 (spring 1979): 91.

(51) Squires, p. 60.

(52) Gross, *Waste disposal,* p. 17.

(53) Delaney, E. T. 1965. *New York's Turtle Bay old & new.* Barre, Mass.: Barre Publishers, p. 35.

(54) Bennet, C. G. "Landfill off S. I. is studied by city." *New York Times,* 7 July 1967, pp. 1f.

(55) Gross, *Waste disposal,* pp. 17-18.

(56) Schlee, J. and Sanko, P. 1975. *Sand and gravel.* MESA New York Bight Atlas Monograph 21. Albany, N. Y.: New York Sea Grant Institute, p. 23.

(57) Swartz, S. M. and Brinkhuis, B. H. 1978. *The impact of dredged holes on oxygen demand in the Lower Bay, New York Harbor.* Special report 17. Stony Brook, N. Y.: Marine Sciences Research Center, State University of New York at Stony Brook.

(58) Albion, *The rise of New York port,* p. 26.

(59) Hammon, *Port Facilities and Commerce,* p. 11.

(60) Olsen, C. R. et al. "A geochemical analysis of the sediments and sedimentation in the Hudson Estuary." *Journal of Sedimentary Petrology* 48. 2 (June 1978): 416.

(61) Gross, *Waste disposal,* p. 10.

(62) Gross, M. G. "New York metropolitan region—a major sediment source." *Bulletin of Water Resources Research* 6. 3 (June 1970): 929.

(63) Freeland, G. L. et al. "Surficial sediments of the NOAA-MESA study areas in the New York Bight." In Gross, M. G., ed. 1976. *Middle Atlantic continental shelf and the New York Bight.* Special Symposia, vol. 2. Lawrence, Kans.: American Society of Limnology and Oceanography, pp. 93-961.

(64) Gross, *Waste disposal,* p. 10.

(65) Ibid., p. 16.

(66) New York (City), *Section 208. . . program,* pp. 1-3.

(67) Heikoff, *Politics,* pp. 1-163.

(68) "People of the State of New York v. State of New Jersey and the Passaic Valley Sewerage Commission." *United States Reports,* vol. 256, 1921, p. 297.

(69) "The New York Harbor Case." *Interstate Commerce Commission Reports,* vol. 47, October/December 1917, p. 747.

(70) "City of New York, Plaintiff, *v.* William R. Willcox et al., Defendants."

Miscellaneous Reports, New York, vol. 115, March/June 1921, pp. 352–353.

(71) Marr, P. 1979. *Jurisdictional zones and governmental responsibilities.* MESA New York Bight Atlas Monograph 22. Albany, N. Y.: New York Sea Grant Institute, p. 11.

(72) United States, Bureau of the Census. 1973. *1970 Census of population,* vol. 1, *Characteristics of the population, p. 32, New Jersey—sect. 1.* Washington, D.C.: Government Printing Office, p. 32–13; also United States, Bureau of the Census. 1973. *1970* Census of Population, vol. 1, Characteristics of the population, p. 34, New York—section 1. Washington, D.C.: Government Printing Office, p. 34–14.

(73) Kavenagh, W. K. 1980. *Vanishing tidelands: land use and the law, Suffolk County, N. Y. 1650–1979.* Albany, N. Y.: New York Sea Grant Institute, p. 38.

(74) Ibid, pp. 97–121.

(75) Marr, p. 16.

(76) Marr, p. 11.

(77) Marr, p. 13.

(78) Marr, p. 18.

(79) Marr, p. 16.

(80) Marr, p. 36.

(81) Marr, p. 34.

Chapter 3. The Resources *(Pages 51–77)*

(1) Dickens, C. 1957. *American notes and Pictures from Italy.* London: Oxford University Press, p. 87.

(2) New York (Colony). 1894. *Colonial laws of New York from the year 1664 to the Revolution.* Albany, N. Y.: James B. Lyon, State Printer, vol. 1, p. 845.

(3) New York (State), Commissioners of Fisheries. 1887. *Second report of the oyster investigation and of the Survey of oyster territory for the years 1885 and 1886,* by Eugene G. Blackford. New York State Legislature, Assembly documents, 1887, no. 28: Albany, N. Y.: Argus Co., p. 8.

(4) Ibid., p. 37.

(5) Loop, A. S. 1964. *History and development of sewage treatment in New York City.* New York: Department of Health of the City of New York, p. 16.

(6) Wright, L. 1960. *Clean and decent, the fascinating history of the bathroom & the water closet and of sundry habits, fashions & accessories of the toilet principally in Great Britain, France & America.* Toronto, Canada: University of Toronto Press, p. 151.

(7) Verber, J. L. 1980. *Shellfish-borne disease outbreaks.* Davisville, R. I.: Department of Health and Human Services, Food and Drug Administration, Northeast Technical Services Unit, p. 3 (mimeo.).

(8) Loop, p. 16.

(9) New York (City), Department of Environmental Protection. 1979. *Section 208 areawide waste treatment management planning program.* New York, p. S–2.

(10) Larkin, P. A. "An epitaph for the concept of maximum sustained yield." *Transactions of the American Fisheries Society* 106. 1 (Jan. 1977): 6.

(11) Rayback, R. J. "The Indian." In Thompson, J. H., ed., 1966. *Geography of New York State*, Syracuse, N. Y.: Syracuse University Press, p. 118.

(12) Ingersoll, E. 1881. *The oyster industry.* Washington, D.C.: Government Printing Office, p. 99 (The history and present condition of the fisheries industries).

(13) McDonald, M. "The fisheries of the Hudson River." In Goode, G. B., ed., 1887. *The fisheries and fishery industries of the United States, sect. V, history and methods of the fisheries.* Washington, D.C.: Government Printing Office, vol. 1, pp. 658–659.

(14) McHugh, J. L. and Ginter, J. J. C. 1978. *Fisheries.* MESA New York Bight Atlas Monograph 16. Albany, N. Y.: New York Sea Grant Institute, pp. 10–12.

(15) Ibid., p. 10.

(16) Ibid., p. 12.

(17) McHugh, J. L. "Atlantic sea clam fishery: a case history." In *Extended fishery jurisdiction: problems and progress, 1977,* Proceedings of the North Carolina Governor's Conference on Fishery Management under Extended Jurisdiction, Raleigh, N. C., 1967, ed. K. M. Jurgensen and A. P. Covington. Raleigh, N. C.: Office of Marine Affairs, North Carolina Department of Administration, Coastal Plains Center for Marine Development Services, p. 79.

(18) Petruny-Lounsbury, M. E. 1981. *Is extended jurisdiction working? An analysis of the surf clam* (Spisula solidissima) *and ocean quahog* (Artica islandica) *management plan.* Master's thesis, State University of New York at Stony Brook, p. 20.

(19) McHugh, "Atlantic sea clam," p. 73.

(20) Rinaldo, R. G. 1977. *Atlantic clam fishery management plan. Environmental Impact Statement.* Prepared by Ronald G. Rinaldo and support staff from National Marine Fisheries Service, Northeast Regional Office and State-Federal Clam Management Subboard and Technical Committee, Mid-Atlantic and New England Regional Fisheries Management Councils. Dover, Del., and Peabody, Mass.

(21) Mid-Atlantic Fishery Management Council. 1977. *Fisheries management plan for surf clam and ocean quahog fisheries.* Dover, Del.

(22) Petruny-Lounsbury, p. 24.

(23) United States, National Marine Fisheries Service. 1981. *Fisheries of the United States, 1980.* (Current fisheries statistics no. 8100) Washington, D.C.: Government Printing Office, p. 2 (hereafter cited as *Fisheries of the United States, 1980*).

(24) Petruny-Lounsbury, p. 51.

(25) Verber, J. L. "Safe shellfish from the sea." In Gross, M. G., ed. 1976. *Middle Atlantic Continental Shelf and the New York Bight.* Special Symposia 2. Lawrence, Kans.: American Society of Limnology and Oceanography, p. 436.

(26) Swanson, R. L. and Sindermann, C. J., ed. 1979. *Oxygen depletion and*

REFERENCES

associated benthic mortalities in New York Bight, 1976. NOAA professional paper 11. Rockville, Md.: U.S. National Oceanic and Atmospheric Administration.

(27) Ropes, J. W. et al. "Impact on clams and scallops, p. 1, Field survey assessments." In Swanson and Sindermann, p. 274.

(28) O'Connor, J. S. "A Perspective on natural and human factors." In Swanson and Sindermann, p. 331.

(29) Longwell, A. C. "Chromosome mutagenesis in developing mackerel eggs sampled from the New York Bight." In Gross, M. G., ed. 1976. *Middle Atlantic Continental Shelf and the New York Bight.* Special Symposia, vol. 2. Lawrence, Kans.: American Society of Limnology and Oceanography, p. 337.

(30) McHugh, J. L. 1977. *Fisheries and fishery resources of New York Bight.* NOAA technical report NMFS circular 401. Washington, D.C.: Government Printing Office, p. 47.

(31) United States, National Marine Fisheries Service. 1979. *Fishery statistics of the United States, 1975.* Statistical Digest No. 69. Washington, D.C.: Government Printing Office, p. 122.

(32) Personal communication with Gerhardt Muller, member of the Regional and Economic Development Task Force, Port of New York and New Jersey Authority, February 1981.

(33) United States, National Marine Fisheries Service. 1979. *Fisheries of the United States, 1978.* Current fishery statistics no. 7800. Washington, D.C.: Government Printing Office, p. 76.

(34) Calculated from information in Chase, D. M. 1979. *Factors relating to the continued development of the commercial fishing industry of New York State.* Calverton, N. Y.: Prepared for the Mid-Atlantic Fisheries Development Foundation [of] Annapolis, Maryland, p. 12 (unpublished ms.).

(35) Destefano, T. and Hosenball, M. "Probers sense something's rotten at Fulton Fish Market." *Supermarket News,* 26 November 1979, p. 8. See also Kaplan, M. and Renner, T. "Probe of Fish Market uncovers a network of organized crime." *Newsday* 41. 247, 10 May 1981, pp. 5f. See also Lubash, A. H. "U.S. prosecutors say mob controls Fulton Market." *New York Times,* 14 February 1982, sect. 1, p. 53.

(36) United States, National Marine Fisheries Service. 1980. *Marine recreational fishery statistics survey, Atlantic and Gulf Coasts, 1979.* Current fishery statistics no. 8063. *Marine recreational fishery statistics survey, Atlantic and Gulf Coasts, 1979.*

(37) Ibid. pp. 35–36.

(38) McHugh, J. L. "Fisheries of New York Bight." In MESA New York Bight Workshop, Williamsburg, Va., 1978. [Background paper] Stony Brook, N. Y.: U. S. National Oceanic and Atmospheric Administration, MESA New York Bight Project, p. 1 (unpubl.).

(39) *Fisheries of the United States, 1980,* p. 41.

(40) Jensen, A. C. "Mangement of New York Bight fisheries is an antagonistic environment." In MESA New York Bight Workshop, Williamsburg, Va., 1978. [Background paper] Stony Brook, N. Y.: U.S. Na-

tional Oceanic and Atmospheric Administration, MESA New York Bight Project, p. 11 (unpubl.).

(41) Freeman, B. L. and Walford, L. A. 1974. *Angler's guide to the United States Atlantic coast: fish, fishing grounds & fishing facilities, sect. III, Block Island to Cape May, New Jersey*. Washington, D.C.: Government Printing Office.

(42) Murray, J. D., Sutherland, J. E., and Gratzer, M. A. J. 1976. *The charter boat industry of New York State: a problem analysis*. Syracuse, N. Y.: College of Environmental Science and Forestry, State University of New York, p. 10.

(43) New York (State), Department of Environmental Conservation. 1977. *Marine related activities: an assessment of the economic impacts of OCS energy development*. [Unpublished report prepared for the NYS Department of State as Task 8.7, 1st OCS Year]. Albany, N. Y., p. 31.

(44) Miller, W. A. "Editorial: Time for reader action on gill net bill." *The Long Island Fishermen*, 18 June 1981.

(45) Hardin, G. "The tragedy of the commons." *Science* 162. 3859, 13 December 1968, p. 1244.

(46) Gordon, H. S., "A rising tide for seaweed." *Chemical Engineering*, 83. 6 December 1976, pp. 92–98.

(47) Squires, D. F. "Broadening our experience with marine biomass." In Proceedings, Bio-Energy '80 World Congress and Exposition, Atlanta, Ga. Washington, D.C.: Bio-Energy Council, pp. 475–476.

(48) Leopold, B. and Marton R. 1975. *Papermaking potential of Zostera and Cladophora, two marine weeds*. Albany, N. Y.: New York Sea Grant Institute.

(49) Hanisak, M. D. "*Codium*: an invading seaweed." *Maritimes*, 24 September 1980, pp. 10–11.

(50) Terry, O. W. 1977. *Aquaculture*. MESA New York Bight Atlas Monograph 17. Albany, N. Y.: New York Sea Grant Institute.

(51) Calculated from information in Poag, C. W. "Stratigraphy and depositional environments of Baltimore Canyon Trough." *American Association of Petroleum Geologists Bulletin* 63. 9 (September 1979): 1560.

(52) Parish, A. J. "New gas discovery is made by Texaco off Jersey's coast." *New York Times*, 24 November 1979, sect. 1, pp. 1f.

(53) Rogers, W. B., Fakundiny, R. H., and Kreidler, W. L. 1973. *Petroleum exploration offshore from New York*. New York State Museum and Science Service, Circular 46. Albany, N. Y.: University of the State of New York, State Education Dept. p. 21.

(54) Ibid.

(55) Schlee, J. and Sanko, P. 1975. *Sand and gravel*. MESA New York Bight Atlas Monograph 21). Albany, N. Y.: New York Sea Grant Institute, p. 23.

(56) Personal communication with James Marotta, New York State Office of General Services.

(57) New York (State), Office of Planning Services. 1970. *Long Island sand and gravel mining*. New York: Metropolitan New York District Office.

(58) Schubel, J. R. and Squires, D. F. "Management of New York Harbor's sand and gravel resources." *Proceedings of the Coastal Society* [in press].

REFERENCES

(59) Kastens, K. A., Fray, C. T., and Schubel, J. R. 1978. *Environmental effects of sand mining in the Lower Bay of New York Harbor: Phase 1.* With a section on Circulation by Robert E. Wilson. Special report 15. Stony Brook, N. Y.: Marine Sciences Research Center, State University of New York, pp. 53 and 70.

(60) Connor, W. G. et al. 1979. *Disposal of dredged material within the New York district, vol. 1, present practices and candidate alternatives.* MITRE technical report MTR-7808. McLean, V. MITRE Corp., Metrek Division, pp. 7–41.

(61) Personal communication with H. B. Bokuniewicz of the Marine Sciences Research Center, State University of New York at Stony Brook, in June 1980.

(62) "Happy anniversary." *Sports Illustrated* 49. 12, 18 September 1978, p. 13.

Chapter 4. Peopling the Bight *(Pages 78–99)*

(1) Thompson, J. H. ed. 1966. *Geography of New York State.* Syracuse, N. Y.: Syracuse University Press, p. 12.

(2) Martin, P. S. "Pleistocene ecology and biogeography of North America." In Hubbs, C. L. 1958. *Zoogeography.* Publication 51. Washington, D.C.: Association for the Advancement of Science, pp. 375–420. See also Martin, P. S. "The discovery of America." *Science* 179. 4077, 9 March 1973, pp. 969–974. See also International Association of Quaternary Research. 1967. Proceedings of the Seventh Congress, vol. 6, *Pleistocene extinctions; the search for a cause,* ed. P. S. Martin and H. E. Wright, Jr. New Haven: Yale University Press. See also Edwards, R. L. and Merrill, A. S. "A reconstruction of the continental shelf areas of eastern North America for the times 9,500 B.P. and 12,500 B.P." *Archaeology of Eastern North America 5* (fall 1977): 1–43.

(3) De Rasieres, I. "Letter of Isaac de Rasieres to Samuel Bloomaert. 1628 (?)." In Jameson, J. F., ed. 1909. *Narratives of New Netherland, 1609–1644.* New York: Charles Scribner's Sons, p. 104.

(4) Van Der Donck, A. "Description of the New Netherlands, 1656." *New York State Historical Society Collections, ser. 2,* vol. 1, 1841, pp. 208–209.

(5) Kroeber, A. L. 1963. *Cultural and natural areas of native North America.* University of California Publications in Archeology and Ethnology, vol. 38. Berkeley and Los Angeles: University of California Press, pp. 143–146 and 166–172.

(6) Salwen, B. "Post-glacial environments and cultural change in the Hudson River Basin." *Man in the Northeast* 10 (fall 1975): 57–58.

(7) Ibid., p. 59.

(8) Van Laer, A. J. F., ed. 1924. *Documents relating to New Netherland 1624–1626 in the Henry E. Huntington Library.* San Marino, Calif.: Henry E. Huntington Library and Art Gallery, p. xix.

(9) O'Callaghan, E. B. 1853. *Documents relative to the colonial history of the State of New York.* Albany, N. Y.: Weed, Parsons & Co.

(10) Salwen, p. 59.

(11) Albion, R. G. 1939. *The rise of New York port: 1815–1860*. New York: Charles Scribner's Sons, p. 2.

(12) Greene, E. B. and Harrington, V. D. 1966. *American population before the federal census of 1970*. Gloucester, Mass.: Peter Smith, p. 40.

(13) De Bow, J. D. B. 1854. *Statistical view of the United States . . . being a compendium of the seventh census*. Washington, D.C.: Beverly Tucker, Senate Printer, pp. 192–195.

(14) United States, Bureau of the Census. 1979. *1977 Population estimates for counties, incorporated places, and minor civil divisions in New York*. Current population reports, series P-25, no. 845. Washington, D.C.: Government Printing Office, pp. 5–16.

(15) Ibid.

(16) United States, Bureau of the Census. 1977. *Population estimates for counties, incorporated places and minor civil divisions in New Jersey*. Current population reports, series P-25, no. 843. Washington, D.C. Government Printing Office, p. 5.

(17) Marr, P. D. 1979. *Jurisdictional zones and governmental responsibilities*. MESA New York Bight Atlas Monograph 22. Albany, N. Y.: New York Sea Grant Institute, p. 10.

(18) Salwen, p. 65.

(19) "Metromarket." *Via Port of New York-New Jersey* 31. 2 (December 1979): 9.

(20) Data for New York counties from United States, Bureau of the Census. 1979. *1977 Census of retail trade: geographic area series, New York*. Washington, D.C.: Government Printing Office, pp. 33–33 to 33–92. Data for New Jersey counties from United States, Bureau of the Census. 1979. *1977 Census of retail trade: geographic area series, New Jersey*. Washington, D. C.: Government Printing Office, pp. 31–40 to 31–60. Data for Fairfield County from United States, Bureau of the Census. 1979. *1977 Census of retail trade: geographic area series, Connecticut*. Washington, D.C.: Government Printing Office, pp. 7–30 to 7–31. Data for the whole United States from United States, Bureau of the Census. 1979. *1977 Census of retail trade: geographic area series, United States*. Washington, D.C.: Government Printing Office, p. 52–10.

(21) Goodman, J., Cappello, S., Koppelman, L., Casler, G., Moss., M., and Chytelo, K. "Consequences of industrialization and urbanization on the New York Bight." In MESA New York Bight Workshop, Williamsburg, Va., 1978. [Summary report] Stony Brook, N. Y.: U. S. National Oceanic and Atmospheric Administration, MESA New York Bight Project, p. 6 (unpubl.).

(22) Ballabon, M. B. and Boddewyn, J. J. "The economic development of the New York Bight coastal zone." In MESA New York Bight Workshop, Williamsburg, Va., 1981. [Summary report] Stony Brook, N. Y.: U. S. National Oceanic and Atmospheric Administration, MESA New York Bight Project, pp. 18, 19 (unpubl.).

(23) United States, Bureau of the Census. 1976. *1972 census of manufactures, vol. III, Area statistics, p. 2. Nebraska – Wyoming*. Washington, D.C.: Government Printing Office, pp. 33–39.

(24) Data for New York counties from United States, Bureau of the Census.

REFERENCES

1977. *1974 Census of agriculture*, vol. 1, p. 32, New York, state and county data. Washington, D.C.: Government Printing Office, p. 289 and p. xii. Data for New Jersey counties from United States, Bureau of the Census. 1977. *1974 Census of agriculture, vol. 1, p. 30, New Jersey, state and county data*. Washington, D.C.: Government Printing Office, p. xii.

(25) Jones, H. G. M., Bronheim, H., and Palmedo, P. F. 1975. *Electricity generation and oil refining*. MESA New York Bight Atlas Monograph 25. Albany, N. Y.: New York Sea Grant Institute, p. 17.

(26) Goodman et al., p. 6.

(27) Ballabon and Boddewyn, p. 18.

(28) Mueller, J. A. and Anderson, A. R. 1978. *Industrial wastes*. MESA New York Bight Atlas Monograph 30. Albany, N. Y.: New York Sea Grant Institute, p. 8.

(29) "Metromarket," p. 10.

(30) United States, Army Corps of Engineers. 1979. *Waterborne commerce of the United States, calendar year 1977, pt. 1, Waterways and harbors, Atlantic Coast*. Vicksburg, Mich.: U. S. Army Engineer Division, Lower Mississippi Valley, p. 48.

(31) Ibid., p. 49.

(32) Port Authority of New York and New Jersey. 1975. *Oceanborne foreign trade: lifeblood of the port*. New York, p. 40.

(33) Ballabon and Boddewyn, p. 73.

(34) Toffler, A. 1970. *Future Shock*. New York: Random House; see also Mumford, L. 1961. *The city in history*. New York: Harcourt Brace & World, pp. 551–555, 561–570.

(35) Calculated from data in Drysdale, F. R. and Calef, C. E. 1977. *The energetics of the United States of America: an atlas*. Upton, N. Y.: Brookhaven National Laboratory (BNL 50501-R).

(36) Jones, Bronheim, and Palmedo, p. 8.

(37) Drysdale and Calef, *op. cit.*

(38) Lillard, R. G. 1947. *The great forest*. New York: Alfred A. Knopf, p. 85.

(39) Bridenbaugh, C. 1955. *Cities in revolt, urban life in America, 1743–1776*. New York: Alfred A. Knopf, p. 26.

(40) Ibid., p. 233.

(41) Klein, M. M., ed. 1976. *New York: the centennial years 1676–1976*. Port Washington, N. Y.: Kennikat Press, pp. 19–20.

(42) Gross, M. G. 1976. *Waste disposal*. MESA New York Bight Atlas Monograph 26. Albany, N. Y.: New York Sea Grant Institute, p. 18.

(43) Schurr, S. H. and Netschert, B. C. 1960. *Energy in the American economy, 1850–1975, an economic study of its history and prospects*. Baltimore, Md.: Published for Resources for the Future, Inc. by the Johns Hopkins Press, p. 44.

(44) Schurr and Netschert, p. 102.

(45) "Survey of operating refineries in the United States." *Oil and gas journal* 73. 17 April 1975, pp. 98–101.

(46) Jones et al., p. 17.

(47) Calculated from Drysdale and Calef, *op cit.*

(48) *Waterborne commerce . . . 1977*, pp. 49–50.

(49) Calculated from data on computer tape, compiled under the Coast Guard's Pollution Incident Reporting System (PIRS). Described in Leotta, J. and Wallace, W. A. "The United States Coast Guard's Pollution Incident Reporting System: its use in program management." In Proceedings, Conference on Prevention and control of oil pollution, 1975. Washington, D.C.: American Petroleum Institute, pp. 201–204.

(50) Mueller, J. A., Jeris, J. S., Anderson, A. R., and Hughes, C. F. 1976. *Contaminant inputs to the New York Bight.* NOAA technical memorandum ERL MESA-6. Boulder, Colo.: Marine Ecosystems Analysis Program Office, p. 92.

(51) Le Lourd, P. "Oil pollution in the Mediterranean Sea." *Ambio* 6. 6 (1977): 319.

(52) Schurr and Netschert, p. 126.

(53) Stotz, L. and Jamison, A. 1938. *History of the gas industry.* New York: Stettiner Bros., p. 69.

(54) Schurr and Netschert, p. 127.

(55) Stotz and Jamison, p. 32.

(56) Ibid., p. 178.

(57) Schurr and Netschert, p. 97.

(58) Stotz and Jamison, p. 9.

(59) Still, B. 1956. *Mirror for Gotham, New York as seen by contemporaries from Dutch days to the present.* New York: New York University Press, p. 209.

(60) Schurr and Netschert, p. 116.

(61) Ibid., p. 117.

(62) Calculated from data in Drysdale and Calef, *op. cit.*

(63) Jones, Bronheim and Palmedo, p. 9.

(64) Ibid.

(65) Crump, L. H. 1977. *Fuels and energy data: United States by states and census divisions, 1974.* Information circular 8739. Washington, C.D.: U. S. Bureau of Mines, pp. 91 and 95.

(66) Woodhead, P. M. J., Duedall, I. W. and Lansing, N. F. 1979. *Coal waste artificial reef program, phase I: FP-1252, Research Project 1341-1, interim report, November 1979.* Prepared by the New York State Energy Research and Development Authority. Palo Alto, Calif.: Electric Power Research Institute, p. 2–1.

(67) Ibid., p. 2–2.

(68) Mohnen, V. A. 1977. *Air quality.* MESA New York Bight Atlas Monograph 28. New York Sea Grant Institute, p. 15.

(69) Wright, L. 1960. *Clean and decent. The fascinating history of the bathroom & the water closet and of sundry habits, fashions & accessories of the toilet principally in Great Britain, France & America.* Toronto, Canada: University of Toronto Press. p. 3.

(70) Squires, D. F. 1981. *The Bight of the Big Apple.* Albany, N. Y.: New York Sea Grant Institute, p. 64.

(71) Blake, N. M. 1956. *Water for the cities, a history of urban water supply problem in the United States.* Maxwell School series, III. Syracuse, N. Y.: Syracuse University Press, p. 70.

(72) Sulzberger, A. O., Jr. "New York area fights complex water woes." *New York Times,* 10 August 1981, p. B6.

(73) Carmody, D. "N.Y.C. problem isn't supply, but high consumption." *New York Times* 15 February 1981, sect. 4, p. 6.

(74) Herbers, J. "Water shortage linked to delay on new projects." *New York Times,* 15 February 1981, pp. 1f.

(75) Sulzberger, *op. cit.*

(76) Hanley, R. "Jersey shortage really goes back a very long way." *New York Times,* 15 February 1981. sect. 4, p. 6.

(77) Herbers, p. 22.

(78) McQuiston, J. T. "Aquifers under L. I. are its liquid asset. *New York Times,* 9 December 1980, p. B2.

(79) Loop, A. S. 1964. *History and development of sewage treatment in New York City.* New York: Department of Health of the City of New York, pp. 9–10.

(80) Tarr, J. A. "The separate vs. combined sewer problem, a case study in urban technology design choice." *Journal of Urban History,* 5. 3 (May 1979): 309.

(81) Tarr, J. A. and McMichael, F. C. "Decisions about wastewater technology: 1850–1932." *Journal of the Water Resources Planning and Management Division . . . American Society of Civil Engineers,* vol. 103 no. WR1, p. 51 (Proceedings Paper 12920).

(82) Loop, p. 56.

(83) Gunnerson, C. G. "Waste disposal in the New York metropolitan area." In Myers, Ed., [in press] *Ocean disposal of municipal wastewaters: the impact on estuarine and coastal waters.* Cambridge, Mass.: Massachusetts Institute of Technology Press.

(84) O'Brien, E. C., "Recreation piers." *Municipal Affairs* 1. 3, (September 1897): 511.

(85) Loop, pp. 44, 47–49.

(86) Kennedy, E. R. and Wilson, J. S. "New York Harbor Corrosion, Port of New York Authority conducts pile survey." *Materials Protection,* 6. 1 January 1967, pp. 53–55.

(87) Mueller and Anderson, pp. 16–17.

Chapter 5. The Law and The Bight *(Pages 100–125)*

(1) Thurow, L. C. 1980. *The zero-sum society: distribution and the possibilities of economic change.* New York: Basic Books.

(2) United States, Congress, Senate, Committee on Commerce. 1976. *Ocean dumping regulation: an appraisal of implementation.* Prepared at the request of . . . the Committee on Commerce and the National Ocean Study Policy

pursuant to S. Res. 222. Washington, D. C.: Government Printing Office, p. 1, 94th Cong. 2d sess., (Committee print) (hereafter cited as *Ocean dumping regulation*).

(3) Ibid.

(4) Personal communication between Peter Anderson, U.S. Environmental Protection Administration, Region II, and Merton Ingham, U.S. National Oceanic and Atmospheric Administration, Office of Marine Pollution assessment, dated 15 June 1981.

(5) Calculated from data in United States, Environmental Protection Agency. 1978. *Final environmental impact statement on the ocean dumping of sewage sludge in the New York Bight*. New York: U. S. Environmental Protection Agency, Region II, table 5 (hereafter cited as *Final environmental impact statement on ocean dumping*).

(6) Public Law 50-496 "An act to prevent obstructive and injurious deposits within the harbor and adjacent waters of New York City." *United States Statues at large*, vol. 25, 1887-1889, p. 209.

(7) Gross, M. G. 1976. *Waste disposal*. MESA New York Bight Atlas Monograph 26. Albany, N. Y.: New York Sea Grant Institute, p. 8, map. 1.

(8) *Ocean dumping regulation*, p. 14.

(9) Calculated from data in *Final environmental impact statement on ocean dumping*, table 5.

(10) Gross, *Waste disposal*, p. 16.

(11) Nixon, R. M. "Control of pollution of the Great Lakes and the oceans; the president's message to the Congress on waste disposal—April 15, 1970." *Weekly Compilation of Presidential Documents*, vol. 6, no. 16, 20 April 1970, p. 526.

(12) United States, Council on Environmental Quality. 1970. *Ocean dumping: a national policy*. Washington, D.C.: Government Printing Office, p. v.

(13) Buelow, R. W., Pringle, B. M., and Verber, J. L. 1968. *Preliminary investigation of waste disposal in the New York Bight*. NERC-NCUIH Report 21. Narragansett, R. I.: Northeastern Marine Health Sciences Laboratory, p. 5. Also, Buelow, R. W., Pringle, B. H. and Verber, J. L. 1968. *Preliminary investigation of sewage sludge dumping off Delaware Bay*. NERC-NCUIH Report 33. Narragansett, R. I.: Northeastern Marine Health Sciences Laboratory, p. 13.

(14) Verber, J. L. "Safe shellfish from the sea." In Gross, M. G., ed. 1976. *Middle Atlantic continental shelf and the New York Bight*. Special Symposia, vol. 2. Lawrence, Kans.: American Society of Limnology and Oceanography, p. 436.

(15) "Public Law 92-532: Marine Protection, Research, and Sanctuaries Act of 1972." *United States Statutes at Large*, vol. 86, 1972, p. 1052.

(16) Ibid., p. 1054.

(17) "Public Law 92-500: Federal Water Pollution Control Act Amendments of 1972." *United States Statutes at Large*, vol. 86, 1972 p. 816.

(18) "Public Law 92-532," p. 1061.

(19) Ibid., p. 1052.

REFERENCES

(20) *Ocean dumping regulation,* p. 45.

(21) "Public Law 92-500," p. 883.

(22) "Environmental Protection Agency—ocean dumping, final regulations and criteria." *Federal Register,* 15 October 1973, pp. 28609-28621.

(23) United States, Environmental Protection Agency. 1975. Decision of the administrator; in the matter of the interim ocean disposal permit no. PA-010 granted to the City of Philadelphia. Washington, D.C. (mimeo.)

(24) "Environmental Protection Agency—ocean dumping: final revision of regulations and criteria." *Federal Register,* 11 January 1977, pp. 2461-2490.

(25) Ibid., p. 2463.

(26) Ibid., p. 2464.

(27) "Legislative history, P.L. 95-153: Authorization, appropriation—Marine Protection, Research, and Sanctuaries Act of 1972." *U.S. Code Congressional and Administrative News,* 95th Cong., 1st Sess., 1977, p. 3265.

(28) Swanson, R. L. et al. "June 1976 pollution of Long Island ocean beaches." *Journal of The Environmental Engineering Division . . . American Society of Civil Engineers,* vol. 104, no. EE6, pp. 1067-1085 (Proceedings paper 14238).

(29) *Ocean dumping regulation.*

(30) United States, Congress, Senate, Committee on Commerce, Science, and Transportation. 1977. *The Tanker and Vessel Safety Act of 1977: report . . . on Senate 682.* Washington, D.C.: Government Printing Office, p. 32, 95th Cong., 1st Sess., Senate report no. 176.

(31) United States, Congress, House, Committee on Science and Technology. 1978. *Amending the Marine Protection, Research and Sanctuaries Act of 1972: report to accompany H.R. 10661.* Washington, D.C.: Government Printing Office, pt. 1, p. 4, 95th Cong., 2d Sess., House report no. 95-1145, pt. 1.

(32) "P.L. 95-273: National Ocean Pollution Research and Development and Monitoring Planning Act of 1978." *United States Statutes at Large,* vol. 92, 1978, p. 229.

(33) United States, National Oceanic and Atmospheric Administration. 1979. *Federal plan for ocean pollution research, development, and monitoring, fiscal years 1979-83.* Washington, D.C.: Government Printing Office, p. 5.

(34) "P. L. 96-381: Marine Protection, Research, and Sanctuaries Act, amendment." *United States Statutes at Large,* vol. 94, 1980, p. 1523.

(35) United States, Congress, House, Committee on Merchant Marine and Fisheries. 1980. *Ocean dumping authorization: fiscal year 1981; report to accompany H.R. 6616.* Washington, D.C.: Government Printing Office, pt. 1, p. 3, 96th Cong., 2d sess., House report no. 96-894, pt. 1.

(36) "P. L. 96-572: Marine Protection, Research, and Sanctuaries Act, title I, reauthorization." *United States Statutes at Large,* vol. 94, 1980, p. 3345.

(37) Testimony of Thomas C. Jorling, assistant administrator for Water and Hazardous Materials, U. S. Environmental Protection Agency, in United States, Congress, House, Committee on Merchant Marine and Fisheries. 1978. *Ocean dumping and pollution: hearings before the Subcommittee on Oceanography and the Subcommittee on Fisheries and Wildlife Conservation and the*

Environment. Serial no. 95–42. Washington, D.C.: Government Printing Office, pp. 69–83.

(38) "P. L. 49–929: An act making appropriations for the construction, repair, and prevention of certain public works on rivers and harbors, and for other purposes." *United States Statutes at Large,* vol. 24, 1885–1887, p. 330.

(39) Williams, S. J. and Duane, D. B. 1974. *Geomorphology and sediments of the inner New York Bight continental shelf.* Technical memorandum no. 45. Ft. Belvoir, Va.: U.S. Army Corps of Engineers, Coastal Engineering Research Center, p. 38.

(40) "P. L. 96–572," p. 1055.

(41) *Ocean dumping regulation,* p. 26.

(42) Conner, W. G. et al. 1979. *Disposal of dredged material within the New York District.* MITRE technical report MTR-7808 vol. 1 and vol. 2. McLean, Va.: MITRE Corp., Metrek Division.

(43) United States, Army Corps of Engineers. 1980. Announcement of an incremental implementation plan for the dredged material disposal management program for the Port of New York and New Jersey and notice of public information meetings. Public notice 10314 (mimeo.). New York: New York District, Corps of Engineers.

(44) "P. L. 87–167: To implement the provisions of the International Convention for the Prevention of the Pollution of the Sea by Oil, 1954." *United States Statutes at Large,* vol. 75, 1961, pp. 402–407.

(45) Marr, P. D., 1979. *Jurisdictional zones and governmental responsibilities.* MESA New York Bight Atlas Monograph 22. Albany, N.Y.: New York Sea Grant Institute, p. 15.

(46) "Convention on the Prevention of Marine Pollution by Dumping of Wastes and Other Matter." *United States Treaties and Other International Agreements,* vol. 26, 1975, pp. 2403–2485.

(47) "P. L. 93–254: To amend the Marine Protection, Research, and Sanctuaries Act of 1972, in order to implement the provisions of the Convention on the Prevention of Marine Pollution by Dumping of Wastes and Other Matter." *United States Statutes at Large,* vol. 88. 1974, pp. 50–51.

(48) Peter, W. G. III. "New York Bight: a case study—Part I." *BioScience* 20. 10, 15 May 1970, p. 617.

(49) Brady, T. F. " 'Dead sea' rising at harbor mouth." *New York Times,* 8 February 1970, sect. 1, pp. 1f.

(50) United States, National Marine Fisheries Service. 1972. *The effects of waste disposal in the New York Bight—Final report.* Highlands, N. J.: Middle Atlantic Coastal Fisheries Center (for sale by National Technical Information Service, Springfield, Va. as AD 739531 through AD 739539).

(51) Peter, p. 617.

(52) Ibid., p. 618.

(53) "P. L. 95–532," p. 1060.

(54) United States, National Oceanic and Atmospheric Administration. 1972. *Marine Ecosystems Analysis (MESA): conceptual plan.* NOAA Program Plan 72 (mimeo.). Rockville, Md.: Office of Marine Resources.

REFERENCES

(55) Interview with R. L. Swanson, director, Office of Marine Pollution Assessment, U.S. National Oceanic and Atmospheric Administration, in Stony Brook, N. Y. on 25 March 1981.

(56) Greenberger, M., Crenson, M. A., Crissey, B. L. 1976. *Models in the policy process: public decision-making in the computer era.* New York: Russell Sage Foundation, p. 79.

(57) United States, National Oceanic and Atmospheric Administration. 1974. *Project Development Plan. MESA New York Bight Project.* Boulder, Colo.: Environmental Research Laboratories (mimeo.).

(58) Memorandum from R. L. Swanson, manager, MESA New York Bight Project, "Review of sewage sludge issue," dated 15 April 1976 (hereafter cited as Swanson memo).

(59) Ibid.

(60) Soucie, G. "Here come de sludge." *Audubon* 76. 4 (July 1974) p: 108–113.

(61) Ibid., p. 110.

(62) Swanson memo, p. 2.

(63) Bird, D. "Sewage sludge nears L.I. beach." *New York Times*, 11 December 1973, pp. 1f. See also Hureta, M. "Dead sea of sludge, a threat to Island?" *Long Island Press*, 23 December 1973. "Officials meet to discuss off-shore sludge." *Newsday*, 18 December 1973; and Shanov, L. "A chain of reactions on sludge discovery." *Newsday*, 12 December 1973.

(64) Swanson memo, p. 2.

(65) Swanson et al., p. 1069.

(66) Ibid., p. 1071.

(67) United States, National Oceanic and Atmospheric Administration. 1977. *Long Island beach pollution: June 1975.* MESA special report. Boulder, Colo.: Environmental Research Laboratories.

(68) Swanson, R. L. and Sindermann, C. J., ed. 1979. *Oxygen depletion and associated benthic mortalities in New York Bight, 1976.* NOAA Professional Paper 11. Rockvile, Md.: U.S. National Oceanic and Atmospheric Administration.

(69) Publications counted by the staff of the MESA New York Bight Project.

(70) Published by the New York Sea Grant Institute in Albany, N. Y.

(71) Gross, M. G., ed. 1976. *Middle Atlantic Continental Shelf and the New York Bight.* Special Symposia, vol. 2. Lawrence, Kans.: American Society of Limnology and Oceanography.

(72) Mueller, J. A., Jeris, J. S., Anderson, A. R., and Hughes, C. F. 1976. *Contaminant inputs to the New York Bight.* NOAA technical memorandum ERL MESA-6. Boulder, Colo.: Marine Ecosystems Analysis Programs Office.

(73) Swanson and Sindermann, *op. cit.*

(74) O'Connor, J. S. and Stanford, H. M., ed. 1979. *Chemical pollutants of the New York Bight, priorities for research.* Boulder, Colo.: U.S. National Oceanic and Atmospheric Administration, Environmental Research Laboratory, p. 7.

(75) United States, National Oceanic and Atmospheric Administration, Environmental Research Laboratories. 1980. *INSTEP achievements—an interim*

report. Miami, Fla.: Atlantic Oceanographic and Meterologic Laboratories, Marine Geology and Geophysics Lab. (mimeo.).

(76) Longwell, A.C. 1976. *Chromosome mutagenesis in developing mackerel eggs sampled form [from] the New York Bight.* NOAA technical memorandum ERL MESA-7. Boulder, Colo.: Marine Ecosystems Analysis Programs Office.

Chapter 6. The Bight As A Dump *(Pages 126–153)*

(1) Shumway, F. M. 1975. *Seaport city: New York in 1775.* New York: South Street Seaport Museum, p. 9.

(2) Mueller, J. A., Jerris, J. S., Anderson, A. R., Hughes, C. F. 1976. *Contaminant Inputs to the New York Bight.* NOAA Technical Memorandum ERL MESA-6. Boulder, Colo.: Marine Ecosystems Analysis Programs Office, p. 49.

(3) Ibid., p. 50.

(4) Ibid., p. 93.

(5) Ibid.

(6) Ibid.

(7) Ibid.

(8) Hetling, L. J., Horn, E., and Tofflemire, J. 1978. *Summary of Hudson River PCB study results.* Technical Paper 51. Albany, N. Y.: Department of Environmental Conservation, Bureau of Water Research.

(9) Mueller et al., p. 93. See also Mueller, J. A. and Anderson, A. R. 1978. *Industrial wastes.* MESA New York Bight Monograph 30. Albany, N. Y.: New York Sea Grant Institute, pp. 30–32.

(10) Pomerantz, S. I. 1938. *New York, an American city, 1783–1803, a study of urban life.* New York: Columbia University Press, p. 277.

(11) Gunnerson, C. G. "Waste disposal in the New York metropolitan area." In Myers, E., ed. [in press] *Ocean disposal of municipal wastewaters: the impact on estuarine and coastal waters.* Cambridge, Mass.: Massachusetts Institute of Technology Press.

(12) Hellman, H. 1981. "The day New York runs out of water." *Science '81,* May 1981, p. 72.

(13) O'Connor, J. and V. Cabelli. [In preparation] *Environmental health.* MESA New York Bight Atlas Monograph 32. Albany, N. Y. New York Sea Grant Institute, tables 1–3.

(14) Mueller and Anderson, p. 20.

(15) Hufeland, O. "Report of sewage disposal in the City of New York—a resume of thirty years' investigations." In Manhattan (Borough), President, *Report of the business and transactions . . . for the year ending December 31, 1924.* New York, p. 52.

(16) Loop, A. S. 1964. *History and development of sewage treatment in New York City.* New York: Department of Health of the City of New York, p. 48.

(17) Ibid.

(18) Loop, p. 49.

REFERENCES

(19) New York (City), Department of Environmental Protection. 1979. *Section 208 areawide waste treatment management planning program.* New York. p. 3.9 (Hereafter cited as New York (City), *Section 208 . . . program*).

(20) Wright, L. 1960. *Clean and decent. The fascinating history of the bathroom & the water closet and of sundry habits, fashions & accessories of the toilet principally in Great Britain, France & America.* Toronto, Canada: University of Toronto Press, p. 149.

(21) Mueller and Anderson, p. 16.

(22) New York (City). *Section 208 . . . program*, p. 4.10.

(23) Anderson, A. R. et al. "Sources." In Proceedings, Workshop on Assimilative Capacity of U. S. Coastal Waters for Pollutants, Crystal Mountain, Wash., 1980, ed. Edward D. Goldberg, rev. ed. Boulder, Colo.: U. S. National Oceanic and Atmospheric Administration, Environmental Research Laboratories, p. 31.

(24) Robbins, W. "Philadelphia ends dumping into ocean." *New York Times*, 23 Nov. 1980, sect. 1, p. 24.

(25) Stanford, O'Connor, and Swanson, p. 59.

(26) O'Connor, J. S. 1981. *Studies on fates and effects of pollutants in the New York Bight.* Copenhagen, Denmark: International Council for the Exploration of the Sea, Marine Environmental Quality Committee (No. C.M. 1981/E:21) (mimeo.).

(27) Mueller and Anderson, p. 32.

(28) Mueller et al., pp. 31–33.

(29) Ibid., p. 93.

(30) Anderson, P. W. and Dewling, R. T. "Industrial ocean dumping in EPA Region II—regulatory aspects." In Ketchum, B. H., Kester, D. R., and Park, P. K., ed. 1981. *Ocean dumping of industrial wastes.* Marine science, vol. 12. New York: Plenum Press, p. 26.

(31) Ibid., p. 30.

(32) Ibid., p. 32.

(33) Ibid., p. 25.

(34) Ibid., p. 33.

(35) "The era of gasoline, 1911–1939." *Lamp* (spring/summer 1957): 21–31.

(36) New York (State), Commissioners of Fisheries. 1887. *Second report of the oyster investigation and of the survey of oyster territory for the years 1885 and 1886*, by Eugene G. Blackford. New York State, Legislature, Assembly documents, 1887, no. 28. Albany, N. Y.: Argus Co., p. 37.

(37) Mueller and Anderson, p. 8.

(38) Ibid., p. 12.

(39) Ibid., p. 8.

(40) Ibid., p. 14.

(41) Calculated from data on computer tape, compiled under the Coast Guard's Pollution Incident Reporting System (PIRS), as described by Leotta, J. and Wallace, W. A. "The United States Coast Guard's Pollution Incident Reporting System: its use in program management." In Proceedings, Conference on prevention and control of oil pollution, 1975. Washington, D.C.: American Petroleum Institute, pp. 201–204.

(42) Anderson and Dewling, p. 32.

(43) Ibid., p. 34.

(44) Ibid., p. 35.

(45) Ibid.

(46) Mellanby, K. 1967. *Pesticides and pollution*. London: Collins, p. 120.

(47) Dunlap, T. R. 1981. *DDT: scientists, citizens and public policy*. Princeton, N. J.: Princeton University Press, p. 18.

(48) Ibid., p. 98. See also Carson, R. 1962. *Silent spring*. New York: Houghton-Miflin.

(49) Henahan, J. F. "Whatever happened to the Cranberry crisis?" *The Atlantic* 239. 3 (March 1977): 29–36.

(50) Hetling, L. J. and Horn, E. G. 1977. *Hudson River PCB study description and detailed work plan*. Albany, N. Y.: Bureau of Water Research, Division of Pure Waters, New York State Department of Environmental Conservation, p. 10.

(51) Tofflemire, T. J., Hetling, L. J. and Quinn, S. O. 1979. *PCB in the Upper Hudson River: sediment distributions, water interactions and dredging*. Technical paper 55. Albany, N.Y.: Department of Environmental Conservation, Bureau of Water Research, p. 1.

(52) Hetling, Horn, and Tofflemire, p. 44.

(53) O'Connor, J. S. and Stanford, H., ed. 1979. *Chemical pollutants of the New York Bight: Priorities for research*. Boulder, Colo.: U.S. National Oceanic and Atmospheric Administration, Environmental Research Laboratories.

(54) Telephone conversation with Joel O'Connor, senior scientist, U. S. National Oceanic and Atmospheric Administration, Office of Marine Pollution Assessment, Northeast Office, in June 1981.

(55) Patterson, C. C., Chow, T. J., and Murozumi, M. "The possibility of measuring variations in the intensity of world-wide lead smelting during medieval and ancient times using lead aerosol deposits in polar snow strata." In Berger, R., ed. 1970. *Scientific methods in medieval archeology*. Berkeley and Los Angeles: University of California Press, p. 3.

(56) Nriagu, J. O. "Properties and the biogeochemical cycle of lead." In Nriagu, J. O., ed. 1978. *The biogeochemistry of lead in the environment*. Amsterdam: Elsevier/North-Holland Biomedical Press, p. 1.

(57) Schroeder, H. A. "Environmental metals: specific effects on the human body." In McKee, W. D., ed. 1974. *Environmental problems in medicine*. Springfield, Ill.: Charles C. Thomas, pp. 656–683.

(58) Smith, W. E. and Smith, A. M. 1975. *Minomata*. New York: Holt, Rinehart and Winston.

(59) Officer, C. B. and Ryther, J. H. "Swordfish and mercury: a case history." *Oceanus* 24. 1 (spring 1981): 36.

(60) Ibid., pp. 34–41.

(61) Cordle, F. "The FDA responds: mercury levels in fish." *Oceanus* 24. 1 (spring 1981): 42–43.

(62) Kneip, T. J. and Hazen, R. E. 1979. *Cadmium in an aquatic ecosystem; final report to the National Science Foundation*. New York: New York University Medical Center, Institute of Environmental Health.

REFERENCES

(63) Kneip, T. J. and O'Connor, J. M. 1979. *Cadmium in Foundry Cove crabs: health hazard assessment: final report to the New York State Health Council.* Tuxedo Park, N. Y.: New York University Medical Center, Institute of Environmental Medicine.

(64) Edward, J. 1893. *Improvement of New York Harbor, 1885 to 1891.* New York: Wynkoop & Hallenback.

(65) Ibid.

(66) Gross, M. G., "Sediment and waste deposition in New York Harbor." *Annals of the New York Academy of Sciences* 250 (1974): 116 (hereafter cited as Gross, "Sediment").

(67) Stanford, O'Connor, and Swanson, p. 60.

(68) Klawoon, p. 133.

(69) Connor, W. G. et al. 1979. *Disposal of dredge material within the New York District.* MITRE Technical Report MTR-7808 vol. 1 and vol. 2. McLean, Va.: MITRE Corp., Metrek Division, vol. 1, p. 2.7.

(70) Mueller and Anderson, p. 32.

(71) O'Connor, J. M., Kneip, T. J., and Nau-Ritter, G. "Chemical ecology of the Hudson-Raritan system: sources and transport of PCBs from the estuary to coastal waters." *Canadian Journal of Aquatic and Fisheries Sciences* [in press]. (Special volume).

(72) Hudson, E. "Dredging delays imperil berthing of liners in port." *New York Times*, 30 January 1980, p. B3.

(73) O'Brien, L. J., Jr. "Sharing the port barrel." *New York Times*, 16 April 1981, p. A31.

(74) New York (City), Department of Sanitation. 1979. *An overview of refuse disposal and resource recovery in New York City: issues and new directions.* New York: The City of New York, p. 18 (hereafter cited as New York (City), *Overview.*

(75) Ibid., p. 19.

(76) Ibid., pp. 27–29.

(77) Ibid., p. 20.

(78) Kelly, K. 1973. *Garbage: The history and future of garbage in America.* New York: Saturday Review Press, p. 150.

(79) New York (City), *Overview*, p. 29.

(80) Kelly, p. 151.

(81) Kelly, p. 121.

(82) New York (City), *Overview*, loco cit.

(84) Gross, M. G. 1976. *Waste disposal.* MESA New York Bight Atlas Monograph 26. Albany, N. Y.: New York Sea Grant Institute, p. 16.

(85) Ibid., p. 17.

(86) New York (City), *Overview*, p. 18.

(87) Gross, *Waste disposal*, p. 16.

(88) Ibid.

(89) Ibid., p. 8.

(90) United States, Army Corps of Engineers. 1935. *Report of the Chief of Engineers, 1935.* Washington, D.C.: Government Printing Office, pt. 1, p. 1726.

(91) New York (City), Deparment of City Planning. 1978. *Coastal zone management; draft New York City regional element of the New York State coastal management program.* New York, p. II.91.

(93) Ibid., p. II.93.

(94) Barbanel, J. "Garbage crisis: after landfills, what?" *New York Times,* 2 Apr. 1978, sect. XI, pp. 1f.

(95) Hanley, R. "Garbage disposal: Byrne vs. Meadows." *New York Times,* 20 May 1979, sect. XI, pp. 1f.

(96) Gross, M. G. "Waste sources and effects." In Gross, M. G., ed. 1976. *Middle Atlantic Continental Shelf and the New York Bight.* Special Symposia, vol. 2. Kans.: Lawrence American Society of Limnology and Oceanography, p. 158.

(97) Bennett, C. G. "Landfill off S.I. is studied by city." *New York Times,* 7 July 1967, pp. 1f.

(98) New York (State), Energy Research and Development Authority. 1978. *Methane recovery from sanitary landfills.* Prepared by New York City Resource Recovery Task Force, Brooklyn Union Gas Company [and] Leonard S. Wegman Co., Inc. Report 78-18. Albany, N. Y., p. 1.

(99) New York (City), *Overview,* pp. 74-82.

(100) Hanley, R. "Utility may tap Jersey park site for its methane." *New York Times,* 2 Apr. 1979, sect. 2, p. 2.

Chapter 7. The Costs of Dumping *(Pages 154-175)*

(1) "Public Law 92-532: Marine Protection, Research, and Sanctuaries Act of 1972." *United States at Large,* vol. 86, 1972, p. 1054.

(2) Anderson, P. W. and Dewling, R. T. "Industrial ocean dumping in EPA Region II—regulatory aspects." In Ketchum, B. H., Kester, D. R., and Park, P. K., ed. 1981. *Ocean dumping of industrial wastes.* Marine science, vol. 12. New York: Plenum Press, p. 26.

(3) Cabelli, V. J. and Heffernan, W. P. "Accumulation of *Escherichia coli* by the northern quahog." *Applied Microbiology* 19. 2 (February 1970): 239-244.

(4) Verger, J. L. 1980. *Shellfish borne disease outbreaks.* Davisville, R. I.: Dept. of Health and Human Services, Food and Drug Administration, Northeast Technical Services Unit, p. 14 (mimeo.).

(5) Ibid., p. 10.

(6) Mirchel, A.C.F. 1980. *Enforcement of hard clam laws on Great South Bay, New York.* Unpublished M.A. thesis, Stony Brook, N. Y.: Marine Sciences Research Center, State University of New York at Stony Brook, p. 78.

(7) Ibid., p. 103.

(8) United States, Food and Drug Administration, State Programs Branch. 1980. *New York shellfish sanitation program appraisal 1978-1979.* Washington, D.C., p. 4 (mimeo.).

(9) Koditschek, L. and Guyre, P. "Antimicrobial-resistant coliforms in New York Bight." *Marine Pollution Bulletin,* 5. (1974): 71-74.

REFERENCES

(10) Koditschek, L. "Antimicrobial resistant bacteria in the New York Bight." In Gross, M. G., ed. 1976. *Middle Atlantic Continental Shelf and the New York Bight.* Special Symposia, vol. 2. Lawrence, Kans.: American Society of Limnology and Oceanography, p. 391.

(11) Kanter, N. "Superbug in sea sludge perils health, Wolff says." *New York News,* 23 February 1975.

(12) O'Connor, J. S. "Contaminant effects on biota of the New York Bight." In Proceedings, Twenty-eighth annual session, Gulf and Caribbean Fisheries Institute, Miami, Fla., 1976, p. 58.

(13) Mahoney, J. B. and McLaughlin, J.J.A. "The association of phytoflagellate blooms in lower New York Bay with hypertrophication." *Journal of Experimental Marine Biology and Ecology* 28. 1 (June 1977): 53.

(14) Cabelli, V. J. et al. "The impact of pollution on marine bathing beaches: An epidemiological study." In Gross, M. G., ed. 1976. *Middle Atlantic continental shelf and the New York Bight.* Special Symposia, vol. 2. Lawrence, Kans.: American Society of Limnology and Oceanography, pp. 424–432.

(15) Baylor, E. et al. "Virus transfer from surf-to-wind" *Science* 198. 4317, 11 November 1977, pp. 575–580.

(16) Heatwole, C. A. and West, N. C. "Race, income and attitude toward beach cleanliness." In Proceedings, Second Symposium on Coastal and Ocean Management, Hollywood, Fla., 1980. vol. 2, pp. 1684–1696.

(17) Swanson, R. L. et al. 1977. *Long Island beach pollution: June 1976.* MESA special report. Boulder, Colo.: U. S. National Oceanic and Atmospheric Administration, Environmental Research Laboratories (hereafter cited as Swanson, *Long Island beach pollution*). See also Swanson, R. L. et al. "June 1976 pollution of Long Island ocean beaches." *Journal of the Environmental Engineering Division, American Society of Civil Engineers* 104. EE6 (December 1978): 1067–1085 (Proceedings paper 14238).

(18) Swanson, *Long Island beach pollution*, pp. 3–5, and 61–62.

(19) Ibid., pp. 10–13.

(20) Ibid., pp. 5–6, 62–63.

(21) New York (State), Long Island Park and Recreation Commission. 1976. *Long Island waste pollution study: An economic analysis.* Prepared in partial fulfillment of Task 8.7 of the New York State Outer Continental Shelf Development Impact Study. Albany, N. Y.: New York State Office of Parks and Recreation, p. 3 (mimeo.).

(22) Ibid., p. 4.

(23) Swanson, *Long Island beach pollution*, pp. 67–75.

(24) Ibid., p. 39.

(25) Ibid., p. 43.

(26) Ibid., p. 35.

(27) Ibid., p. 37.

(28) Ibid., p. 31.

(29) Ibid.

(30) Ibid.

(31) Ibid.

(32) Personal communication between R. L. Swanson, head, U.S. National Oceanic and Atmospheric Administration, MESA New York Bight Project, and W. Librizzi, U.S. Environmental Protection Administration, Region II.

(33) United States, Coast Guard, Public Affairs Office, undated. "Why pick on me?" Springfield, Va.: National Technical Information Service (G-WEP-3/1).

(34) Swanson, *Long Island beach pollution*, p. 35.

(35) Ibid., p. 38.

(36) New York (State), Governor's Special Long Island Sanitary Commission. 1931. *Report of the . . . Nassau County, May 15, 1931*. Albany, N. Y.: J. B. Lyon Co., Printers, pp. 55–56.

(37) Brongersma-Sanders, M. 1957. "Mass mortalities in the sea." In Hedgepeth, J. W., ed. *Treatise on Marine Ecology and Paleoecology*. Memoir 67. New York: Geological Society of America, pp. 941–1010.

(38) Swanson, R. L. and Sindermann, C. J., ed. 1979. *Oxygen depletion and associated benthic mortalities in New York Bight, 1976*. NOAA professional paper 11. Rockville, Md.: U.S. National Oceanic and Atmospheric Administration.

(39) Sindermann, C. J. and Swanson, R. L. "Historical and regional perspective." In Swanson, R. L. and Sindermann, C. J., ed. 1979. *Oxygen depletion and associated benthic mortalities in New York Bight, 1976*. NOAA professional paper 11. Rockville, Md.: U.S. National Oceanic and Atmospheric Administration, p. 1.

(40) "Court limits citizen suits based on 2 pollution laws." *New York Times*, 26 June 1981, p. B3.

(41) Han, G., Hansen D. V., and Cantillo, A. "Diagnostic model of water and oxygen transport." In Swanson, R. L. and Sindermann, C. J., ed. 1979. *Oxygen depletion and associated benthic mortalities in New York Bight, 1976*. NOAA professional paper 11. Rockville, Md.: U.S. National Oceanic and Atmospheric Administration, p. 191.

(42) Perlmutter, A. "Mystery on Long Island." *The New York State Conservationist* 6. 4 (February–March 1952): 11.

(43) Sinderman and Swanson, p. 9.

(44) Malone, T. C., Esaias, W., and Falkowski, P. "Plankton dynamics and nutrient cycling: part 1, water column processes." In Swanson, R. L. and Sindermann, C. J., ed. 1979. *Oxygen depletion and associated benthic mortalities in New York Bight, 1976*. NOAA professional paper 11. Rockville, Md.: U.S. National Oceanic and Atmospheric Administration, p. 213.

(45) Ibid., p. 212.

(46) O'Connor, J. S. "A perspective on natural and human factors." In Swanson, R. L. and Sindermann, C. J., ed. 1979. *Oxygen depletion and associated benthic mortalities in New York Bight, 1976*. Rockville, Md.: U.S. National Oceanic and Atmospheric Administration, p. 324 (NOAA professional paper 11).

(47) Ibid., p. 330.

(48) Swanson, R. L., Sindermann, C. J. and Han, G. "Oxygen depletion and the future: an evaluation." In Swanson, R. L. and Sindermann, C. J., ed.

REFERENCES

1979, *Oxygen depletion and associated benthic mortalities in New York Bight, 1976.* Rockville, Md.: U.S. National Oceanic and Atmospheric Administration, pp. 335–345 (NOAA professional paper 11).

(49) Steimle, F. Jr. and Radosh, D. J. "Effects on the benthic invertebrate community." In Swanson, R.L. and Sindermann, C. J., ed, 1979. *Oxygen depletion and associated benthic mortalities in New York Bight, 1976.* Rockville, Md.: U.S. National Oceanic and Atmospheric Administration, p. 283 (NOAA professional paper 11).

(50) Murchelano, R. and Ziskowski, J. "Fin rot disease studies in New York Bight." In Gross, M. G., ed. 1976. *Middle Atlantic Continental Shelf and the New York Bight.* Special Symposia, vol. 2. Lawrence, Kans.: American Society of Limnology and Oceanography, p. 333.

(51) O'Connor, J. S. 1981. *Studies on fates and effects of pollutants in the New York Bight.* Copenhagen, Denmark: International Council for the Exploration of the Sea, Marine Environmental Quality Committee (No. C.M. 1981/E:21) (mimeo.), p. 5.

(52) Ibid., p. 6.

(53) Longwell, A. "Chromosome mutagenesis in developing mackerel eggs sampled from the New York Bight." In Gross, M. G., ed. 1976. *Middle Atlantic Continental Shelf and the New York Bight.* Special Symposia, vol. 2. Lawrence, Kans.: American Society of Limnology and Oceanography, p. 337.

(54) Longwell, A. C. 1976. *Chromosome mutagenesis in developing mackerel eggs sampled from the New York Bight.* NOAA Technical Memorandum ERL MESA-7. Boulder, Colo.: Marine Ecosystems Analysis Program Office, p. 11.

(55) Boesch, D. F. "Ecosystem consequences of alterations of benthic community structure and function in the New York Bight region." In Mayer, G. S., ed. 1982. *Ecological stress and the New York Bight: science and management.* Columbia, S. C.: Estuarine Research Foundation.

(56) Figley, W., Pyle, B. and Halgren B. "Socioeconomic impacts." In Swanson R. L. and Sindermann, C. J., ed. 1979. *Oxygen depletion and associated benthic mortalities in New York Bight, 1976.* Rockville, Md.: U.S. National Oceanic and Atmospheric Administration, p. 316 (NOAA) professional paper 11).

(57) Ibid., p. 321.

(58) Ibid., p. 317.

(59) Ibid.

(60) Ibid., p. 318.

(61) Ibid.

(62) Ibid.

(63) Ibid., p. 321.

(64) Ibid.

(65) New York (State), Long Island Park and Recreation Commission, p. 18.

(66) Ibid., p. 20.

(67) The Port Authority of New York and New Jersey. 1981. *Foreign Trade 1980: The Port of New York and New Jersey,* New York, p. 40.

(68) "Excerpts from City's statement in bond offering." *New York Times,* 20 July 1981, p. B6.

Chapter 8. The Bight in Our Future *(Pages 176–191)*

(1) Segar, D. A. "Contamination of populated estuaries and adjacent coastal ocean—a global review." In MESA New York Bight Workshop, Williamsburg, Va., 1980 [Background paper] Stony Brook, N. Y.: U.S. National Oceanic and Atmospheric Administration, MESA New York Bight Project (unpubl.).

(2) Goldberg, E. D. "Assimilative capacity of U.S. coastal waters for pollutants: overview and summary." In Proceedings, Workshop on Assimilative Capacity of U.S. Coastal Waters for Pollutants, Crystal Mountain, Wash., 1980, ed. Edward D. Goldberg, rev. ed. Boulder, Colo.: U.S. National Oceanic and Atmospheric Administration, Environmental Research Laboratories, p. 1.

(3) Ibid.

(4) Ibid., p. 2.

(5) United States, National Advisory Committee on Oceans and Atmosphere. 1981. *Tenth Annual Report to the President and the Congress.* Washington, D.C., p. 35.

(6) Ibid., 37–38.

(7) Ibid., p. 38.

(8) United States, District Court, Southern District of New York. 1981. The City of New York, Plaintiff, against United States Environmental Protection Agency, Douglas M. Costle as Administrator, United States Environmental Protection Agency, and Charles Warren as Regional Administrator, United States Environmental Protection Agency, Region II, Defendants. New York. (80 Civ. 1677 ADS) (unpubl.).

(9) Ibid., see footnote 21. p. v–vi.

(10) Kamlet, K.S. "Court decision makes future of sewage sludge ocean dumping uncertain." *Coastal Ocean Pollution Assessment News; Man and Environment* 1. 3 (spring 1981): 47. Marine Sciences Research Center, State University of New York at Stony Brook.

(11) Perlee, J. "Koch says ban on dumping sludge would close harbor." *New York Times,* 24 March 1982, p. B1.

(12) Personal communication between D. F. Squires and Harold Stanford, head, Hudson/Raritan Estuarine Project, U.S. National Oceanic and Atmospheric Administration, on 4 February 1982.

(13) Kantrowitz, B. 1978. "Marine education: Bringing the mountain to Mohammed." In *The second wave and other tales.* Albany, N. Y.: New York Sea Grant Institute, p. 8.

(14) Letter from J. S. O'Connor, senior scientist, Northeast Office, Office of Marine Pollution Assessment, U.S. National Oceanic and Atmospheric Administration, to D. F. Squires, 21 April 1982.

Index

Acid waste dump, 136, 139
Airplanes: effect on Port of New York, 39
Agriculture: early, 79; effect on erosion, 80
Aggregate mining, 74
Aquaculture, 70
Ambrose Channel, 44, 145
Assimilative capacity, 181

Barrier Islands: defined, 22; formation of, 25; flora and fauna of, 25; inlets, 23; washover, 23; wetlands, 26
Beach: development of, 20; erosion, 22; formation of, 22; littoral drift, 22; protection devices, 24, 27; protection policies, 28; rates of erosion, 24-25
Benthos, 10, 12
Bight. See Middle Atlantic Bight; New York Bight
Bioaccumulation, 160
Bioconcentration, 156
Black gill "disease", 171

Cadmium, 143, 144, 148
Carson, Rachael, 140
Cellar dirt: defined, 42, 103, 149. See also Mud dump grounds
Ceratium, role in fish kill, 167-69
Channel: dredging, 43, 44, 145; spoil disposal, 44, 102, 145
Clams. See Shellfish
Clean Water Act. See Federal Water Pollution Control Act, Amended
Cold pool, the, 8
Coliform bacteria, 157, 158, 163. See also Superbug

Combined sewers, 95, 164
Commons, problem of, 54, 58, 66, 75-76, 188
Communities, biological, 12; degraded, 172
Consolidated Edison, origins, 91
Construction debris: disposal of, 44; islands formed (Hoffman, Swineborne, Rikers, Governors), 43, 150. See also Cellar dirt
Containerization, 38
Contaminants: atmosphere as source, 129; "most serious" list of, 123; runoff as source, 130; sewage sludge as source, 135; wastewater as source, 130
Contiguous zones, 48
Corps of Engineers, U.S. Army: harbor drift project, 39, 162; research on spoil dumping, 114; shore protection, 28; spoil disposal permits, 44, 102, 105, 111, 114, 148
Council on Environmental Quality, 104
Cousteau, Jacques Yves: quoted, 187

DDT, 16, 140
Dead Sea, issue of, 114
Deep water dump site. See Industrial waste dump site
Dickens, Charles: quoted, 52
Dredge spoils: contaminants from, 45, 147; defined, 127; disposal of, 44, 102, 127, 145; disposal alternatives, 75, 112; as landfill, 43; ocean dumping, 102
Dump sites: ocean, 102. See also Acid waste dump; Cellar dirt; Deep water

dump site; Industrial waste dump
site; Mud dump grounds; sewage
sludge dump site; Wreck dump site

East River: development of, 36; dissolved oxygen, 132; tidal flow, 34
Ecosystem: defined, 4
Eelgrass, 69
Encephalitis, Eastern Equine, 16
Energy, consumption of, 87; sources of:
coal, 89; electricity, 92; natural gas,
90; oil, 89; water power, 88; wood, 88;
waste disposal: ash, 88; coal ash, 92;
scrubber sludge, 92
Environmental Conservation, NYS
Department of, 144, 157
Environmental Protection Agency: guide-
lines, ocean dumping, 106; permit
authority, 105, 185; termination of
ocean dumping, 106, 108, 111, 120,
136
EPA. See Environmental Protection
Agency
Epifauna, 12
Erie Canal, 36
Estuaries: circulation, estuarine, 32;
described, 32; tidal river, 32

Federal Water Pollution Control Act,
Amended, 105, 114; section 208, 186
Fin rot, 15, 171
Fish and Wildlife Coordination Act, 114
Fish and Wildlife, U.S. Service, 114
Fish kill of 1976, 59, 120, 123, 166;
economic costs of, 173; other fish
kills, 167
Fishery: conservation zone, 55; Fishery
Conservation and Management Act,
49, 55; foreign fleets, 55; history of,
54–55; management of, 60; surf clam
fishery, management of, 58
Fishermen: charter and partyboat, 66;
commercial, 60, 62; recreational, 63
Floatables event, 107, 120, 161–66;
economic costs of, 174
Food and Drug Administration, U.S.,
59, 104, 114, 144, 158
Fuller, Buckminister: quoted, 4
Fulton Fish Market, 62

Garbage. See Landfill
Gedney Channel, 44, 145
General Electric Company, 130, 141
Gunnerson, Charles: quoted, 131

Halocline: defined, 8
Harbor drift project, 39, 162
Health, human, 53, 155; sewage treat-
ment, 133; shellfish-related, 157;
water-related epidemics, 93, 158
Heikoff, Joseph: quoted, 27
Hepatitis, from shellfish, 158
High seas, 49
Hudson-Raritan Estuary: circulation, 34;
defined, 31, 33; modification of, 41–42;
PCB in, 142; as pollutant trap, 35;
wastewater discharged into, 35. See
also Port of New York
Hudson River, 33; development of, 36;
PCB pollution, 141
Hurricanes. See storms

Industrial development, 82; of Long
Island, 85; of New Jersey, 85; of
New York City, 84
Industrial wastes: defined, 111, 151;
history of, 136. See also Wastewater,
industrial
Industrial waste dump site, 103, 136,
139; alternative disposal, 139
Infauna, 12
Interstate Sanitation Commission, 46, 49
International Conventions on ocean
pollution, 112–13

Juet, John: quoted, 1
Jurisdictions: contiguous zones, 48;
federal, 49; High Seas, 49; interstate,
49; marine, 48; Territorial Sea, 48;
tidal boundaries, 48; 200-mile limit,
55

Kamlet, Kenneth: quoted, 185–86

Land grants, 46–47
Landfill: garbage dumps, 45, 137, 149,
150; industrial wastes in, 146;
methane from, 152; pierhead filling,
42, 147, 150; as source of pollution,
151, 165
Lang, Martin, 116
Lead, 16, 129, 143, 148
Legislation, coastal, 101
Limit, 200-mile. See Fishery, conservation zone
Littoral drift: defined, 23
Long Island, beaches described, 24;
floatables, 162; sewage, 96, 132; water
supply, 94; wetlands lost, 29

Marine Protection, Research, and Sanctuaries Act, 115; described, 104
Marshes. *See* Wetlands
McHugh, John L.: quoted, 63
Mercury, 16, 143
MESA. *See* National Oceanic and Atmospheric Administration
Middle Atlantic Bight, 5
Middle Atlantic Fisheries Management Council, 59
Minor civil divisions: of New York Bight region, 46–49
Mud dump grounds, 44, 147, 181
Mutagenicity, 172

National Advisory Committee on Oceans and Atmosphere, 184
National Marine Fisheries Service, 123; fish-kill study, 166
National Oceanic and Atmospheric Administration, 115; fish-kill study, 166; Marine Ecosystem Analysis Program, 115–25; ocean dumping research responsibility, 110
National Ocean Pollution Research and Development and Monitoring Planning Act, 10
National Park Service, 28
New Jersey: beaches described, 24; erosion policy, 28; fish-kill, 166; sewage, 132; water supply, 94; wetlands lost, 29. *See also* Port of New York
New York Bight: benthos, 10, 12; biology, 6, 9; birds, 15; circulation, 7; climatology, 7; compared, 178; defined, 4; dumping, 102; dump sites; fishes, 14; fishery, 15; geology, 4; jurisdictions, 48; mammals, 18; oceanography, 6; phytoplankton, 9; salinity, 8–9; water temperatures, 8; zooplankton, 10. *See also* Acid waste dump; Fishery; Industrial waste dump site; Mud dump grounds; Sewage sludge dump site
New York Bight region: development of, 49; energy consumption, 87; industrial development, 84; minor civil divisions of, 47
New York City: abandoned piers, 39; dumping suit, 185; growth by shoreline filling, 42; industrial development, 84; land and coastal use, 41; minor civil divisions, 40; sewage treatment facilities, 133; sewerage, 95, 132; water supply, 93. *See also* Port of New York

New York State: erosion policy, 28. *See also* Long Island; New York City; Port of New York
NOAA. *See* National Oceanic and Atmospheric Administration

O'Connor, Joel, 117; quoted, 190
Ocean Dumping Act. *See* Marine Protection, Research, and Sanctuaries Act
Ocean dumping, 101; research on, 113; termination of, 106; volumes of, 102, 103. *See also* Dump sites
OCS. *See* Petroleum
Oil spills, 16, 79, 90, 137, 163; in ocean, 73
Oysters. *See* Shellfish

PCB, 16, 130, 141, 160
Petroleum, 71; consumption of, 89; outercontinental shelf (OCS) development, 72
Phytoplankton, 9
Pollution: compared, 178; effects on biota, 12, 15, 59, 124, 170, 172; health effects of, 159
Pomerantz, S. I.: quoted, 131
Population, growth of, 80–82
Port Authority of New York and New Jersey, 38, 39, 49; formation of, 47
Port of New York: channel dredging, 148; colonial history, 36; early trade, 36–38; port facilities, 38; role in region's economy, 86. *See also* Channel
Pycnocline, 167; defined, 8

Refuse: defined, 127, 148; from boats, ships, 164; ocean dumping of, 150; reclamation of, 149; volumes of, 148
River and Harbor Act, 102, 111
Runoff, 129; contaminants in, 130

Salt hay (*Spartina*), 69
Salwen, Bert: quoted, 82
Sand and gravel, 74
Sandy Hook: formation of, 25; erosion rates, 24
Sanitary landfills. See Landfill
Sea level changes, 22
Seafood industry, 62; Fulton Fish Market, 62
Seaweeds, 68; biomass, 69; introduction of exotic, 70
Sewage, 96; discharge amounts, 97; discharge to estuary, Bight, 99; health effects of, 159; nutrients from, 134; pollution by, 96; treatment of, 96, 133

Sewage sludge, 96, 134–36, 162, 165; contaminants from, 102; defined, 102; termination of dumping of, 108
Sewage sludge dump site, 102, 135; closure of shellfishery, 104; effects on benthic communities of, 12, 135; ocean dumping of, 135; volumes of, 135
Sewers, 95; combined, 95, 164; development of, 95, 132
Shelf edge front, 8
Shellfish: effects of pollution on, 29, 52, 156, 157; shellfishery, 52; over-harvesting of, 53; surf clam, management of, 58
Shumway, Floyd: quoted, 126
Sludge Monster, 119, 120, 163
Smithsonian Institution, 114
Sofaer, Judge Abraham: quoted, 185
Spilhaus, Athelstan: quoted, 186
Spoils. See Dredge spoils
Sportfishery, 63; economic value of, 66; numbers of participants, 66
State University of New York at Stony Brook, 118
Storms, 29–30
Superbug, 158
Surf clam: closure of, fishery, 59; mortality of, in fish kill, 59; production of, 58

Swanson, Commander R. Lawrence, 116, 118, 185; quoted, 119

Territorial Sea, 48
Thermocline, defined, 7
Toxic wastes, 139, 142, 159; effects on biota, 170
Train, Russell: quoted, 106
Two-hundred mile limit. See Fishery, conservation zone
Typhoid fever, from shellfish, 53, 157

Verrazano, Giovanni da: quoted, 1
Virginian Biogeographic Province, 6

Wastewater: chlorine in, 134, 159; contaminants in, 130; domestic, defined, 127; floatables from, 164; industrial, 136–39; volume discharged, 132
Water: consumption, 94; discharge, 95; supplies, 93, 131
Westway Project, 42, 74
Wetlands: ditching of, 26; Long Island, 29; New Jersey, 29; New York City, remaining, 41; rate of loss, 29, 150
Wreck dump site, 103

Zooplankton, 10